BERLITZ®

W9-BSR-715

FRENCH
for travellers

By the staff of Berlitz Guides

How best to use this phrase book

● We suggest that you start with the **Guide to pronunciation** (pp. 6–9), then go on to **Some basic expressions** (pp. 10–15). This gives you not only a minimum vocabulary, but also helps you get used to pronouncing the language. The phonetic transcription throughout the book enables you to pronounce every word correctly.

● Consult the **Contents** pages (3–5) for the section you need. In each chapter you'll find travel facts, hints and useful information. Simple phrases are followed by a list of words applicable to the situation.

● Separate, detailed contents lists are included at the beginning of the extensive **Eating out** and **Shopping guide** sections (Menus, p. 39, Shops and services, p. 97).

● If you want to find out how to say something in French, your fastest look-up is via the **Dictionary** section (pp. 164–189). This not only gives you the word, but is also cross-referenced to its use in a phrase on a specific page.

● If you wish to learn more about constructing sentences, check the **Basic grammar** (pp. 159–163).

● Note the **colour margins** are indexed in French and English to help both listener and speaker. And, in addition, there is also an **index in French** for the use of your listener.

● Throughout the book, this symbol 🖝 suggests phrases your listener can use to answer you. If you still can't understand, hand this phrase book to the French-speaker to encourage pointing to an appropriate answer. The English translation for you is just alongside the French.

Copyright © 1970, 1986 by Berlitz Guides, a division of Macmillan S.A., Avenue d'Ouchy 61, 1000 Lausanne 6, Switzerland. All rights reserved. No part of this book may be reproduced or transmitted in any form or by any means, electronic or mechanical, including photocopying, recording or by any information storage and retrieval system, without permission in writing from the publisher. Berlitz Trademark Reg. U.S. Patent Office and other countries—Marca Registrada.
Library of Congress Catalog Card No. 85-81370

Second revised edition—10th printing 1989
Printed in Hungary

Contents

Acknowledgments
We are particularly grateful to Gérard Chaillon for his help in the preparation of this book, and to Dr. T.J.A. Bennett who devised the phonetic transcription.

Guide to pronunciation

This and the following chapter are intended to make you familiar with the phonetic transcription we devised and to help you get used to the sounds of French.

As a minimum vocabulary for your trip, we've selected a number of basic words and phrases under the title "Some basic expressions" (pages 10–15).

An outline of the spelling and sounds of French

You'll find the pronunciation of the French letters and sounds explained below, as well as the symbols we're using for them in the transcriptions. Note that French has some diacritical marks—accents on letters, the cedilla—which we don't have in English.

The imitated pronunciation should be read as if it were English except for any special rules set out below. It is based on Standard British pronunciation, though we have tried to take into account General American pronunciation as well. Of course, the sounds of any two languages are never exactly the same; but if you follow carefully the indications supplied here, you'll have no difficulty in reading our transcriptions in such a way as to make yourself understood.

Consonants

Letter	Approximate pronunciation	Symbol	Example	
b, c, d, f, k, l, m, n, p, s, t, v, x, z	as in English			
ch	like **sh** in **shut**	sh	**chercher**	shehrshay

ç	like **s** in sit	s	**ça**	sah
g	1) before **e, i, y**, like **s** in pleasure	zh	**manger**	mahngzhay
	2) before **a, o, u**, like **g** in **go**	g	**garçon**	gahrsawng
gn	like **ni** in onion	ñ	**ligne**	leeñ
h	always silent		**homme**	om
j	like **s** in pleasure	zh	**jamais**	zhahmeh
qu	like **k** in **k**ill	k	**qui**	kee
r	rolled in the back of the mouth, rather like gargling	r	**rouge**	roozh
w	usually like **v** in **v**oice	v	**wagon**	vahgawng

Vowels

a, à or **â**	between the **a** in hat and the **a** in father	ah	**mari**	mahree
é, er, ez	like **a** in late, but a pure vowel, not a diphthong	ay	**été**	aytay
è, ê, e	like **e** in get	eh	**même**	mehm
e	sometimes (when at the end of a syllable or of a one-syllable word), like **er** in other (quite short)	er*	**je**	zher
i	like **ee** in meet	ee	**il**	eel
o	generally like **o** in hot but sometimes like **o** in wrote	o/ oa	**donner** **rose**	donnay roaz
ô	like **o** in wrote	oa	**Rhône**	roan
u	no equivalent in English. Round your lips and try to say **ee**; this should sound more or less correct	ew	**cru**	krew

---

* The **r** should not be pronounced when reading this transcription.

Sounds spelt with two or more letters

ai, ay, ey	can be pronounced as **a** in late	ay	**j'ai**	zhay
aient, ais, ait, aî	like **e** in get	eh	**chaîne**	shehn
(e)au	similar to **o** in wrote	oa	**chaud**	shoa
ei	like **e** in get	eh	**peine**	pehn
eu, eû, œu	like **ur** in fur, but with lips rounded, not spread	ur*	**peu**	pur
oi, oy	like **w** followed by the **a** in hat	wah	**moi**	mwah
ou, oû	like **oo** in look	oo	**nouveau**	noovoa
ui	approximately like **wee** in between	wee	**traduire**	trahdweer

Nasal sounds

French contains nasal vowels, which we transcribe with a vowel symbol plus **ng**. This **ng** should *not* be pronounced, and serves solely to indicate nasal quality of the preceding vowel. A nasal vowel is pronounced simultaneously through the mouth and the nose.

am, an	something like **arn** in tarnish	ahng	**tante**	tahngt
em, en	generally like the previous sound	ahng	**enchanté**	ahngshahngtay
ien	sounds like **yan** in yank	yang	**bien**	byang
im, in, aim, ain, eim, ein	approximately like **ang** in rang	ang	**instant**	angstahng
om, on	approximately like **ong** in song	awng	**maison**	mayzawng
um, un	approximately like **ang** in rang	ang	**brun**	brang

---

* The **r** should not be pronounced when reading this transcription.

Liaison

Normally, the final consonants are not pronounced in French. However, when a word ending in a consonant is followed by one beginning with a vowel, they are often run together, and the consonant is pronounced as if it began the following word. For instance, **nous** *(we)* is pronounced **noo**, but, in the sentence "**Nous avons un enfant**" *(We have a child)*, the **s** of **nous** is pronounced, and the sentence sounds something like: **noo zahvawng zang nahngfahng**. Another example: "**comment**" is pronounced **kommahng**, but the **t** is pronounced in "**Comment allez-vous?**" *(How are you)*, which sounds something like: **kommahng tahlay voo**.

Stress

Unlike English, all syllables in French have more or less the same degree of stress (loudness), although in some short and common words the vowel "e" tends to be pronounced only very weakly. For French ears, there is a slightly heavier stress on the last syllable of a word-group, but as this is a fine distinction, stress has not been indicated in the transcription of this book. Each syllable should be pronounced with equal stress.

	Pronunciation of the French alphabet						
A	ah	**H**	ahsh	**O**	oa	**V**	vay
B	bay	**I**	ee	**P**	pay	**W**	doobler vay
C	say	**J**	zhee	**Q**	kew	**X**	eex
D	day	**K**	kah	**R**	ehr	**Y**	ee grehk
E	er	**L**	ehl	**S**	ehss	**Z**	zehd
F	ehf	**M**	ehm	**T**	tay		
G	zhay	**N**	ehn	**U**	ew		

Some basic expressions

Yes.	**Oui.**	wee
No.	**Non.**	nawng
Please.	**S'il vous plaît.**	seel voo pleh
Thank you.	**Merci.**	mehrsee
Thank you very much.	**Merci beaucoup.**	mehrsee boakoo
Not at all/You're welcome.	**De rien/Il n'y a pas de quoi.**	der ryang/eel nee ah pah der kwah

Greetings *Salutations*

Good morning.	**Bonjour.**	bawngzhoor
Good afternoon.	**Bonjour.**	bawngzhoor
Good evening.	**Bonsoir.**	bawngsswahr
Good night.	**Bonne nuit.**	bon nwee
Good-bye.	**Au revoir.**	oa rervwahr
See you later.	**A tout à l'heure.**	ah too tah lurr
This is Mr./Mrs./ Miss ...	**Je vous présente Monsieur/Madame/ Mademoiselle ...**	zher voo prayzahngt mursyur/mahdahm/ mahdmwahzehl
How do you do? (Pleased to meet you.)	**Enchanté(e).***	ahngshahngtay
How are you?	**Comment allez-vous?**	kommahng tahlay voo
Very well, thanks. And you?	**Très bien, merci. Et vous?**	treh byang mehrsee. ay voo

---

* The final **-e** in the written form shows that the writer is a woman. Pronunciation remains the same, however, whether the speaker is a man or a woman.

How's life?	**Comment ça va?**	kommahng sah vah
Fine.	**Bien.**	byang
I beg your pardon?	**Pardon?**	pahrdawng
Excuse me. (May I get past?)	**Excusez-moi!/ Pardon!**	ehxkewzay mwah/ pahrdawng
Sorry!	**Désolé(e).**	dayzolay

Questions *Questions*

Where?	**Où?**	oo
How?	**Comment?**	kommahng
When?	**Quand?**	kahng
What?	**Quoi?**	kwah
Why?	**Pourquoi?**	poorkwah
Who?	**Qui?**	kee
Which?	**Lequel/Laquelle?**	lerkehl/lahkehl
Where is ...?	**Où est/ Où se trouve ...?**	oo eh/oo ser troov
Where are ...?	**Où sont/ Où se trouvent ...?**	oo sawng/oo ser troov
Where can I find/ get ...?	**Où puis-je trouver ...?**	oo pweezh troovay
How far?	**A quelle distance?**	ah kehl deestahngss
How long?	**Combien de temps?**	kawngbyang der tahng
How much/ How many?	**Combien?**	kawngbyang
How much does this cost?	**Combien coûte ceci?**	kawngbyang koot serssee
When does ... open/ close?	**A quelle heure ouvre/ ferme ...?**	ah kehl urr oovr/fehrm
What do you call this/that in French?	**Comment appelle-t-on ceci/cela en français?**	kommahng tahpehl tawng serssee/serlah ahng frahngsseh
What does this/that mean?	**Que veut dire ceci/ cela?**	ker vur deer serssee/ serlah

Do you speak ...? *Parlez-vous ...?*

Do you speak English?	**Parlez-vous anglais?**	pahrlay voo ahnggleh
Is there anyone here who speaks English?	**Y a-t-il quelqu'un qui parle anglais ici?**	ee ahteel kehlkang kee pahrl ahnggleh eessee
I don't speak (much) French.	**Je ne parle pas (bien) français.**	zher ner pahrl pah (byang) frahngsseh
Could you speak more slowly?	**Pourriez-vous parler plus lentement?**	pooryay voo pahrlay plew lahngtermahng
Could you repeat that?	**Pourriez-vous répéter?**	pooryay voo raypaytay
Could you spell it?	**Pourriez-vous me l'épeler?**	pooryay voo mer layperlay
Please write it down.	**Ecrivez-le, s'il vous plaît.**	aykreevay ler seel voo pleh
Can you translate this for me?	**Pouvez-vous me traduire ceci?**	poovay voo mer trahdweer serssee
Can you translate this for us?	**Pouvez-vous nous traduire ceci?**	poovay voo noo trahdweer serssee
Please point to the word/phrase/ sentence in the book.	**Montrez-moi le mot/ l'expression/la phrase dans le livre, s'il vous plaît.**	mawngtray mwah ler moa/ lehxprehssyawng/lah frahz dahng ler leevr seel voo pleh
Just a minute. I'll see if I can find it in this book.	**Un instant. Je vais voir si je la trouve dans ce livre.**	ang nangstahng. zher vay vwahr see zher lah troov dahng ser leevr
I understand.	**Je comprends.**	zher kawngprahng
I don't understand.	**Je ne comprends pas.**	zher ner kawngprahng pah
Do you understand?	**Comprenez-vous?**	kawngprernay voo

Can/May ...? *Puis-je ...?*

Can I have ...?	**Puis-je avoir ...?**	pweezh ahvwahr
Can we have ...?	**Pouvons-nous avoir ...?**	poovawng noo ahvwahr
Can you show me ...?	**Pouvez-vous m'indiquer ...?**	poovay voo mangdeekay

I can't.	**Je ne peux pas.**	zher ner pur pah
Can you tell me...?	**Pouvez-vous me dire ...?**	poovay voo mer deer
Can you help me?	**Pouvez-vous m'aider?**	poovay voo mehday
Can I help you?	**Puis-je vous aider?**	pweezh voo zehday
Can you direct me to ...?	**Pouvez-vous m'indiquer la direction de ...?**	poovay voo mangdeekay lah deerehkssyawng der

Wanting ... *Je voudrais ...*

I'd like ...	**Je voudrais ...**	zher voodreh
We'd like ...	**Nous voudrions ...**	noo voodreeyawng
What do you want?	**Que désirez-vous?**	ker dayzeeray voo
Give me ...	**Donnez-moi ...**	donnay mwah
Give it to me.	**Donnez-le-moi.**	donnay ler mwah
Bring me ...	**Apportez-moi ...**	ahportay mwah
Bring it to me.	**Apportez-le-moi.**	ahportay ler mwah
Show me ...	**Montrez-moi ...**	mawngtray mwah
Show it to me.	**Montrez-le-moi.**	mawngtray ler mwah
I'm looking for ...	**Je cherche ...**	zher shehrsh
I'm hungry.	**J'ai faim.**	zhay fang
I'm thirsty.	**J'ai soif.**	zhay swahf
I'm tired.	**Je suis fatigué(e).**	zher swee fahteegay
I'm lost.	**Je me suis perdu(e).**	zher mer swee pehrdew
It's important.	**C'est important.**	seh tangportahng
It's urgent.	**C'est urgent.**	seh tewrzhahng
Hurry up!	**Dépêchez-vous.**	daypehshay voo

It is/There is ... *C'est/Il y a ...*

It is ...	**C'est ...**	seh
Is it ...?	**Est-ce ...?**	ehss
It isn't ...	**Ce n'est pas ...**	ser neh pah

Here it is.	**Le voici/La voici.**	ler vwahssee/lah vwahssee
Here they are.	**Les voici.**	lay vwahssee
There it is.	**Le voilà/La voilà.**	ler vwahlah/lah vwahlah
There they are.	**Les voilà.**	lay vwahlah
There is/There are ...	**Il y a ...**	eel ee ah
Is there/Are there ...?	**Y a-t-il ...?**	ee ahteel
There isn't/aren't ...	**Il n'y a pas ...**	eel nee ah pah
There isn't/aren't any.	**Il n'y en a pas.**	eel nee ahng nah pah

It's ... *C'est ...*

big/small	**grand/petit***	grahng/pertee
quick/slow	**rapide/lent**	rahpeed/lahng
hot/cold	**chaud/froid**	shoa/frwah
full/empty	**plein/vide**	plang/veed
easy/difficult	**facile/difficile**	fahsseel/deefeesseel
heavy/light	**lourd/léger**	loor/layzhay
open/shut	**ouvert/fermé**	oovehr/fehrmay
right/wrong	**juste/faux**	zhewst/foa
old/new	**ancien/nouveau (nouvelle)**	ahngssyang/noovoa (noovehl)
old/young	**vieux (vieille)/jeune**	vyur (vyehy)/zhurn
next/last	**prochain/dernier**	proshang/dehrnyay
beautiful/ugly	**beau (belle)/laid**	boa (behl)/leh
free (vacant)/ occupied	**libre/occupé**	leebr/okkewpay
good/bad	**bon/mauvais**	bawng/moaveh
better/worse	**meilleur/pire**	mehyurr/peer
early/late	**tôt/tard**	toa/tahr
cheap/expensive	**bon marché/cher**	bawng mahrshay/shehr
near/far	**près/loin**	preh/lwang
here/there	**ici/là**	eessee/lah

Quantities *Quantités*

a little/a lot	**un peu/beaucoup**	ang pur/boakoo
few/a few	**peu de/quelques**	pur der/kehlker
much	**beaucoup**	boakoo

---

* For feminine and plural forms, see grammar section page 160 (adjectives).

many	**beaucoup de**	boakoo der
more/less	**plus/moins**	plew(ss)/mwang
more than/less than	**plus que/moins que**	plewss ker/mwang ker
enough/too	**assez/trop**	ahssay/troa
some/any	**de, de la, du, des**	der der lah dew day

A few more useful words *Autres mots utiles*

at	**à**	ah
on	**sur**	sewr
in	**dans**	dahng
to	**à**	ah
after	**après**	ahpreh
before (time)	**avant**	ahvahng
before (place)	**devant**	dervahng
for	**pour**	poor
from	**de**	der
with/without	**avec/sans**	ahvehk/sahng
through	**à travers**	ah trahvehr
towards	**vers**	vehr
until	**jusqu'à**	zhewskah
during	**pendant**	pahngdahng
next to	**à côté de**	ah koatay der
near	**près de**	preh der
behind	**derrière**	dehryehr
between	**entre**	ahngtr
since	**depuis**	derpwee
above	**au-dessus (de)**	oa derssew (der)
below	**au-dessous (de)**	oa derssoo (der)
under	**sous**	soo
inside/outside	**dedans/dehors**	derdahng/deror
up/upstairs	**en haut**	ahng oa
down/downstairs	**en bas**	ahng bah
and	**et**	ay
or	**ou**	oo
not	**ne ... pas**	ner ... pah
never	**ne ... jamais**	ner ... zhahmeh
nothing	**rien**	ryang
none	**aucun, aucune**	oakang oakewn
very	**très**	treh
too (also)	**aussi**	oassee
yet	**encore**	ahngkor
soon	**bientôt**	byangtoa
now	**maintenant**	mangternahng
then	**ensuite**	ahngssweet
perhaps	**peut-être**	purtehtr

Arrival

CONTRÔLE DES PASSEPORTS
PASSPORT CONTROL

Here's my passport.	**Voici mon passeport.**	vwahssee mawng pahsspor
I'll be staying ...	**Je resterai ...**	zher rehsterray
a few days	**quelques jours**	kehlker zhoor
a week	**une semaine**	ewn sermehn
a month	**un mois**	ang mwah
I don't know yet.	**Je ne sais pas encore.**	zher ner seh pah zahngkor
I'm here on holiday.	**Je suis en vacances.**	zher swee zahng vahkahngss
I'm here on business.	**Je suis en voyage d'affaires.**	zher swee zahng vwahyahzh dahfehr
I'm just passing through.	**Je suis de passage.**	zher swee der pahssahzh

If things become difficult:

| I'm sorry, I don't understand. | **Excusez-moi, je ne comprends pas.** | ehxkewzay mwah zher ner kawngprahng pah |
| Is there anyone here who speaks English? | **Y a-t-il quelqu'un qui parle anglais?** | ee ahteel kehlkang kee pahrl ahnggleh |

DOUANE
CUSTOMS

After collecting your baggage at the airport (*l'aéroport* – lahayropor) you have a choice: follow the green arrow if you have nothing to declare. Or leave via a doorway marked with a red arrow if you have items to declare.

articles à déclarer
goods to declare

rien à déclarer
nothing to declare

The chart below shows what you can bring in duty-free (visitors from overseas are allowed greater concessions as regards duty-free cigarettes and tobacco).*

	Cigarettes	Cigars	Tobacco	Spirits (liquor)	Wine
France ⎰ Belgium ⎱ Switzerland	[1]300 or [2]200 or 200 or	75 or 50 or 50 or	400 gr. 250 gr. 250 gr.	1½ l. and 1 l. and 1 l. and	5 l. 2 l. 2 l.

[1]Visitors arriving from EEC countries with non-tax-free items
[2]Visitors arriving from EEC countries with tax-free items

I've nothing to declare.	Je n'ai rien à déclarer.	zher nay ryang nah dayklahray
I've ...	J'ai ...	zhay
a carton of cigarettes	une cartouche de cigarettes	ewn kahrtoosh der seegahreht
a bottle of whisky	une bouteille de whisky	ewn bootehy der whisky
It's for my personal use.	C'est pour mon usage personnel.	seh poor mawng newzahzh pehrsonnehl

Votre passeport, s'il vous plaît.	Your passport, please.
Avez-vous quelque chose à déclarer?	Do you have anything to declare?
Pouvez-vous ouvrir ce sac?	Please open this bag.
Il y a des droits de douane sur cet article.	You'll have to pay duty on this.
Avez-vous d'autres bagages?	Do you have any more luggage?

Arrivée

* All allowances subject to change without notice.

Baggage—Porter *Bagages – Porteur*

These days porters are only available at airports or the railway stations of large cities. Where no porters are available you'll find luggage trolleys for the use of the passengers.

Porter!	**Porteur!**	porturr
Please take (this/my) ...	**Prenez ..., s'il vous plaît.**	prernay ... seel voo pleh
luggage	**mes bagages**	may bahgahzh
suitcase	**ma valise**	mah vahleez
(travelling) bag	**mon sac (de voyage)**	mawng sahk (der vwahyahzh)
That's mine.	**C'est à moi.**	seh tah mwah
Take this luggage ...	**Portez ces bagages ...**	portay say bahgahzh
to the bus	**à l'arrêt du bus**	ah lahreh dew bewss
to the luggage lockers	**à la consigne automatique**	ah lah kawngseeñ oatomahteek
How much is that?	**C'est combien?**	seh kawngbyang
There's one piece missing.	**Il en manque un/une.**	eel ahng mahngk ang/ewn
Where are the luggage trolleys (carts)?	**Où sont les chariots à bagages?**	oo sawng lay shahryoa ah bahgahzh

Changing money *Change*

Where's the currency exchange office?	**Où se trouve le bureau de change?**	oo ser troov ler bewroa der shahngzh
Can you change these traveller's cheques (checks)?	**Pouvez-vous changer ces chèques de voyage?**	poovay voo shahngzhay say shehk der vwahyahzh
I want to change some dollars/pounds.	**Je voudrais changer des dollars/livres.**	zher voodreh shahngzhay day dollahr/leevr
Can you change this into ...?	**Pouvez-vous changer ceci en ...?**	poovay voo shahngszhay serssee ahng
Belgian francs	**francs belges**	frahng behlzh
French francs	**francs français**	frahng frahngsseh
Swiss francs	**francs suisses**	frahng sweess
What's the exchange rate?	**Quel est le cours du change?**	kehl eh ler koor dew shahngzh

BANK – CURRENCY, see page 129

Where is ...? *Où est ...?*

Where is the ...?	**Où est ...?**	oo eh
booking office	**le bureau de réservation**	ler bewroa der rayzehrvahssyawng
car hire	**l'agence de location de voitures**	lahzhahngss der lokah-ssyawng der vwahtewr
duty-free shop	**le magasin hors-taxe**	ler mahgahzang or tahks
newsstand	**le kiosque à journaux**	ler kyosk ah zhoornoa
restaurant	**le restaurant**	ler rehstoarahng
How do I get to ...?	**Comment puis-je aller à ...?**	kommahng pweezh ahlay ah
Is there a bus into town?	**Y a-t-il un bus pour aller en ville?**	ee ahteel ang bewss poor ahlay ahng veel
Where can I get a taxi?	**Où puis-je trouver un taxi?**	oo pweezh troovay ang taxi
Where can I hire a car?	**Où puis-je louer une voiture?**	oo pweezh looay ewn vwahtewr

Hotel reservation *Réservation d'hôtel*

Do you have a hotel guide?	**Avez-vous un guide des hôtels?**	ahvay voo ang geed day zoatehl
Could you reserve a room for me at a hotel/boarding house?	**Pourriez-vous me réserver une chambre dans un hôtel/une pension?**	pooryay voo mer rayzehrvay ewn shahngbr dahng zang noatehl/zewn pahngssyawng
in the centre	**dans le centre**	dahng ler sahngtr
near the railway station	**près de la gare**	preh der lah gahr
a single room	**une chambre pour une personne**	ewn shahngbr poor ewn pehrson
a double room	**une chambre pour deux personnes**	ewn shahngbr poor dur pehrson
not too expensive	**pas trop chère**	pah troa shehr
Where is the hotel/boarding house?	**Où est l'hôtel/la pension?**	oo eh loatehl/lah pahngssyawng
Do you have a street map?	**Avez-vous un plan de ville?**	ahvay voo ang plahng der veel

HOTEL/ACCOMMODATION, see page 22

Car hire (rental)   *Location de voitures*

To hire a car you must produce a valid driving licence (held for at least one year) and your passport. Some firms set a minimum age at 21, other 25. Holders of major credit cards are normally exempt from deposit payments, otherwise you must pay a substantial (refundable) deposit for a car. Third-party insurance is usually automatically included.

I'd like to hire (rent) a car.	**Je voudrais louer une voiture.**	zher voodreh looay ewn vwahtewr
small car	**une petite voiture**	ewn perteet vwahtewr
medium-sized car	**une voiture moyenne**	ewn vwahtewr mwahyehn
large car	**une grande voiture**	ewn grahngd vwahtewr
automatic car	**une voiture automatique**	ewn vwahtewr oatomahteek
I'd like it for a day/ a week.	**Je l'utiliserai un jour/ une semaine.**	zher lewteeleezerray ang zhoor/ewn sermehn
Are there any week-end arrangements?	**Existe-t-il des forfaits de fin de semaine?**	ehxeest teel day forfeh der fang der sermehn
Do you have any special rates?	**Proposez-vous des tarifs spéciaux?**	propoazay voo day tahreef spayssyoa
What's the charge per day/week?	**Quel est le tarif par jour/semaine?**	kehl eh ler tahreef pahr zhoor/sermehn
Is mileage included?	**Le kilométrage est-il compris?**	ler keeloamehtrahzh ehteel kawngpree
What's the charge per kilometre?	**Quel est le tarif par kilomètre?**	kehl eh ler tahreef pahr keeloamehtr
I want to hire the car here and leave it in ...	**Je voudrais prendre la voiture ici et la rendre à ...**	zher voodreh prahngdr lah vwahtewr eessee ay lah rahngdr ah
I want full insurance.	**Je voudrais une assurance tous risques.**	zher voodreh zewn ahssewrahngss too reesk
What's the deposit?	**A combien s'élève la caution?**	ah kawngbyang saylehv lah koassyawng
I've a credit card.	**J'ai une carte de crédit.**	zhay ewn kahrt der kraydee
Here's my driving licence	**Voici mon permis de conduire.**	vwahssee mawng pehrmee der kawngdweer

CAR, see page 75

Taxi *Taxi*

Taxis are clearly marked and available in all the larger towns. If the cab is unmetered, or you have a fair distance to go, ask the fare beforehand. Special rates for night journeys, baggage etc. should be posted on an official fare chart.

Where can I get a taxi?	Où puis-je trouver un taxi?	oo pweezh troovay ang tahksee
Please get me a taxi.	Appelez-moi un taxi, s'il vous plaît.	ahperlay mwah ang tahksee seel voo pleh
What's the fare to ...?	Quel est le tarif pour ...?	kehl eh ler tahreef poor
How far is it to ...?	A quelle distance se trouve ...?	ah kehl deestahngss ser troov
Take me to ...	Conduisez-moi ...	kawngdweezay mwah
this address	à cette adresse	ah seht ahdrehss
the airport	à l'aéroport	ah lahayropor
the town centre	au centre de la ville	oa sahngtr der lah veel
the ... Hotel	à l'hôtel ...	ah loatehl
the railway station	à la gare	ah lah gahr
Turn ... at the next corner.	Tournez ... au prochain coin de rue.	toornay ... oa proshang kwang der rew
left/right	à gauche/à droite	ah goash/ah drwaht
Go straight ahead.	Tout droit.	too drwah
Please stop here.	Arrêtez-vous ici, s'il vous plaît.	ahrehtay voo eessee seel voo pleh
I'm in a hurry.	Je suis pressé(e).	zher swee prehssay
Could you drive more slowly?	Pourriez-vous conduire moins vite, s'il vous plaît?	pooryay voo kawngdweer mwang veet seel voo pleh
Could you help me carry my luggage?	Pouvez-vous m'aider à porter mes bagages, s'il vous plaît?	poovay voo mehday ah portay may bahgahzh seel voo pleh
Could you wait for me?	Pourriez-vous m'attendre?	pooryay voo mahtahngdr
I'll be back in 10 minutes.	Je serai de retour dans 10 minutes.	zher serray der rertoor dahng 10 meenewt

TIPPING, see inside back-cover

Hotel—Other accommodation

Early reservation and confirmation are essential in most major tourist centres during the high season. Most towns and arrival points have a tourist information office (*le syndicat d'initiative*—ler sangdeekah deeneessyahteev), and that's the place to go if you're stuck without a room.

Hôtel
(oatehl)

Hotels are officially classified into five categories by the *Direction du Tourisme*. Room prices, fixed according to amenities, size and to the hotel's star rating, must be posted visibly at reception desks and behind each room door. *Hôtel garni* means that only a room and breakfast are offered.

Note: Hôtel de Ville is not a hotel, but the town hall.

Château-Hôtel
(shahtoa oatehl)

A chain of castles and mansions covering all of France and offering many tempting possibilities. All are four-star establishments.

Relais de campagne
(rerleh der kahngpahñ)

A similar chain offering a wider variety of hotels in country settings, from two- to four-star establishments. Some are genuine, old-time stagecoach inns. Both *châteaux-hôtels* and *relais* are listed jointly in a free booklet published annually.

**Logis de France/
Auberge rurale**
(lozhee der frahngss/
oabehrzh rewrahl)

Government-sponsored hotels, often on the outskirts or outside of towns. *Logis de France* are in the one- and two-star bracket; *auberges rurales* are three- or four-star establishments.

Motel
(motehl)

Motels are being increasingly found near motorways (expressways) and other major roads.

Auberge
(oabehrzh)

A country inn providing simple accommodation at economical boarding rates.

Pension
(pahngssyawng)

Boarding house offering full or half board.

**Auberge de
jeunesse**
(oabehrzh der
zhurnehss)

Youth hostel; in season, some local student associations operate dormitories to accommodate the influx of foreign students.

Checking in—Reception *A la réception*

My name is ...	**Je m'appelle ...**	zher mahpehl
I've a reservation.	**J'ai fait réserver.**	zhay feh rayzehrvay
We've reserved two rooms, a single and a double.	**Nous avons réservé deux chambres – une pour une personne, et l'autre pour deux.**	noo zahvawng rayzehrvay dur shahngbr – ewn poor ewn pehrson ay loatr poor dur
Here's the confirmation.	**Voici la confirmation.**	vwahssee lah kawngfeermahssyawng
Do you have any vacancies?	**Avez-vous des chambres disponibles?**	ahvay voo day shahngbr deesponeebl
I'd like a ... room ...	**Je voudrais une chambre ...**	zher voodreh ewn shahngbr
single	**pour une personne**	poor ewn pehrson
double	**pour deux personnes**	poor dur pehrson
with twin beds	**avec des lits jumeaux**	ahvehk day lee zhewmoa
with a double bed	**avec un grand lit**	ahvehk ang grahng lee
with a bath	**avec salle de bains**	ahvehk sahl der bang
with a shower	**avec douche**	ahvehk doosh
with a balcony	**avec balcon**	ahvehk bahlkawng
with a view	**avec vue**	ahvehk vew
We'd like a room ...	**Nous voudrions une chambre ...**	noo voodreeyawng ewn shahngbr
in the front	**qui donne sur la rue**	kee don sewr lah rew
at the back	**qui donne sur la cour**	kee don sewr lah koor
facing the sea	**qui donne sur la mer**	kee don sewr lah mehr
It must be quiet.	**Une chambre tranquille.**	ewn shahngbr trahngkeel
Is there ...?	**Y a-t-il ...?**	ee ahteel
air conditioning	**la climatisation**	lah kleemahteezahssyawng
heating	**le chauffage**	ler shoafahzh
a radio/television in the room	**un poste de radio/ télévision dans la chambre**	ang post der rahdyoa/ taylayveezyawng dahng lah shahngbr
a laundry service	**une blanchisserie**	ewn blahngsheesserree
room service	**le service d'étage**	ler sehrveess daytahzh
hot water	**l'eau chaude**	loa shoad
running water	**l'eau courante**	loa koorahngt
a private toilet	**des toilettes privées**	day twahleht preevay

CHECKING OUT, see page 31

| Could you put an extra bed in the room? | **Pourriez-vous installer un autre lit dans la chambre?** | pooryay voo angstahllay ang noatr lee dahng lah shahngbr |

How much? *Combien?*

What's the price ...?	**Quel est le prix ...?**	kehl eh ler pree
per night	**par nuit**	pahr nwee
per week	**par semaine**	pahr sermehn
for bed and breakfast	**avec petit déjeuner**	ahvehk pertee dayzhurnay
excluding meals	**sans les repas**	sahng lay rerpah
for full board (A.P.)	**en pension complète**	ahng pahngssyawng kawngpleht
for half board (M.A.P.)	**en demi-pension**	ahng dermee pahngssyawng
Does that include ...?	**Ce prix comprend-il ...?**	ser pree kawngprahng teel
breakfast	**le petit déjeuner**	ler pertee dayzhurnay
service	**le service**	ler sehrveess
value-added tax (VAT)*	**la T.V.A.**	lah tay-vay-ah
Is there any reduction for children?	**Y a-t-il une réduction pour les enfants?**	ee ahteel ewn raydewksyawng poor lay zahngfahng
Do you charge for the baby?	**Faut-il payer pour le bébé?**	foateel pehyay poor ler baybay
That's too expensive.	**C'est trop cher.**	seh troa shehr
Haven't you anything cheaper?	**N'avez-vous rien de meilleur marché?**	nahvay voo ryang der mehyurr mahrshay

How long? *Combien de temps?*

We'll be staying ...	**Nous resterons ...**	noo rehsterrawng
overnight only	**juste cette nuit**	zhewst seht nwee
a few days	**quelques jours**	kehlker zhoor
a week (at least)	**une semaine (au moins)**	ewn sermehn (oa mwang)
I don't know yet.	**Je ne sais pas encore.**	zher ner seh pah zahngkor

---

* Americans note: a type of sales tax in Belgium and France

NUMBERS, see page 147

Decision *Décision*

May I see the room?	**Puis-je voir la chambre?**	pweezh vwahr lah shahngbr
That's fine. I'll take it.	**D'accord. Je la prends.**	dahkor. zher lah prahng
No. I don't like it.	**Non, elle ne me plaît pas.**	nawng ehl ner mer pleh pah
It's too ...	**Elle est trop ...**	ehl eh troa
cold/hot	**froide/chaude**	frwahd/shoad
dark/small	**sombre/petite**	sawngbr/perteet
noisy	**bruyante**	brweeyahngt
I asked for a room with a bath.	**J'avais demandé une chambre avec salle de bains.**	zhahveh dermahngday ewn shahngbr ahvehk sahl der bang
Do you have anything ...?	**Avez-vous quelque chose ...?**	ahvay voo kehlker shoaz
better	**de mieux**	der myur
bigger	**de plus grand**	der plew grahng
cheaper	**de meilleur marché**	der mehyurr mahrshay
quieter	**de plus tranquille**	der plew trahngkeel
Do you have a room with a better view?	**Auriez-vous une chambre avec une meilleure vue?**	oaryay voo ewn shahngbr ahvehk ewn mehyurr vew

Registration *Enregistrement*

Upon arrival at a hotel or boarding house you'll be asked to fill in a registration form (*une fiche*—ewn feesh).

Nom/Prénom	Name/First name
Lieu de domicile/Rue/N°	Home address/Street/Number
Nationalité/Profession	Nationality/Profession
Date/Lieu de naissance	Date/Place of birth
Venant de .../Allant à ...	From .../To...
Numéro du passeport	Passport number
Lieu/Date	Place/Date
Signature	Signature

What does this mean?	**Que signifie ceci?**	ker seeñeefee serssee

Votre passeport, s'il vous plaît.	May I see your passport, please?
Voudriez-vous remplir cette fiche?	Would you mind filling in this registration form?
Signez ici, s'il vous plaît.	Please sign here.
Combien de temps resterez-vous?	How long will you be staying?

What's my room number?	**Quel est le numéro de ma chambre?**	kehl eh ler newmehroa der mah shahngbr
Will you have our luggage sent up?	**Pouvez-vous faire monter nos bagages?**	poovay voo fehr mawngtay noa bahgahzh
Where can I park my car?	**Où puis-je garer ma voiture?**	oo pweezh gahray mah vwahtewr
Does the hotel have a garage?	**L'hôtel a-t-il un garage?**	loatehl ahteel ang gahrahzh
I'd like to leave this in your safe.	**Je voudrais déposer ceci dans votre coffre-fort.**	zher voodreh daypoazay serssee dahng votr kofr for

Hotel staff   *Personnel hôtelier*

hall porter	**le concierge**	ler kawngssyehrzh
maid	**la femme de chambre**	lah fahm der shahngbr
manager	**le directeur**	ler deerehkturr
page (bellboy)	**le chasseur**	ler shahssurr
porter	**le bagagiste**	ler bahgahzheest
receptionist	**le réceptionnaire**	ler rayssehpssyonnehr
switchboard operator	**la standardiste**	lah stahngdahrdeest
waiter	**le garçon**	ler gahrsawng
waitress	**la serveuse**	lah sehrvurz

Call the members of the staff *madame* (mahdahm), *mademoiselle* (mahdmwahzehl) or *monsieur* (mursyur). Address the waiter as *garçon* (gahrsawng) when calling for service.

General requirements *Questions générales*

The key, please.	**La clé, s'il vous plaît.**	lah klay seel voo pleh
Will you please wake me at ...?	**Pourriez-vous me réveiller à ...?**	pooryay voo mer ray-vehyay ah
Is there a bath on this floor?	**Y a-t-il une salle de bains à cet étage?**	ee ahteel ewn sahl der bang ah seht aytahzh
What's the voltage here?	**Quel est le voltage?**	kehl eh ler voltahzh
Where's the socket (outlet) for the shaver?	**Où est la prise pour le rasoir?**	oo eh lah preez poor ler rahzwahr
Can you find me a ...?	**Pouvez-vous me procurer ...?**	poovay voo mer prokewray
babysitter	**une garde d'enfants**	ewn gahrd dahngfahng
secretary	**une secrétaire**	ewn serkraytehr
typewriter	**une machine à écrire**	ewn mahsheen ah aykreer
May I have a/an/ some ...?	**Puis-je avoir ...?**	pweezh ahvwahr
ashtray	**un cendrier**	ang sahngdryay
bath towel	**une serviette de bain**	ewn sehrvyeht der bang
extra blanket	**une couverture supplémentaire**	ewn koovehrtewr sewplay-mahngtehr
envelopes	**des enveloppes**	day zahngverlop
(more) hangers	**(d'autres) cintres**	(doatr) sangtr
hot-water bottle	**une bouillotte**	ewn booyot
ice cubes	**des glaçons**	day glahssawng
extra pillow	**encore un oreiller**	ahngkor ang norehyay
needle and thread	**une aiguille et du fil**	ewn aygweey ay dew feel
reading-lamp	**une lampe de chevet**	ewn lahngp der sherveh
soap	**du savon**	dew sahvawng
writing-paper	**du papier à lettres**	dew pahpyay ah lehtr
Where's the ...?	**Où est ...?**	oo eh
bathroom	**la salle de bains**	lah sahl der bang
dining-room	**la salle à manger**	lah sahl ah mahngzhay
emergency exit	**la sortie de secours**	lah sortee der serkoor
hairdresser's	**le salon de coiffure**	ler sahlawng der kwahfewr
lift (elevator)	**l'ascenseur**	lahssahngssurr
Where are the toilets?	**Où sont les toilettes?**	oo sawng lay twahleht

BREAKFAST, see page 38

Telephone—Post (mail)   *Téléphone – Courrier*

Can you get me Paris..., please.	**Passez-moi le... à Paris, s'il vous plaît.**	pahssay mwah ler... ah pahree seel voo pleh
Do you have stamps?	**Avez-vous des timbres?**	ahvay voo day tangbr
Would you please mail this for me?	**Pourriez-vous mettre ceci à la poste?**	pooryay voo mehtr ser-ssee ah lah post
Is there any mail for me?	**Y a-t-il du courrier pour moi?**	ee ahteel dew kooryay poor mwah
Are there any messages for me?	**Y a-t-il des messages pour moi?**	ee ahteel day mehssahzh poor mwah
How much are my telephone charges?	**A combien se monte ma note de téléphone?**	ah kawngbyang ser mawngt mah not der taylayfon

Difficulties   *Difficultés*

The ... doesn't work.	**... ne fonctionne pas.**	ner fawngksyon pah
air conditioner	**le climatiseur**	ler kleemahteezurr
bidet	**le bidet**	ler beedeh
fan	**le ventilateur**	ler vahngteelahturr
heating	**le chauffage**	ler shoafahzh
light	**la lumière**	lah lewmyehr
radio	**la radio**	lah rahdyoa
television	**la télévision**	lah taylayveezyawng
The tap (faucet) is dripping.	**Le robinet fuit.**	ler robeeneh fwee
There's no hot water.	**Il n'y a pas d'eau chaude.**	eel nee ah pah doa shoad
The wash-basin is blocked.	**Le lavabo est bouché.**	ler lahvahboa eh booshay
The window is jammed.	**La fenêtre est coincée.**	lah fernehtr eh kwangssay
The curtains are stuck.	**Les rideaux sont coincés.**	lay reedoa sawng kwangssay
The bulb is burned out.	**L'ampoule est grillée.**	lahngpool eh greeyay
My room has not been made up.	**Ma chambre n'a pas été faite.**	mah shahngbr nah pah aytay feht

POST OFFICE AND TELEPHONE, see page 132

The ... is broken.	... est cassé(e).	eh kahssay
blind	le store	ler stor
lamp	la lampe	lah lahngp
plug	la fiche	lah feesh
shutter	le volet	ler voleh
switch	l'interrupteur	langtehrewpturr
Can you get it repaired?	Pouvez-vous le faire réparer?	poovay voo ler fehr raypahray

Laundry—Dry cleaner's *Blanchisserie – Teinturerie*

I want these clothes ...	Je voudrais faire ... ces vêtements.	zher voodreh fehr ... say vehtermahng
cleaned	nettoyer	nehtwahhyay
ironed	repasser	rerpahssay
pressed	repasser à la vapeur	rerpahssay ah lah vahpurr
washed	laver	lahvay
When will they be ready?	Quand seront-ils prêts?	kahng serrawng teel preh
I need them ...	Il me les faut ...	eel mer lay foa
today	aujourd'hui	oazhoordwee
tonight	ce soir	ser swahr
tomorrow	demain	dermang
before Friday	avant vendredi	ahvahng vahngdrerdee
Can you ... this?	Pouvez-vous ... ceci?	poovay voo ... serssee
mend	raccommoder	rahkommoday
patch	rapiécer	rahpyayssay
stitch	recoudre	rerkoodr
Can you sew on this button?	Pouvez-vous coudre ce bouton?	poovay voo koodr ser bootawng
Can you get this stain out?	Pouvez-vous faire partir cette tache?	poovay voo fehr pahrteer seht tahsh
Is my laundry ready?	Mon linge est-il prêt?	mawng langzh ehteel preh
This isn't mine.	Ce n'est pas à moi.	ser neh pah zah mwah
There's something missing.	Il me manque quelque chose.	eel mer mahngk kehlker shoaz
There's a hole in this.	Ce vêtement a un trou.	ser vehtermahng ah ang troo

Hairdresser—Barber *Coiffeur*

Is there a hairdresser/ beauty salon in the hotel?	Y a-t-il un coiffeur/ salon de beauté à l'hôtel?	ee ahteel ang kwahfurr/ salawng der boatay ah loatehl
Can I make an appointment for sometime on Thursday?	Puis-je prendre rendez-vous pour jeudi?	pweezh prahngdr rahngday voo poor zhurdee
I'd like it cut and shaped.	Je voudrais une coupe et une mise en plis.	zher voodreh ewn koop eh ewn meez ahng plee
I want a haircut, please.	Une coupe de cheveux, s'il vous plaît.	ewn koop der shervur seel voo pleh
bleach	une décoloration	ewn daykolorahssyawng
blow-dry	un brushing	ang ''brushing''
colour rinse	une coloration	ewn kolorahssyawng
dye	une teinture	ewn tangtewr
face-pack	un masque de beauté	ang mahsk der boatay
manicure	une manucure	ewn mahnewkewr
permanent wave	une permanente	ewn pehrmahnahngt
setting lotion	un fixatif	ang feeksahteef
shampoo and set	un shampooing et une mise en plis	ang shahngpwang eh ewn meez ahng plee
with a fringe (bangs)	avec une frange	ahvehk ewn frahngzh
I'd like a shampoo for ... hair.	Je voudrais un shampooing pour ...	zher voodreh ang shahngpwang poor
normal/dry/ greasy (oily)	cheveux normaux/ secs/gras	shervur normoa/ sehk/grah
Do you have a colour chart?	Avez-vous un nuancier?	ahvay voo ang newahngssya
Don't cut it too short.	Pas trop court, s'il vous plaît.	pah troa koor seel voo pleh
A little more off the ...	Dégagez un peu plus ...	daygahzhay ang pur plewss
back	derrière	dehryehr
neck	la nuque	lah newk
sides	les côtés	lay koatay
top	le haut de la tête	ler oa der lah teht
I don't want any hairspray.	Je ne veux pas de laque.	zher ner vur pah der lahk

DAYS OF THE WEEK, see page 151

I'd like a shave.	**Je voudrais me faire raser.**	zher voodreh mer fehr rahzay
Would you please trim my ...?	**Pourriez-vous me rafraîchir ...?**	pooryay voo mer rahfrehsheer
beard	**la barbe**	lah bahrb
moustache	**la moustache**	lah moostash
sideboards (sideburns)	**les favoris**	lay fahvorree

Checking out *Départ*

May I please have my bill?	**Puis-je avoir ma note, s'il vous plaît?**	pweezh ahvwahr mah not seel voo pleh
I'm leaving early in the morning. Please have my bill ready.	**Je pars demain de bonne heure. Veuillez préparer ma note.**	zher pahr dermang der bonurr. vuryay praypahray mah not
We'll be checking out around noon.	**Nous partirons vers midi.**	noo pahrteerawng vehr meedee
I must leave at once.	**Je dois partir immédiatement.**	zher dwah pahrteer eemaydyahtermahng
Is everything included?	**Tout est compris?**	too teh kawngpree
Can I pay by credit card?	**Puis-je payer avec une carte de crédit?**	pweezh pehyay ahvehk ewn kahrt der kraydee
You've made a mistake in this bill, I think.	**Je crois qu'il y a une erreur dans la note.**	zher krwah keel ee ah ewn ehrurr dahng lah not
Can you get us a taxi?	**Pouvez-vous nous appeler un taxi?**	poovay voo noo zahperlay ang tahksee
Would you send someone to bring down our luggage?	**Pourriez-vous faire descendre nos bagages?**	pooryay voo fehr dehssahngdr noa bahgahzh
Here's the forwarding address.	**Faites suivre mon courrier à cette adresse.**	feht sweevr mawng kooryay ah seht ahdrehss
You have my home address.	**Vous avez mon adresse habituelle.**	voo zahvay mawng nahdrehss ahbeetewehl
It's been a very enjoyable stay.	**Le séjour a été très agréable.**	ler sayzhoor ah aytay treh zahgrayahbl

TIPPING, see inside back-cover

Camping *Camping*

Camping is extremely popular and very well organized in France. The sites are classified from one to four stars depending on their amenities. In the summer season, it's important to book in advance. If you camp on private property, ask the landowner for permission. A *camping interdit* notice means the site is forbidden to campers.

Is there a camp site near here?	**Y a-t-il un camping près d'ici?**	ee ahteel ang kahngpeeng preh deessee
Can we camp here?	**Pouvons-nous camper ici?**	poovawng noo kahngpay eessee
Have you room for a tent/caravan (trailer)?	**Avez-vous de la place pour une tente/une caravane?**	ahvay voo der lah plahss poor ewn tahngt/ewn kahrahvahn
What's the charge ...?	**Quel est le tarif ...?**	kehl eh ler tahreef
per day	**par jour**	pahr zhoor
per person	**par personne**	pahr pehrson
for a car	**par voiture**	pahr vwahtewr
for a tent	**par tente**	pahr tahngt
for a caravan (trailer)	**par caravane**	pahr kahrahvahn
Is the tourist tax included?	**La taxe de séjour est-elle comprise?**	lah tahks der sayzhoor ehtehl kawngpreez
Is there/Are there (a) ...?	**Y a-t-il ...?**	ee ahteel
drinking water	**l'eau potable**	loa potahbl
electricity	**l'électricité**	laylehktreesseetay
playground	**un terrain de jeu**	ang tehrrang der zhur
restaurant	**un restaurant**	ang rehstoarahng
shopping facilities	**des commerces**	day kommehrs
swimming pool	**une piscine**	ewn peesseen
Where are the showers/toilets?	**Où sont les douches/ toilettes?**	oo sawng lay doosh/twahleht
Where can I get butane gas?	**Où puis-je trouver du butane?**	oo pweezh troovay dew bewtahn
Is there a youth hostel near here?	**Y a-t-il une auberge de jeunesse dans les environs?**	ee ahteel ewn oabehrzh der zhurnehss dahng lay zahngveerawng

CAMPING EQUIPMENT, see page 106

Eating out

There are many types of places where you can eat and drink.

Auberge
(oabehrzh)

An inn, often in the country; serves full meals and drink.

Bar
(bahr)

Bar; can be found on virtually every street corner; coffee and drinks served, sometimes light meals, too.

Bar à café
(bahr ah kahfay)

Coffee shop; alcoholic beverages aren't served, but light meals are (Switzerland).

Bistrot
(beestroa)

The nearest equivalent to an English pub or an American tavern though the atmosphere may be very different; usually only serves a few "dishes of the day", sometimes the choice is bigger.

Brasserie
(brahsserree)

A large café serving food and drink.

Buffet
(bewfeh)

A restaurant found in principal train stations; food is generally quite good.

Cabaret
(kahbahreh)

Features supper and show including song and dance acts, vaudeville patter and political satire.

Café
(kahfay)

Nowadays, a lot of cafés serve snacks and complete meals. At least you'll be able to get a crescent roll with your morning coffee. Cafés always serve beer, wine and liquor but don't ask for any fancy cocktails or highballs.

Carnotzet
(kahrnotzeh)

A cozy cellar restaurant found in French-speaking Switzerland; cheese specialities like *fondue* (fawngdew) and *raclette* (rahkleht) are the principal fare as well as locally produced cured, dried beef, sausages and the region's wine.

Hostellerie
(ostehlerree)

A handsome country restaurant furnished in a traditional style; the cuisine will usually please a gourmet's palate but the prices may be a bit steep.

Relais (de campagne)
(rerleh [der kahngpahñ])

A country inn; menus range from a snack to a banquet; food can be superb.

Restaurant
(rehstoarahng)

These are rated by scores of professional and amateur gourmets. You'll encounter restaurants classified by stars, forks and knives and endorsed by everyone including travel agencies, automobile associations and gastronomic guilds. Bear in mind that any form of classification is relative.

Restoroute
(rehstoaroot)

A large restaurant just off a motorway (expressway); table and/or cafeteria service is available.

Rôtisserie
(roateesserree)

Originally, such restaurants specialized in grilled meats and chicken. Today the word is frequently used synonymously with *restaurant*. You can usually count on a *rôtisserie* being smart and a bit on the expensive side.

Routier
(rootyay)

Roughly equivalent to a roadside diner; the food is simple but can be surprisingly good if you happen to hit upon the right place.

Salon de thé
(sahlawng der tay)

(*Tea-Room,* in Switzerland). Serves ice-cream and pastries in addition to nonalcoholic beverages. Some even serve snacks and full meals.

Snack bar

The French have taken over the word though you may see *buffet-express* (bewfeh ehxprehss) which is the same type of place.

Meal times *Heures de repas*

Breakfast (*le petit déjeuner*—ler pertee dayzhurnay): from 7 to 10 a.m.

Lunch (*le déjeuner*—ler dayzhurnay) is generally served from noon until 2 p.m.

Dinner (*le dîner*—ler deenay) is usually served later than at home, seldom beginning before 8 p.m. and until around 10.

The French like to linger over a meal, so service may seem on the leisurely side.

French cuisine *Cuisine française*

In 1825, Brillat-Savarin, a well-known gastronomic writer, declared that "cookery is the oldest form of art"; this is truly illustrated by the French, who have developed their culinary skills with brio throughout the centuries. There are few countries in the world where you can spend more delightful hours just eating. For, apart from many regional specialities which do ample justice to the local produce, you can sample, among others, gastronomic *haute cuisine*—sophisticated dishes made according to time-honoured recipes—or *nouvelle cuisine,* where a more refined preparation enhances the delicate flavours of the food. But most restaurants offer homely cooking and well-balanced, tasty menus: *hors-d'œuvre,* main dish, cheese and/or dessert. As for the famous French wines—they certainly live up to their reputation!

Que prendrez-vous?	What would you like?
Je vous recommande ceci.	I recommend this.
Que boirez-vous?	What would you like to drink?
Nous n'avons pas ...	We haven't got ...
Voulez-vous ...?	Do you want ...?

Hungry? *Avez-vous faim?*

I'm hungry/I'm thirsty.	**J'ai faim/J'ai soif.**	zhay fang/zhay swahf
Can you recommend a good restaurant?	**Pouvez-vous m'indiquer un bon restaurant?**	poovay voo mangdeekay ang bawng rehstoarahng
Are there any inexpensive restaurants around here?	**Y a-t-il des restaurants bon marché dans les environs?**	ee ahteel day rehstoarahng bawng mahrshay dahng lay zahngveerawng

If you want to be sure of getting a table in well-known restaurants, it may be better to telephone in advance.

I'd like to reserve a table for 4.	Je voudrais réserver une table pour 4 personnes.	zher voodreh rayzehrvay ewn tahbl poor 4 pehrson
We'll come at 8.	Nous viendrons à 8 heures.	noo vyangdrawng ah 8 urr
Could we have a table ...?	Pouvons-nous avoir une table ...?	poovawng noo ahvwahr ewn tahbl
in the corner	dans un angle	dahng zang nahngl
by the window	près de la fenêtre	preh der lah fernehtr
outside	dehors	deror
on the terrace	sur la terrasse	sewr lah tehrahss
in a non-smoking area	dans un endroit pour non-fumeurs	dahng zang nahngdrwah po nawng fewmurr

Asking and ordering *Demandes et commandes*

Waiter/Waitress!	Garçon/ Mademoiselle!	gahrsawng/ mahdmwahzehl
I'd like something to eat/drink.	Je voudrais manger/ boire quelque chose.	zher voodreh mahngzhay/ bwahr kehlker shoaz
May I have the menu, please?	Puis-je avoir la carte?	pweezh ahvwahr lah kahrt
Do you have a set menu/local dishes?	Avez-vous un menu/ des spécialités locales?	ahvay voo ang mernew/ day spayssyahleetay lokahl
What do you recommend?	Que me recomman- dez-vous?	ker mer rerkommahngday voo
I'd like ...	Je voudrais ...	zher voodreh
Could we have a/ an ..., please?	Pourrions-nous avoir ...?	pooryawng noo ahvwahr
ashtray	un cendrier	ang sahngdryay
cup	une tasse	ewn tahss
fork	une fourchette	ewn foorsheht
glass	un verre	ang vehr
knife	un couteau	ang kootoa
napkin (serviette)	une serviette	ewn sehrvyeht
plate	une assiette	ewn ahssyeht
spoon	une cuillère	ewn kweeyehr
May I have some ...?	Pourrais-je avoir ...?	poorehzh ahvwahr
bread	du pain	dew pang
butter	du beurre	dew burr

lemon	**du citron**	dew seetrawng
mustard	**de la moutarde**	der lah mootahrd
oil	**de l'huile**	der lweel
pepper	**du poivre**	dew pwahvr
salt	**du sel**	dew sehl
seasoning	**des condiments**	day kawngdeemahng
sugar	**du sucre**	dew sewkr
vinegar	**du vinaigre**	dew veenehgr

Some useful expressions for dieters and special requirements:

I have to live on a diet.	**Je suis au régime.**	zher swee oa rayzheem
I mustn't eat food containing ...	**Je dois éviter les plats contenant ...**	zher dwah ayveetay lay plah kawngternahng
flour/fat	**de la farine/du gras**	der lah fahreen/dew grah
salt/sugar	**du sel/du sucre**	dew sehl/dew sewkr
Do you have ... for diabetics?	**Avez-vous ... pour diabétiques?**	ahvay voo ... poor dyahbayteek
cakes	**des gâteaux**	day gahtoa
fruit juice	**du jus de fruits**	dew zhew der frwee
special menu	**un menu spécial**	ang mernew spayssyahl
Do you have vegetarian dishes?	**Avez-vous des plats végétariens?**	ahvay voo day plah vayzhaytahryang
Could I have ... instead of the dessert?	**Pourrais-je avoir ... à la place du dessert?**	poorehzh avwahr ... ah lah plahss dew dehssehr
Can I have an artificial sweetener?	**Puis-je avoir de l'édulcorant?**	pweezh avwahr der laydewlkorahng

And ...

I'd like some more.	**J'en voudrais encore.**	zhahng voodreh ahngkor
Can I have more ..., please.	**Puis-je avoir encore un peu de ...**	pweezh avwahr ahngkor ang pur der
Just a small portion.	**Juste une petite portion.**	zhewst ewn perteet porsyawng
Nothing more, thanks.	**Je suis servi(e), merci.**	zher swee sehrvee mehrssee
Where are the toilets?	**Où sont les toilettes?**	oo sawng lay twahleht

Breakfast *Petit déjeuner*

The French breakfast consists of coffee, rolls (*petits pains*
—pertee pang), *croissants* (krwahssahng—flaky pastry in
the form of a crescent) and jam, seldom marmalade. Most
of the larger hotels, however, are now used to providing an
English or American breakfast.

I'd like breakfast, please.	**Je voudrais prendre mon petit déjeuner.**	zher voodreh prahngdr mawng pertee dayzhurnay
I'll have a/an/ some …	**Je prendrai …**	zher prahngdray
bacon and eggs	**des œufs au bacon**	day zur oa baykon
boiled egg	**un œuf à la coque**	ang nurf ah lah kok
soft/hard	**mollet/dur**	molleh/dewr
cereal	**des céréales**	day sayrayahl
eggs	**des œufs**	day zur
fried eggs	**des œufs au plat**	day zur oa plah
scrambled eggs	**des œufs brouillés**	day zur brooyay
fruit juice	**un jus de fruits**	ang zhew der frwee
grapefruit	**pamplemousse**	pahngplermooss
orange	**orange**	orahngzh
ham and eggs	**des œufs au jambon**	day zur oa zhahngbawng
jam	**de la confiture**	der lah kawngfeetewr
marmalade	**de la marmelade**	der lah mahrmerlahd
toast	**du pain grillé**	dew pang greeyay
yoghurt	**un yaourt/yoghourt**	ang yahoort/yogoort
May I have some …?	**Pourrais-je avoir …?**	poorehzh ahvwahr
bread	**du pain**	dew pang
butter	**du beurre**	dew burr
(hot) chocolate	**un chocolat (chaud)**	ang shokolah (shoa)
coffee	**un café**	ang kahfay
caffein-free	**décaféiné**	daykahfayeenay
black/with milk	**noir/au lait**	nwahr/oa leh
honey	**du miel**	dew myehl
milk	**du lait**	dew leh
cold/hot	**froid/chaud**	frwah/shoa
pepper	**du poivre**	dew pwahvr
rolls	**des petits pains**	day pertee pang
salt	**du sel**	dew sehl
tea	**du thé**	dew tay
with milk	**au lait**	oa leh
with lemon	**au citron**	oa seetrawng
(hot) water	**de l'eau (chaude)**	der loa (shoad)

What's on the menu? *Qu'y a-t-il au menu?*

Most restaurants display a menu *(la carte)* outside. Besides ordering à la carte, you can order a fixed-price menu *(le menu)*. Cheaper meals often run to three courses, with or without wine, but service is always included. More expensive menus stretch to four or even five courses, but hardly ever include wine. Words like *maison* or *du chef* next to a dish listed on the menu are clues that the dish is a speciality of the restaurant.

Under the headings below you'll find alphabetical lists of dishes that might be offered on a French menu with their English equivalent. You can simply show the book to the waiter. If you want some fruit, for instance, let *him* point to what's available on the appropriate list. Use pages 36 and 37 for ordering in general.

EATING OUT

Reading the menu *Pour lire la carte*

Menu à prix fixe	Set menu
Plat du jour	Dish of the day
Boisson comprise	Drink included
Le chef vous propose …	The chef proposes …
Spécialités locales	Local specialities
Garniture au choix	Choice of vegetable accompaniment
Toutes nos viandes sont servies avec une garniture	All our meat dishes are accompanied by vegetables
Supplément pour changement de garniture	Extra charge for alternative vegetable accompaniment
Sur commande	Made to order
Supplément/En sus	Extra charge
En saison	In season
Selon arrivage	When available
Attente: 15 min	Waiting time: 15 minutes
Pour deux personnes	For two

boissons	bwahssawng	drinks
crustacés	krewstahssay	shellfish
desserts	dehssehr	desserts
entrées	ahngtray	first course
fromages	fromahzh	cheese
fruits	frwee	fruit
fruits de mer	frwee der mehr	seafood
gibier	zheebyay	game
glaces	glahss	ice-cream
grillades	greeyahd	grilled meat
légumes	laygewm	vegetables
pâtes	paht	pasta
pâtisseries	pahteesserree	pastries
poissons	pwahssahng	fish
potages	potahzh	soups
riz	ree	rice
salades	sahlahd	salads
viandes	vyahngd	meat
vins	vang	wine
volailles	volahy	poultry

Restaurant

Starters (Appetizers)   *Hors-d'œuvre*

I'd like an appetizer.	**Je voudrais un hors-d'œuvre.**	zher voodreh ang ordurvr
What do you recommend?	**Que nous/me recommandez-vous?**	ker noo/mer rerkommahng-day voo

assiette anglaise	ahssyeht ahngglehz	assorted cold cuts
assiette de charcuterie	ahssyeht der shahrkewterree	assorted pork products
cervelas	sehrverlah	type of sausage
crudités	krewdeetay	mixed raw vegetable salad
hors-d'œuvre variés	ordurvr vahryay	assorted appetizers
jambon (de Bayonne)	zhahngbawng (der bahyon)	(Bayonne) ham
jambonneau	zhahngbonnoa	cured pig's knuckle
jus de tomate	zhew der tomaht	tomato juice
mortadelle	mortahdehl	Bologna sausage
œufs à la diable	ur ah lah dyahbl	devilled eggs
olives	oleev	olives
farcies/noires/ vertes	fahrsee/nwahr/ vehrt	stuffed/black/ green
saucisson	soasseessawng	cold sausage
viande séchée	vyahngd sayshay	cured dried beef

andouille(tte)
(ahngdooy [eht])
: seasoned, aromatic sausage made from tripe, served grilled or fried

bouchée à la reine
(booshay ah lah rehn)
: pastry shell usually filled with creamed sweetbreads and mushrooms

crépinette
(kraypeeneht)
: small, flat sausage, highly seasoned

pâté
(pahtay)
: an exquisite liver purée which may be blended with other meat like a *pâté de campagne*; *pâté de fois gras* indicates a fine paste of duck or goose liver, often with truffles *(truffé)*; *pâté en croûte* would be enveloped in a pastry crust.

quenelles
(kernehl)
: light dumplings made of fish, fowl or meat, served with a velvety sauce. The best known are *quenelles de brochet,* made of pike.

quiche
(keesh)
: a flan or open-faced tart with a rich, creamy filling of cheese, vegetables, meat or seafood; *quiche lorraine* (keesh lorehn), the best known of the *quiches*, is garnished with bacon.

rillettes de porc (reeyeht der por)		minced pork, cooked in its own fat and served chilled in earthenware pots
soufflé (sooflay)		a puffy, brown dish made of egg whites delicately flavoured with cheese, vegetables or seafood
terrine (tehreen)		the same as a *pâté* but sliced and served from its *terrine* (traditionally an earthenware pot). It may resemble a perfectly flavoured meat loaf and be made of any meat including game or fowl.

Salads *Salades*

A green or mixed salad is usually eaten after the main course
—never with it. Other salads may be very well ordered as a
first course.

What salads do you have?	**Quelles salades servez-vous?**	kehl sahlahd sehrvay voo
salade mêlée	sahlahd mehlay	mixed salad
salade de museau de bœuf	sahlahd der mewzoa der berf	marinated brawn (beef headcheese)
salade russe	sahlahd rewss	diced vegetable salad
salade de thon	sahlahd der tawng	tunny (tuna) salad
salade verte	sahlahd vehrt	green salad
salade niçoise (sahlahd neeswahz)		a Riviera combination salad which includes tuna, anchovies, olives and vegetables.

Omelets *Omelettes*

A classic French *omelette* isn't merely scrambled eggs but
is shaped like a smooth, slightly swelling golden oval. It
should be tender and creamy inside and served either plain
or flavoured with one or more ingredients:

omelette (nature)	omerleht (nahtewr)	(plain) omelet
aux champignons	oa shahngpeeñawng	mushroom
aux fines herbes	oa feen zehrb	herb
au fromage	oa fromahzh	cheese
au jambon	oa zhahngbawng	ham

Soups *Potages et soupes*

You may see one of any number of words for a type of soup on the menu, some of which may be main-course fare.

aïgo bouïdo	aheegoa bweedoa	garlic soup (Provençal speciality)
bisque	beesk	seafood stew (chowder)
d'écrevisses	daykrerveess	crayfish
de homard	der omahr	lobster
bouillabaisse	booyahbehss	fish and seafood stew (Marseilles speciality)
bouillon	booyawng	bouillon
de poule	der pool	chicken
consommé	kawngssommay	consommé
à l'œuf	ah lurf	with a raw egg
au porto	oa portoa	with port wine
crème	krehm	cream of ...
d'asperges	dahspehrzh	asparagus
de bolets	der boleh	boletus mushrooms
de volaille	der volahy	chicken
garbure	gahrbewr	cabbage soup, often with salt pork or preserved goose
pot-au-feu	po toa fur	stew of meat and vegetables
potage	potahzh	soup
à l'ail	ah lahy	garlic
au cresson	oa krehssawng	watercress
bonne femme	bon fahm	potato, leek and sometimes bacon
Condé	kawngday	mashed red beans
julienne	zhewlyehn	shredded vegetables
Parmentier	pahrmahngtyay	potato
soupe	soop	soup
à l'ail	ah lahy	garlic
aux choux	oa shoo	cabbage
du jour	dew zhoor	day's soup
à l'oignon	ah lonyawng	French onion soup
au pistou	oa peestoo	Provençal vegetable soup
velouté	verlootay	cream of ...
de tomates	der tomaht	tomato
de volaille	der volahy	chicken

Fish and seafood *Poissons et fruits de mer*

Don't miss the opportunity to sample some of the wide variety of fresh fish and seafood in coastal areas. Fish is most commonly baked or poached until just done, then dressed with a delicate sauce. Trout are often made *au bleu* which means they're freshly poached in a simmering bouillon.

I'd like some fish.	**Je voudrais du poisson.**	zher voodreh dew pwahssawng
What kinds of seafood do you have?	**Quel genre de fruits de mer servez-vous?**	kehl zhahngr der frwee der mehr sehrvay voo
aiglefin (aigrefin)	ehglerfang	haddock
anchois	ahngshwah	anchovies
anguille	ahnggeey	eel
bar	bahr	bass
barbue	bahrbew	brill
baudroie	boadrwah	angler
blanchaille	blahngshahy	whitebait
brochet	brosheh	pike
cabillaud	kahbeeyoa	(fresh) cod
calmars	kahlmahr	squid
carpe	kahrp	carp
carrelet	kahrerleh	plaice
crabe	krahb	crab
crevettes	krerveht	shrimp
cuisses de grenouilles	kweess der grernooy	frog's legs
daurade	doarahd	sea bream
écrevisses	aykrerveess	crayfish
éperlans	aypehrlahng	smelt
escargots	ehskahrgoa	snails
féra	fayrah	lake salmon
goujons	goozhawng	gudgeon
grondin	grawngdang	gurnet
harengs	ahrahng	herring
homard	omahr	lobster
huîtres	weetr	oysters
lamproie	lahngprwah	lamprey
langouste	lahnggoost	spiny lobster
langoustines	lahnggoosteen	Dublin bay prawns, scampi
lotte	lot	burbot
lotte de mer	lot der mehr	angler

loup	loo	sea bass
maquereau	mahkerroa	mackerel
merlan	mehrlahng	whiting
morue	morew	cod
moules	mool	mussels
omble (chevalier)	awngbl (shervahlyay)	char
palourdes	pahloord	clams
perche	pehrsh	perch
plie	plee	plaice
poulpes	poolp	octopus
rascasse	rahskahss	fish used in *bouillabaisse*
rouget	roozheh	red mullet
sardines	sahrdeen	sardines
saumon	soamawng	salmon
scampi	skahngpee	prawns
sole	sol	sole
thon	tawng	tunny (tuna)
truite	trweet	trout
turbot	tewrboa	turbot

baked	**au four**	oa foor
fried	**frit**	free
grilled	**grillé**	greeyay
marinated	**mariné**	mahreenay
poached	**poché**	poshay
sautéed	**sauté**	soatay
smoked	**fumé**	fewmay
steamed	**cuit à la vapeur**	kwee ah lah vahpurr

bourride
(boorreed)
fish stew (chowder) from Marseilles

brandade de morue
(brahngdahd der morew)
creamed salt cod

coquilles St-Jacques
(kokeey sang zhahk)
scallops served in a creamy sauce on the half shell

homard à l'américaine
(omahr ah lahmayree-kehn)
sautéed diced lobster, flamed in cognac and then simmered in wine, aromatic vegetables, herbs and tomatoes

matelote
(mahterlot)
fish (especially eel) stew with wine

Meat *Viandes*

I'd like some ...	Je voudrais ...	zher voodreh
beef/lamb	**du bœuf/de l'agneau**	dew burf/der lahñoa
pork/veal	**du porc/du veau**	dew por/dew voa
boulettes	booleht	meatballs
carré d'agneau	kahray dahñoa	rack of lamb
cervelle	sehrvehl	brains
charcuterie	shahrkewterree	assorted pork products
cochon de lait	koshawng der leh	suck(l)ing pig
côte	koat	rib
côtelettes	koaterleht	chops
épaule	aypoal	shoulder
escalope	ehskahlop	cutlet, scallop
foie	fwah	liver
gigot	zheegoa	leg
jambon	zhahngbawng	ham
jambonneau	zhahngbonnoa	pig's knuckle
jarret	zhahreh	knuckle
langue	lahngg	tongue
lard	lahr	bacon
médaillon	maydahyawng	a tenderloin steak (lamb, pork or veal)
pieds	pyay	trotters (feet)
ris de veau	ree der voa	veal sweetbreads
rognons	roñawng	kidneys
rosbif	rosbeef	roast beef
saucisses	soasseess	sausages
selle	sehl	saddle
steak/steack	stehk	steak (always beef)

Meat is cut differently in France than at home. Here are the names of some commonly seen cuts of beef with their approximate English equivalents:

chateaubriand	shahtoabryahng	double fillet steak (tenderloin of porterhouse steak)
contre-filet	kawngtr feeleh	loin strip steak
côte de bœuf	koat der burf	T-bone steak
entrecôte	ahngtrerkoat	rib or rib-eye steak
filet	feeleh	fillet steak
tournedos	toornerdoa	tenderloin of T-bone steak

baked	**au four**	oa foor
baked in grease-proof paper	**en chemise**	ahng shermeez
boiled	**bouilli**	booyee
braised	**braisé**	brehzay
fried	**frit**	free
grilled	**grillé**	greeyay
roast	**rôti**	roatee
sautéed	**sauté**	soatay
stewed	**à l'étouffée**	ah laytoofay
very rare	**bleu**	blur
underdone (rare)	**saignant**	sehñahng
medium	**à point**	ah pwang
well-done	**bien cuit**	byang kwee

Meat dishes *Plats de viande*

In many restaurants, meat is dressed with some sort of creamy sauce or gravy—sometimes prepared at your table. Some establishments customarily serve low-calorie *nouvelle cuisine* sauces to go with their dishes.

bœuf bourguignon
(burf boorgeeñawng)
a rich beef stew with vegetables, braised in red Burgundy wine

carbon(n)ade flamande
(kahrbonnahd flah-mahngd)
beef slices and onions braised in beer (a Belgian speciality)

cassoulet toulousain
(kahssooleh tooloozang)
a casserole of white beans, mutton or salt pork, sausages and preserved goose

choucroute garnie
(shookroot gahrnee)
a mound of sauerkraut served with sausages and cured pork

ragoût
(rahgoo)
a meat stew, generally served in a delicate gravy with vegetables; *ragoût* will be followed by words like *de bœuf* which will tell you it's a beef stew

tripes à la mode de Caen
(treep ah lah mod der kahng)
tripe baked with calf's trotters (calf's feet), vegetables, apple brandy or cider

Game and poultry   *Gibier et volailles*

Chicken, duck and turkey can be found at any time of the year on a French menu. But the hunting season is a unique period in which to sample wild boar, venison or pheasant. Some game is roasted and braised with fruits and vegetables while other game is jugged and stewed. *Civet*—as in *civet de lièvre*—will tell you that the preparation has been jugged. *Terrines, pâtés* and *galantines* are often made of game or fowl. We've also listed below some other seasonal delicacies.

I'd like some game.	**Je voudrais du gibier.**	zher voodreh dew zheebyay
alouette	ahlooeht	lark
bécasse	baykahss	woodcock
bécassine	baykahsseen	snipe
cabri	kahbree	kid goat
caille	kahy	quail
canard (sauvage)	kahnahr (soavahzh)	(wild) duck
caneton	kahnertawng	duckling
cerf	sehr	venison (red deer)
chapon	shahpawng	capon
chevreuil	shervrury	venison (roe deer)
coq de bruyère	kok der brweeyehr	woodgrouse
dinde	dangd	turkey
dindonneau	dangdonnoa	young turkey (cock)
faisan	fehzahng	pheasant
grive	greev	thrush
lapin	lahpang	rabbit
lièvre	lyehvr	wild hare
marcassin	mahrkahssang	young wild boar
oie	wah	goose
ortolan	ortolahng	ortolan bunting
perdreau	pehrdroa	young partridge
perdrix	pehrdree	partridge
pigeon	peezhawng	pigeon
pigeonneau	peezhonnoa	squab
pintade	pangtahd	guinea fowl
pintadeau	pangtahdoa	young guinea cock
poularde	poolahrd	fattened pullet
poule	pool	stewing fowl
poulet	pooleh	chicken
poussin	poossang	spring chicken
sanglier	sahngglyay	wild boar

sarcelle	sahrsehl	teal
suprême de volaille	sewprehm der volahy	chicken breast
volaille	volahy	fowl

canard (or **caneton**) **à l'orange**
(kahnahr [kahnertawng] ah lorahngzh)

the best known of the French duck recipes; it's braised with oranges and orange liqueur

coq au vin
(kok oa vang)

chicken stewed in red wine. Sometimes the menu will tell exactly what kind of wine was used, for instance, *coq au Chambertin*.

poule au pot
(pool oa poa)

stewed chicken with vegetables

Vegetables   *Légumes*

artichaut	ahrteeshoa	artichoke
asperges	ahspehrzh	asparagus
aubergines	oabehrzheen	aubergines (eggplant)
betterave	behterrahv	beet(root)
bolets	boleh	boletus mushrooms
cardon	kahrdawng	cardoon
carottes	kahrot	carrots
céleri (-rave)	sehlerree (rahv)	celery root
cèpes	sehp	flap mushrooms
champignons (de Paris)	shahngpeeñawng (der pahree)	mushrooms
chicorée	sheekoray	endive (Am. chicory)
chou (rouge)	shoo (roozh)	(red) cabbage
choucroute	shookroot	sauerkraut
chou-fleur	shoo flurr	cauliflower
choux de Bruxelles	shoo der brewssehl	Brussels sprouts
concombre	kawngkawngbr	cucumber
cornichons	korneeshawng	gherkins (pickles)
courgette	koorzheht	courgette (zucchini)
cresson	krehssawng	watercress
endives	ahngdeev	chicory (Am. endive)
épinards	aypeenahr	spinach
fenouil	fernooy	fennel
fèves	fehv	broad beans
flageolets	flahzholeh	small kidney beans
haricots blancs	ahreekoa blahng	haricot beans, white kidney beans
haricots verts	ahreekoa vehr	French (green) beans

laitue	lehtew	lettuce
lentilles	lahngteey	lentils
maïs	maheess	sweet corn (corn)
morilles	moreey	morels
navets	nahveh	turnips
oignons	oñawng	onions
petits pois	pertee pwah	peas
poireaux	pwahroa	leeks
pois mange-tout	pwah mahngzh too	string-peas
poivrons	pwahvrawng	sweet peppers
pommes (de terre)	pom (der tehr)	potatoes
potiron	poteerawng	pumpkin
radis	rahdee	radishes
raifort	rayfor	horseradish
tomates	tomaht	tomatoes
truffes	trewf	truffles

- One popular vegetable dish comes from Provence:

| ratatouille | a casserole of stewed eggplant, onions, green |
| (rahtahtooy) | peppers and vegetable marrow (zucchini) |

Spices and herbs *Epices et fines herbes*

ail	ahy	garlic
aneth	ahneht	dill
anis	ahneess	aniseed
basilic	bahzeeleek	basil
cannelle	kahnehl	cinnamon
câpres	kahpr	capers
cerfeuil	sehrfery	chervil
ciboulette	seebooleht	chives
clous de girofle	kloo der zheerofl	clove
cumin	kewmang	caraway
échalote	ayshahlot	shallot
estragon	ehstrahgawng	tarragon
fines herbes	feen zehrb	mixture of herbs
gingembre	zhangzhahngbr	ginger
laurier	loryay	bay leaf
marjolaine	mahrzholehn	marjoram
menthe	mahngt	mint
moutarde	mootahrd	mustard
noix (de) muscade	nwah (der) mewskahd	nutmeg
origan	oreegahng	oregano
persil	pehrsee	parsley
piment	peemahng	pimiento

poivre	pwahvr	pepper
romarin	roamahrang	rosemary
safran	sahfrahng	saffron
sauge	soazh	sage
thym	tang	thyme

Potatoes, rice and noodles *Pommes de terre, riz et pâtes*

pâtes	paht	pasta
nouilles	nooy	noodles
pommes (de terre)	pom (der tehr)	potatoes
allumettes	ahlewmeht	matchsticks
chips	''chips''	crisps (Am. potato chips)
dauphine	doafeen	mashed in butter and egg-yolks, mixed in seasoned flour and deep-fried
duchesse	dewshehss	mashed with butter and egg-yolks
en robe des champs	ahng rob day shahng	in their jackets
frites	freet	chips (french fries)
mousseline	moosserleen	mashed
nature	natewr	boiled, steamed
nouvelles	noovehl	new
vapeur	vahpurr	steamed, boiled
riz	ree	rice
pilaf	peelahf	rice boiled in a bouillon with onions

Sauces and preparations *Sauces et préparations*

What would French cuisine be without its infinite variety of sauces, dressings and gravies? Some of them are creamy and velvety with the delicate taste of herbs, wine and other flavourings. Others are tangy and spicy. Below are a few common names of sauces and garnishes with a hint as to what they're made of.

aïoli	garlic mayonnaise
américaine	white wine, brandy, garlic, shallots, tomatoes, shrimp or lobster flavouring
béarnaise	a creamy sauce flavoured with vinegar, egg yolks, white wine, shallots, tarragon

béchamel	white sauce
beurre blanc	butter, shallots, vinegar, white wine
beurre noir	browned butter, vinegar and/or lemon juice
bigarade	with oranges
bordelaise	boletus mushrooms, red wine, shallots, beef marrow
bourguignonne	red wine, herbs
café de Paris	a butter flavoured with cognac, herbs
chasseur	wine, mushrooms, onions, shallots, herbs
chaud-froid	dressing containing gelatine
diable	hot-pepper sauce
duxelles	with mushrooms
financière	Madeira wine, truffles, olives, mushrooms
fines herbes	with herbs
florentine	with spinach
forestière	with mushrooms
hollandaise	egg yolks, butter, vinegar
indienne	curry sauce
lyonnaise	with onions
madère	with Madeira wine
maître d'hôtel	butter, parsley, lemon juice
marchand de vin	red wine, shallots
marinière	white wine, mussel broth thickened with egg yolks
meunière	brown butter, parsley, lemon juice
Mornay	cheese sauce
mousseline	mayonnaise with cream
moutarde	mustard sauce
normande	mushrooms, eggs and cream
Parmentier	with potatoes
Périgueux	with a goose—or duck—liver purée and truffles
poivrade	pepper sauce
porto	with port wine
provençale	onions, tomatoes, garlic
rémoulade	sauce flavoured with mustard and herbs
Soubise	onion-cream sauce
suprême	thickened chicken broth
tartare	mayonnaise flavoured with mustard and herbs
veloutée	thickened chicken or meat stock
verte	mayonnaise with spinach, watercress and/or herbs
vinaigrette	vinegar dressing

Cheese *Fromages*

Below are the names of just a few of the most popular cheeses of France and Switzerland.

mild	beaufort, beaumont, belle étoile, boursin, brie, cantal, comté, coulommiers, mimolette, reblochon, saint-paulin, tomme de Savoie
sharp, tangy	bleu de Bresse, camembert, livarot, fromage au marc, munster, pont-l'évêque, roquefort
goat's milk cheese	st-marcellin, valençay
Swiss cheeses	emmenthal (which we call Swiss cheese), gruyère, vacherin; Swiss cheeses are almost all mild

The following dishes in French-speaking Switzerland make a meal in themselves:

fondue (fawngdew)	a hot, bubbly mixture of melted cheese, white wine, a drop of kirsch and a hint of garlic; each guest dips a bite-size piece of bread on a fork into the pot of cheese.
raclette (rahkleht)	a half round of a firm cheese which is heated against a fire or grilled until the surface begins to melt; the melting cheese is then scraped off onto a warmed plate and eaten with boiled potatoes, gherkins and pickled pearl onions.

And here are some cheese snacks which are favourites among the French and Swiss:

croque-monsieur (krok mersyur)	toasted ham and cheese sandwich
croûte au fromage (kroot oa fromahzh)	hot, melted cheese served over a slice of toast, sometimes with ham and topped by a fried egg
ramequin (rahmerkang)	cheese ramekin (small cheese tart)
tarte au fromage (tahrt oa fromahzh)	cheese tart

Fruit *Fruits*

Fruit is generally served after the cheese.

Do you have fresh fruit?	**Avez-vous des fruits frais?**	ahvay voo day frwee freh
I'd like a (fresh) fruit cocktail.	**Je voudrais une salade de fruits (frais).**	zher voodreh ewn sahlahd der frwee (freh)

abricot	ahbreekoa	apricot
amandes	ahmahngd	almonds
ananas	ahnahnahss	pineapple
banane	bahnahn	banana
brugnon	brewñawng	nectarine
cacahouètes	kahkahooeht	peanuts
cassis	kahsseess	blackcurrants
cerises (noires)	serreez (nwahr)	(black) cherries
citron	seetrawng	lemon
dattes	daht	dates
figues	feeg	figs
fraises	frehz	strawberries
framboises	frahngbwahz	raspberries
fruits secs	frwee sehk	dried fruit
groseilles	grozehy	redcurrants
à maquereau	ah mahkerroa	gooseberries
mandarine	mahngdahreen	tangerine
marrons	mahrawng	chestnuts
melon	merlawng	melon
mûres	mewr	mulberries, blackberries
myrtilles	meerteey	bilberries, blueberries
noisettes	nwahzeht	hazelnuts
noix	nwah	walnuts
noix de coco	nwah der kokoa	coconut
orange	orahngzh	orange
pamplemousse	pahngplermooss	grapefruit
pastèque	pahstehk	watermelon
pêche	pehsh	peach
poire	pwahr	pear
pomme	pom	apple
pruneaux	prewnoa	prunes
prunes	prewn	plums
raisin	rehzang	grapes
blanc/noir	blahng/nwahr	green/blue
raisins secs	rehzang sehk	raisins
rhubarbe	rewbahrb	rhubarb

Dessert   *Desserts*

I'd like a dessert, please.	**Je prendrai un dessert, s'il vous plaît.**	zher prahngdray ang dehssehr seel voo pleh
What do you recommend?	**Que me/nous recommandez-vous?**	ker mer/noo rerkommahngday voo
Something light, please.	**Quelque chose de léger, s'il vous plaît.**	kehlker shoaz der layzhay seel voo pleh
Just a small portion.	**Une petite portion, s'il vous plaît.**	ewn perteet porsyawng seel voo pleh

barquette (bahrkeht)	small boat-shaped pastry shell garnished with fruit
crêpe suzette (krehp sewzeht)	large, thin pancakes simmered in orange juice and flambéd with orange liqueur
poire Belle Hélène (pwahr behl aylehn)	pear with vanilla ice-cream and chocolate sauce
profiterole (profeeterrol)	puff pastry filled with whipped cream or custard
sabayon (sahbahyawng)	creamy dessert of egg yolks, wine, sugar and flavouring

colonel	kolonehl	lemon (water ice) doused with vodka
coupe (glacée)	koop glahssay	often means a sundae
crème caramel	krehm kahrahmehl	caramel pudding
crème Chantilly	krehm shahngteeyee	whipped cream
flan	flahng	custard
gâteau au chocolat	gahtoa oa shokolah	chocolate cake
glace aux fraises/ à la vanille	glahss oa frehz/ah lah vahneey	strawberry/vanilla ice-cream
mousse au chocolat	mooss oa shokolah	chocolate pudding
omelette norvégienne	omerleht norvayzhyehn	baked Alaska
sorbet	sorbeh	water ice (Am. sherbet)
soufflé au Grand-Marnier	sooflay oa grahng mahrnyay	soufflé made of orange liqueur
tarte aux pommes	tahrt oa pom	apple tart (pie)
tartelette	tahrterleht	small tart
tourte	toort	layer cake
vacherin glacé	vahsherrang glahssay	ice-cream cake

Aperitifs *Apéritifs*

For most Frenchmen, the aperitif is just as important as our cocktail or highball. Often bittersweet, some aperitifs have a wine and brandy base with herbs and bitters (like Amer Picon, Byrrh, Dubonnet), others called *pastis* have an aniseed base (like Pernod, Ricard) or a vegetable base (like Cynar produced from artichoke). An aperitif may also be simply vermouth (like Noilly Prat) or a liqueur drink like *blanc-cassis* or *"kir"* (chilled white wine mixed with a black-currant syrup). An aperitif is rarely drunk neat (straight) but usually with ice or seltzer water.

I'd like a Cynar ...	**Je voudrais un Cynar ...**	zher voodreh ang seenahr
neat (straight)	**sec**	sehk
on the rocks	**avec des glaçons**	ahvehk day glahssawng
with (seltzer) water	**à l'eau (au siphon)**	ah loa (oa seefawng)

> **À VOTRE SANTÉ**
> (ah votr sahngtay)
> YOUR HEALTH!/CHEERS!

Beer *Bières*

Beer is a popular drink in some French-speaking areas. You may like to sample some of the local brews, for instance *Kronenbourg* in France, *Stella Artois* in Belgium and *Cardinal* in Switzerland.

I'd like a beer, please.	**Je voudrais une bière, s'il vous plaît.**	zher voodreh ewn byehr seel voo pleh
Do you have ... beer?	**Avez-vous de la bière ...?**	ahvay voo der lah byehr
bottled	**en bouteilles**	ahng bootehy
draught	**pression**	prehssyawng
foreign	**étrangère**	aytrahngzehr
light/dark	**blonde/brune**	blawngd/brewn

Wine *Vins*

France is the world's greatest producer of fine wine so naturally the matter is taken quite seriously. However, you needn't be frightened off by an impressive list of expensive wines. There are a few rules of thumb to bear in mind, and the rest is largely up to your personal taste.

French cuisine and wine are inseparable components. The one complements the other. The enjoyment of a delicately flavoured *pâte de foie gras,* for instance, can be all the more enhanced with the proper wine.

There are some dishes, however, with which no wine should be drunk. Don't drink wine with salads or other dishes with vinegar preparations. Combining the two could result in a strange taste. Wine doesn't necessarily accompany soup. But if wine is an ingredient in the soup, like *consommé au porto,* then you could have the same wine—port wine in that case—with your soup.

Otherwise, the time-honoured general guideline has it that white wine goes well with fish, fowl and light meats while dark meats call for a red wine. A good rosé or dry champagne goes well with almost anything and can accompany the whole meal.

Everyone's heard of *Bordeaux* (we call it claret) and *Bourgogne* (burgundy) wine. But France has hundreds of kinds of wine going all the way from its prestigious *premiers crus* to the more humble *vins ordinaires.* Don't miss the opportunity to sample local wine. Much of it doesn't travel well and is therefore never exported. The wine of each region is imbued with the character of that district.

The chart on the next page will help to identify some of the good regional wine. Fine provincial cooking is well accompanied by local wine whereas exquisite cuisine calls for a noble wine.

Restaurant

Type of wine	Examples	Accompanies
sweet white wine	best known are those in the Sauternes family; the noblest is Château-Yquem	desserts, especially custard, pudding, cake, sweet soufflé, pâté—at one time popular with oysters
light, dry white wine	Alsatian, Muscadet, Riesling, Sancerre; some types of Pouilly fumé, Pouilly-Fuissé, Chablis; local white wine and Swiss wine often fall into this category	oysters, cold meat or shellfish, grilled fish, boiled meat, egg dishes, first courses, Swiss raclette and fondue
full-bodied, dry white wine	white Burgundy, dry Côtes-du-Rhône, Graves	fish, fowl, veal served in creamy sauces, foie gras
rosé	Rosé d'Anjou	goes with almost anything but especially cold dishes, pâtés, eggs, pork, lamb
light-bodied red wine	Bordeaux from Médoc or Graves districts; a Beaujolais, local or Swiss wine often fits into this selection	roast chicken, turkey, veal, lamb, beef fillet, ham, liver, quail, pheasant, foie gras, soft-textured cheeses, stews, steaks
full-bodied red wine	any of the fine Burgundies or Châteauneuf-du-Pape; certain Bordeaux	duck, goose, kidneys, most game, tangy cheese like bleu — in short, any strong-flavoured preparations
extra dry champagne	any of this category	goes with anything, may be drunk as an aperitif or as the climax to the dinner
dry champagne	any of this category	as an aperitif, shellfish, foie gras, nuts and dried fruit
sweet champagne	any of this category	dessert and pastry

May I have the wine list, please?	**Puis-je avoir la carte des vins?**	pweezh ahvwahr lah kahrt day vang
I'd like a bottle of white/red wine.	**J'aimerais une bouteille de vin blanc/rouge.**	zhehmerreh ewn bootehy der vang blahng/roozh
a carafe	**une carafe**	ewn kahrahf
a half bottle	**une demi-bouteille**	ewn dermee bootehy
a glass	**un verre**	ang vehr
A bottle of champagne, please.	**Une bouteille de champagne, s'il vous plaît.**	ewn bootehy der shangpahñ seel voo pleh
Please bring me another ...	**Apportez-m'en encore ...**	ahportay mahng ahngkor
Where does this wine come from?	**De quelle région vient ce vin?**	der kehl rayzhyawng vyang ser vang

red	**rouge**	roozh
white	**blanc**	blahng
rosé	**rosé**	roazay
dry	**sec**	sehk
light	**léger**	layzhay
full-bodied	**corsé**	korsay
sparkling	**mousseux**	moossur
very dry	**brut**	brewt
sweet	**doux**	doo

Other alcoholic drinks *Autres boissons alcoolisées*

You'll certainly want to take the occasion to sip a fine cognac after a meal. We usually consider cognac and brandy as being synonymous. In the strict sense of the word, cognac is the famed wine-distilled brandy from the Charente-Maritime region. Try one of these: *Courvoisier, Hennessy, Rémy-Martin*. Other areas are noted for their fruit-distilled brandies like *quetsche* (plum), *marc* (grape), *calvados* (apple), *kirsch* (cherry), *poire Williams* (pear).

Are there any local specialities?	**Avez-vous des spécialités locales?**	ahvay voo day spayssyahleetay lokahl

I'd like to try a glass of ..., please.	**Je voudrais goûter un verre de ...**	zher voodreh gootay ang vehr der
A (double) whisky, please.	**Un whisky (double), s'il vous plaît.**	ang "whisky" (doobl) seel voo pleh
brandy	**un cognac**	ang koñyahk
gin and tonic	**un gin-tonic**	ang "gin-tonic"
liqueur	**une liqueur**	ewn leekurr
port	**un porto**	ang portoa
rum	**un rhum**	ang rom
sherry	**un sherry**	ang "sherry"
vermouth	**un vermouth**	ang vehrmoot
vodka	**une vodka**	ewn vodka
neat (straight)	**sec**	sehk
on the rocks	**avec des glaçons**	ahvehk day glahssawng

Nonalcoholic drinks   *Boissons sans alcool*

apple juice	**un jus de pomme**	ang zhew der pom
(hot) chocolate	**un chocolat (chaud)**	ang shokolah (shoa)
coffee	**un café**	ang kahfay
black	**noir**	nwahr
with cream	**crème**	krehm
with milk	**au lait**	oa leh
caffein-free	**décaféiné**	daykahfayeenay
espresso coffee	**un express**	ang nehxprehss
fruit juice	**un jus de fruits**	ang zhew der frwee
grapefruit juice	**un jus de pample-mousse**	ang zhew der pahngpler-mooss
herb tea	**une tisane**	ewn teezahn
lemon juice	**un citron pressé**	ang seetrawng prehssay
lemonade	**une limonade**	ewn leemonahd
milk	**un lait**	ang leh
milkshake	**un frappé**	ang frahpay
mineral water	**de l'eau minérale**	der loa meenayrahl
fizzy (carbonated)	**gazeuse**	gahzurz
still	**non gazeuse**	nawng gahzurz
orange juice	**un jus d'orange**	ang zhew dorahngzh
orangeade	**une orangeade**	ewn orahngzhahd
tea	**un thé**	ang tay
cup of tea	**une tasse de thé**	ewn tahss der tay
with milk/lemon	**crème/citron**	krehm/seetrawng
iced tea	**un thé glacé**	ang tay glahssay
tomato juice	**un jus de tomate**	ang zhew der tomaht
tonic water	**un Schweppes**	ang "Schweppes"

Complaints *Réclamations*

There is a plate/glass missing.	Il manque une assiette/un verre.	eel mahngk ewn ahssyeht/ ang vehr
I have no knive/fork/ spoon.	Je n'ai pas de couteau/fourchette/ cuillère.	zher nay pah der kootoa/ foorsheht/kweeyehr
That's not what I ordered.	Ce n'est pas ce que j'ai commandé.	ser neh pah ser ker zhay kommahngday
I asked for ...	J'ai demandé ...	zhay dermahngday
There must be some mistake.	Il doit y avoir une erreur.	eel dwah ee avwahr ewn ehrurr
May I change this?	Pourriez-vous me changer ceci?	pooryay voo mer shahngzhay serssee
I asked for a small portion (for the child).	J'avais demandé une petite portion (pour cet enfant).	zhahveh dermahngday ewn perteet porsyawng (poor seht ahngfahng)
The meat is ...	La viande est ...	lah vyahngd eh
overdone	trop cuite	troa kweet
underdone	pas assez cuite	pah zahssay kweet
too rare	trop saignante	troa sehñahngt
too tough	trop dure	troa dewr
This is too ...	C'est trop ...	seh troa
bitter/salty/sweet	amer/salé/sucré	ahmehr/sahlay/sewkray
I don't like this.	Je n'aime pas ceci.	zher nehm pah serssee
The food is cold.	C'est tout froid.	seh too frwah
This isn't fresh.	Ce n'est pas frais.	ser neh pah freh
What's taking you so long?	Pourquoi y a-t-il autant d'attente?	poorkwah ee ahteel oatahng dahtahngt
Have you forgotten our drinks?	Avez-vous oublié nos boissons?	ahvay voo zoobleeyay noa bwahssawng
The wine tastes of cork.	Ce vin a un goût de bouchon.	ser vang ah ang goo der booshawng
This isn't clean.	Ce n'est pas propre.	ser neh pah propr
Would you ask the head waiter to come over?	Envoyez-moi donc le maître d'hôtel.	ahngvwahyay mwah dawngk ler mehtr doatehl

The bill (check)   *L'addition*

A service charge is generally included automatically in restaurant bills. Anything extra for the waiter is optional. Credit cards may be used in an increasing number of restaurants. Signs are posted indicating which cards are accepted.

I'd like to pay.	**L'addition, s'il vous plaît.**	lahdeessyawng seel voo pleh
We'd like to pay separately.	**Nous voudrions payer chacun notre part.**	noo voodreeyawng pehyay shahkang notr pahr
I think you made a mistake in this bill.	**Je crois qu'il y a une erreur dans l'addition.**	zher krwah keel ee ah ewn ehrurr dahng lahdeessyawng
What is this amount for?	**Que représente ce montant?**	ker rerprayzahngt ser mawngtahng
Is service included?	**Est-ce que le service est compris?**	ehss ker ler sehrveess eh kawngpree
Is the cover charge included?	**Est-ce que le couvert est compris?**	ehss ker ler koovehr eh kawngpree
Is everything included?	**Est-ce que tout est compris?**	ehss ker too teh kawngpree
Do you accept traveller's cheques?	**Acceptez-vous les chèques de voyage?**	ahksehptay voo lay shehk der vwahyahzh
Can I pay with this credit card?	**Puis-je payer avec cette carte de crédit?**	pweezh pehyay ahvehk seht kahrt der kraydee
Thank you, this is for you.	**Merci. Voici pour vous.**	mehrsee. vwahssee poor voo
Keep the change.	**Gardez la monnaie.**	gahrday lah monneh
That was a delicious meal.	**Le repas était délicieux.**	ler rerpah ayteh dayleessyur
We enjoyed it, thank you.	**C'était très bon, merci.**	sayteh treh bawng mehrsee

---

SERVICE COMPRIS
SERVICE INCLUDED

TIPPING, see inside back-cover

Snacks—Picnic   *Casse-croûte – Pique-nique*

Cafés serve hearty sandwiches of long hunks of French bread filled with ham, cheese, pâté, tomatoes, green salad or hardboiled eggs. Thin-sliced sandwich bread *(pain de mie)* is used for *croque-monsieur* (toasted ham-and-cheese sandwich). Omelettes are always reliable fare, and so are the excellent thin-crusted pizzas (all flavours). The delicious *crêpes,* paper-thin pancakes dusted with sugar or filled with jam, are sold at small street stands.

I'll have one of these, please.	**J'en voudrais un de ceux-ci, s'il vous plaît.**	zhahng voodreh ang der surssee seel voo pleh
Give me two of these and one of those.	**Donnez-moi deux de ceux-ci et un de ceux-là.**	donnay mwah dur der surssee ay ang der surlah
to the left/right above/below	**à gauche/à droite au-dessus/au-dessous**	ah goash/ah drwaht oa derssew/oa derssoo
It's to take away.	**C'est pour emporter.**	seh poor ahngportay
I'd like a/some ...	**Je voudrais ...**	zher voodreh
chicken	**un poulet**	ang pooleh
half a roasted chicken	**un demi-poulet grillé**	ang dermee pooleh greeyay
chips (french fries)	**des frites**	day freet
pancake	**une crêpe**	ewn krehp
with sugar	**au sucre**	oa sewkr
with jam	**à la confiture**	ah lah kawngfeetewr
sandwich	**un sandwich**	ang "sandwich"
cheese	**au fromage**	oa fromahzh
ham	**au jambon**	oa zhahngbawng
vegetable salad	**des crudités**	day krewdeetay

Here's a basic list of food and drink that might come in useful when shopping for a picnic.

Please give me a/an/ some ...	**Donnez-moi ..., s'il vous plaît.**	donnay mwah ... seel voo pleh
apples	**des pommes**	day pom
bananas	**des bananes**	day bahnahn
biscuits (Br.)	**des biscuits**	day beeskwee
beer	**de la bière**	der lah byehr

bread	du pain	dew pang
butter	du beurre	dew burr
cake	un gâteau	ang gahtoa
cheese	du fromage	dew fromahzh
chips (Am.)	des chips	day "chips"
chocolate bar	une plaque de chocolat	ewn plahk der shokolah
coffee	du café	dew kahfay
cold cuts	de la charcuterie	der lah shahrkewterree
cookies	des biscuits	day beeskwee
crackers	des biscuits salés	day beeskwee sahlay
crisps	des chips	day "chips"
eggs	des œufs	day zur
gherkins (pickles)	des cornichons	day korneeshawng
grapes	du raisin	dew rehzang
ham	du jambon	dew zhahngbawng
ice-cream	de la glace	der lah glahss
lemon	un citron	ang seetrawng
milk	du lait	dew leh
mustard	de la moutarde	der lah mootahrd
oranges	des oranges	day zorahngzh
pastries	des pâtisseries	day pahteesserree
pepper	du poivre	dew pwahvr
roll	un petit pain	ang pertee pang
salt	du sel	dew sehl
sausage	une saucisse	ewn soasseess
soft drink	une boisson non alcoolisée	ewn bwahssawng nawng nahlkoleezay
sugar	du sucre	dew sewkr
tea	du thé	dew tay
yoghurt	un yoghourt (yaourt)	ang yogoort (yahoort)

... plus a choice of French bread:

baguette	bahgeht	long thin loaf of French bread
ficelle	feessehl	same as *baguette*, but thinner
pain	pang	bread
blanc/bis	blahng/bee	white/brown
complet	kawngpleh	wholemeal (whole-wheat)
de seigle	der sehgl	rye
petit pain	pertee pang	roll
au cumin	oa kewmang	with caraway seeds
aux pavots	oa pahvoa	with poppy seeds

Travelling around

Plane *Avion*

Is there a flight to Paris?	**Y a-t-il un vol pour Paris?**	ee ahteel ang vol poor pahree
Is it a direct flight?	**Est-ce un vol direct?**	ehss ang vol deerehkt
When's the next flight to Lyons?	**Quand part le prochain avion pour Lyon?**	kahng pahr ler proshang nahvyawng poor lyawng
Do I have to change planes?	**Est-ce que je dois changer d'avion?**	ehss ker zher dwah shahngzhay dahvyawng
Is there a connection to Geneva?	**Puis-je avoir une correspondance pour Genève?**	pweezh ahvwahr ewn korrehspawngdahngss poor zhernehv
I'd like a ticket to Brussels.	**Je voudrais un billet pour Bruxelles.**	zher voodreh ang beeyeh poor brewssehl
single (one-way)	**aller**	ahlay
return (roundtrip)	**aller-retour**	ahlay rertoor
What time do we take off?	**A quelle heure part l'avion?**	ah kehl urr pahr lahvyawng
What time do I have to check in?	**A quelle heure est l'enregistrement?**	ah kehl urr eh lahngrerzheestrermahng
Is there a bus to the airport?	**Y a-t-il un bus pour l'aéroport?**	ee ahteel ang bewss poor lahayropor
What's the flight number?	**Quel est le numéro du vol?**	kehl eh ler newmayroa dew vol
What time do we arrive?	**A quelle heure arrivons-nous?**	ah kehl urr ahreevawng noo
I'd like to … my reservation on flight no …	**Je voudrais … ma réservation sur le vol …**	zher voodreh … mah rayzehrvahssyawng sewr ler vol
cancel	**annuler**	ahnnewlay
change	**changer**	shahngzhay
confirm	**confirmer**	kawngfeermay

ARRIVÉE ARRIVAL	**DÉPART** DEPARTURE

Train *Train*

Rail travel in France is usually fast on the main lines, and the trains (diesel and electric) run on time. Unless otherwise indicated, the terms below apply equally to France, Belgium and Switzerland.

TGV (tay zhay vay)	Extra-high-speed train *(Train à Grande Vitesse)* operating on some routes; reservation compulsory, surcharge sometimes payable
EuroCity (urrossiti)	International express train
Rapide (rahpeed)	Long-distance express stopping only at main stations; luxury coaches; additional fare sometimes required (France)
Intercity (angtehrseetee)	Inter-city express with very few stops
Express (ehxprehss)	Ordinary long-distance train, stopping at main stations (France)
Direct (deerehkt)	The equivalent of the French *express* (Switzerland and Belgium)
Omnibus (omneebewss)	Local train stopping at all stations (France and Belgium)
Train régional (trang rayzhyonahl)	Local train stopping at all stations (Switzerland)
Autorail (oatorahy)	Small diesel used on short runs

Here are a few more useful terms which you may need:

Wagon-restaurant* (vahgawng rehstoarahng)	Dining-car
Wagon-lit* (vahgawng lee)	Sleeping-car with individual compartments (single or double) and washing facilities
Couchette (koosheht)	Berth (converted from seats) with blankets and pillows. You may want a *couchette supérieure* (koosheht sewpayryurr—upper berth) or a *couchette inférieure* (koosheht angfayryurr—lower berth)

---

* The term *voiture* (vwahtewr) is often used instead of *wagon*.

To the railway station *Pour aller à la gare*

Where's the railway station?	**Où se trouve la gare?**	oo ser troov lah gahr
Taxi!	**Taxi!**	tahksee
Take me to the railway station.	**Conduisez-moi à la gare.**	kawngdweezay mwah ah lah gahr
What's the fare?	**C'est combien?**	say kawngbyang

ENTRÉE	ENTRANCE
SORTIE	EXIT
ACCÈS AUX QUAIS	TO THE PLATFORMS
RENSEIGNEMENTS	INFORMATION

Where's the ...? *Où est ...?*

Where is/are the ...?	**Où est ...?**	oo eh
bar	**le bar**	ler bahr
booking office	**le bureau de réservation**	ler bewroa der rayzehrvahssyawng
currency exchange office	**le bureau de change**	ler bewroa der shahngzh
left-luggage office (baggage check)	**la consigne**	lah kawngsseeñ
lost property (lost and found) office	**le bureau des objets trouvés**	ler bewroa day zobzheh troovay
luggage lockers	**la consigne automatique**	lah kawngsseeñ oatomahteek
newsstand	**le kiosque à journaux**	ler kyosk ah zhoornoa
platform 7	**le quai 7**	ler kay 7
reservations office	**le bureau de réservation**	ler bewroa der rayzehrvahssyawng
restaurant	**le restaurant**	ler rehstoarahng
snack bar	**le buffet-express**	ler bewfeh exprehss
ticket office	**le guichet**	ler geesheh
waiting-room	**la salle d'attente**	lah sahl dahtahngt
Where are the toilets?	**Où sont les toilettes?**	oo sawng lay twahleht

TAXI, see page 21

Inquiries *Renseignements*

In Belgium, France and Switzerland | i | means information office.

When is the ... train to Nice?	Quand part le ... train pour Nice?	kahng pahr ler ... trang poor neess
first/last next	premier/dernier prochain	prermyay/dehrnyay proshang
What time does the train to Calais leave?	A quelle heure part le train pour Calais?	ah kehl urr pahr ler trang poor kahleh
What's the fare to Avignon?	Quel est le prix du billet pour Avignon?	kehl eh ler pree dew beeyeh poor ahveeñawng
Is it a through train?	Est-ce un train direct?	ehss ang trang deerehkt
Is there a connection to ...?	Est-ce qu'il existe une correspondance pour ...?	ehss keel ehxeest ewn korrehspawngdahngss poor
Do I have to change trains?	Dois-je changer (de train)?	dwahzh shahngzhay (der trang)
Is there sufficient time to change?	A-t-on le temps de changer?	ahtawng ler tahng der shahngzhay
Will the train leave on time?	Est-ce que le train partira à l'heure?	ehss ker ler trang pahrteerah ah lurr
What time does the train arrive at Bordeaux?	A quelle heure le train arrive-t-il à Bordeaux?	ah kehl urr ler trang ahreev teel ah bordoa
Is there a dining-car/ sleeping-car on the train?	Y a-t-il un wagon-restaurant/un wagon-lit?	ee ahteel ang vahgawng rehstoarahng/ang vahgawng lee
Does the train stop in Mâcon?	Est-ce que le train s'arrête à Mâcon?	ehss ker ler trang sahreht ah mahkawng
What platform does the train to Strasbourg leave from?	De quel quai part le train pour Strasbourg?	der kehl kay pahr ler trang poor strahsboor
What platform does the train from Geneva arrive at?	Sur quel quai arrive le train de Genève?	sewr kehl kay ahreev ler trang der zhernehv
I'd like to buy a time-table.	Je voudrais acheter un horaire.	zher voodreh ahshertay ang norrehr

C'est un train direct.	It's a through train.
Changez à ...	You have to change at ...
Changez à ... et prenez un omnibus.	Change at ... and get a local train.
Le quai 7 se trouve ...	Platform 7 is ...
là-bas/en haut	over there/upstairs
à gauche/à droite	on the left/on the right
Il y a un train pour ... à ...	There's a train to ... at ...
Votre train partira du quai 8.	Your train will leave from platform 8.
Le train a un retard de ... minutes.	There'll be a delay of ... minutes.
Première classe en tête/ au milieu/en queue.	First class at the front/in the middle/at the end.

Tickets *Billets*

I want a ticket to Nice.	**Je voudrais un billet pour Nice.**	zher voodreh ang beeyeh poor neess
single (one-way)	**aller**	ahlay
return (roundtrip)	**aller-retour**	ahlay rertoor
first/second class	**première/deuxième classe**	prermyehr/durzyehm klahss
half price	**demi-tarif**	dermee tahreef

Reservation *Réservation*

I want to book a ...	**Je voudrais réserver ...**	zher voodreh rayzehrvay
seat (by the window)	**une place (côté fenêtre)**	ewn plahss (koatay fernehtr)
berth	**une couchette**	ewn koosheht
upper	**supérieure**	sewpayryurr
middle	**au milieu**	oa meelyur
lower	**inférieure**	angfayryurr
berth in the sleeping car	**une place en wagon-lit**	ewn plahss ang vahgawng lee

All aboard *En voiture*

Is this the right platform for the train to Paris?	**Est-ce bien de ce quai que part le train pour Paris?**	ehss byang der ser kay ker pahr ler trang poor pahree
Is this the right train to Marseilles?	**C'est bien le train pour Marseille, n'est-ce pas?**	seh byang ler trang poor mahrsehy nehss pah
Excuse me. May I get by?	**Pardon. Puis-je passer?**	pahrdawng pweezh pahssay
Is this seat taken?	**Cette place est-elle occupée?**	seht plahss ehtehl okkewpay

FUMEURS SMOKER	**NON-FUMEURS** NONSMOKER

I think that's my seat.	**Je crois que c'est ma place.**	zher krwah ker seh mah plahss
Would you let me know before we get to Liège?	**Pourriez-vous m'avertir quand nous arriverons à Liège?**	pooryay voo mahvehrteer kahng noo zahreeverrawng ah lyehzh
What station is this?	**A quelle gare sommes-nous?**	ah kehl gahr som noo
How long does the train stop here?	**Combien de temps le train s'arrête-t-il ici?**	kawngbyang der tahng ler trang sahreht teel eessee
When do we get to Orleans?	**Quand arriverons-nous à Orléans?**	kahng tahreevrawng noo ah orlayahng

Sleeping *En wagon-lit*

Are there any free compartments in the sleeping-car?	**Y a-t-il des compartiments libres dans le wagon-lit?**	ee ahteel day kawngpahr-teemahng leebr dahng ler vahgawng lee
Where's the sleeping-car?	**Où se trouve le wagon-lit?**	oo ser troov ler vahgawng lee
Where's my berth?	**Où est ma couchette?**	oo eh mah koosheht

I'd like a lower berth.	**Je voudrais une couchette inférieure.**	zher voodreh ewn koosheht angfayryurr
Would you make up our berths?	**Pourriez-vous installer nos couchettes?**	pooray voo angstahlay noa koosheht
Would you wake me at 7 o'clock?	**Pourriez vous me réveiller à 7 heures?**	pooray voo mer rayvehyay ah 7 urr

Eating *Au wagon-restaurant*

You can get snacks and drinks in the buffet-car and in the dining-car when it's not being used for main meals. On some trains an attendant comes around with snacks, coffee, tea, and soft drinks.

| Where's the dining-car? | **Où est le wagon-restaurant?** | oo eh ler vahgawng rehstoarahng |

Baggage and porters *Bagages et porteurs*

Porter!	**Porteur?**	porturr
Can you help me with my luggage?	**Pouvez-vous m'aider à porter mes bagages?**	poovay voo mehday ah portay may bahgahzh
Where are the luggage trolleys (carts)?	**Où sont les chariots à bagages?**	oo sawng lay shahryoa ah bahgahzh
Where are the luggage lockers?	**Où est la consigne automatique?**	oo eh lah kawngseeñ oatomahteek
Where's the left-luggage office (baggage check)?	**Où est la consigne?**	oo eh lah kawngseeñ
I'd like to leave my luggage, please.	**Je voudrais déposer mes bagages, s'il vous plaît.**	zher voodreh daypoazay may bahgahzh seel voo pleh
I'd like to register (check) my luggage.	**Je voudrais faire enregistrer mes bagages.**	zher voodreh fehr ahngrergeestray may bahgahzh

ENREGISTREMENT DES BAGAGES
REGISTERING (CHECKING) BAGGAGE

PORTERS, see also page 18

Coach (long-distance bus) *Car*

You'll find information on destinations and timetables at the coach terminals, usually situated near railway stations. Many companies offer coach tours, as do the French National Railways.

When's the next coach to ...?	**A quelle heure est le prochain car pour ...?**	ah kehl urr eh ler proshang kahr poor
Does this coach stop at ...?	**Ce car s'arrête-t-il à ...?**	ser kahr sahreht teel ah
How long does the journey (trip) take?	**Combien de temps dure le trajet?**	kawngbyang der tahng dewr ler trahzheh

Note: Most of the phrases on the previous pages can be used or adapted for travelling on local transport.

Bus—Tram (streetcar) *Bus – Tram*

Many cities have introduced an automatic system of fare-paying whereby you insert the exact change into a ticket dispenser at the bus or tram stop or have the machine validate your prepaid ticket.

If you're planning to get around a lot in one city by bus, tram, or *métro* (see next page), enquire about a booklet of tickets or special runabout tickets, such as the *carte* or *abonnement d'un jour* (one-day ticket), *carte orange* (valid a week or a month, in Paris) or *billet touristique* (special tourist ticket for two or more days).

I'd like a booklet of tickets.	**J'aimerais un carnet de tickets.**	zhehmerreh ang kahrneh der teekeh
Where can I get a bus to the opera?	**Où puis-je prendre le bus pour l'Opéra?**	oo pweezh prahngdr ler bewss poor lopayrah
What bus do I take for Montmartre?	**Quel bus dois-je prendre pour aller à Montmartre?**	kehl bewss dwahzh prahngdr poor ahlay ah mawngmahrtr
Where's the bus stop?	**Où se trouve l'arrêt de bus?**	oo ser troov lahreh der bewss

When is the ... bus to St. Germain?	Quand part le ... bus pour Saint-Germain?	kawng pahr ler ... bewss poor sang zhehrmang
first/last/next	premier/dernier/ prochain	prermyay/dehrnyay/ proshang
How much is the fare to ...?	Quel est le prix du trajet jusqu'à ...?	kehl eh ler pree dew trahzheh zhewskah
Do I have to change buses?	Dois-je changer de bus?	dwahzh shahngzhay der bewss
How many bus stops are there to ...?	Combien y a-t-il d'arrêts jusqu'à ...?	kawngbyang ee ahteel dahreh zhewskah
Will you tell me when to get off?	Pourriez-vous me dire quand je dois descendre?	pooryay voo mer deer kahng zher dwah dehssahngdr
I want to get off at Notre-Dame	Je voudrais descendre à Notre-Dame.	zher voodreh dehssahngdr ah notrer dahm

| ARRÊT FIXE | REGULAR BUS STOP |
| ARRÊT SUR DEMANDE | STOPS ON REQUEST |

Underground (subway) *Métro*

The *métros* (maytroa) in Paris and Brussels correspond to the London underground or the New York subway. In both cities, the fare is always the same, irrespective of the distance you travel. There's first and second class. Big maps in every Métro station make the system easy to use.

Where's the nearest underground station?	Où se trouve la station de métro la plus proche?	oo ser troov lah stah-ssyawng der maytroa lah plew prosh
Does this train go to ...?	Est-ce que cette rame va à ...?	ehss ker seht rahm vah ah ah
Where do I change for ...?	Où faut-il changer pour aller à ...?	oo foateel shahngzhay poor ahlay ah
Is the next station ...?	La prochaine gare est-elle bien ...?	lah proshehn gahr ehtehl byang
Which line should I take for ...?	Quelle ligne dois-je prendre pour ...?	kehl leeñ dwahzh prahngdr poor

74

Boat service *Bateau*

When does the next boat for ... leave?	A quelle heure part le prochain bateau pour ...?	a kehl urr pahr ler proshang bahtoa poor
Where's the embarkation point?	Où s'effectue l'embarquement?	oo sehffehktew lahngbahrkermahng
How long does the crossing take?	Combien de temps dure la traversée?	kawngbyang der tahng dewr lah trahvehrsay
At which port(s) do we stop?	Quel(s) port(s) dessert ce bateau?	kehl por dehssehr ser bahtoa
I'd like to take a cruise.	Je voudrais faire une croisière.	zher voodreh fehr ewn krwahzyehr
boat	le bateau	ler bahtoa
cabin	la cabine	lah kahbeen
single/double	pour une personne/ deux personnes	poor ewn pehrson/ dur pehrson
deck	le pont	ler pawng
ferry	le ferry	ler ''ferry''
hovercraft	l'aéroglisseur	lahayrogleessurr
hydrofoil	l'hydroptère	leedroptehr
life belt/boat	la ceinture/le canot de sauvetage	la sangtewr/ler kahnoa der soavertahzh
ship	le navire	ler nahveer

Bicycle hire *Location de bicyclettes*

French National Railways operate a cycle-hire service at major stations. Bicycles may be hired at one station and returned at another.

| I'd like to hire a bicycle. | Je voudrais louer une bicyclette. | zher voodreh looay ewn beesseekleht |

Other means of transport *Autres moyens de transport*

cable car	la télécabine	lah taylaykahbeen
helicopter	l'hélicoptère	layleekoptehr
moped	le vélomoteur	ler vayloamoturr
motorbike/scooter	la moto/le scooter	lah moto/ler skootehr

Or perhaps you prefer:

| to hitchhike | faire de l'auto-stop | fehr der loatostop |
| to walk | marcher | mahrshay |

Car *Voiture*

In general roads are good in Belgium, France and Switzerland. Motorways (expressways) are subject to tolls *(le péage)* in France, they are free in Belgium. If you use the motorways in Switzerland you must purchase a sticker (valid for one year) to be displayed on the windscreen.

A red reflector warning triangle must be carried for use in case of a breakdown, and seat belts *(la ceinture de sécurité)* are obligatory.

Where's the nearest filling station?	**Où est la station-service la plus proche?**	oo eh lah stahssyawng sehrveess lah plew prosh
Full tank, please.	**Le plein, s'il vous plaît.**	ler plang seel voo pleh
Give me ... litres of petrol (gasoline).	**Donnez-moi ... litres d'essence.**	donnay mwah ... leetr dehssahngss
super (premium)/ regular/unleaded/ diesel	**du super/de la normale/sans plomb/ gas-oil**	dew sewpehr/der lah normahl/sahng plawng/ gahzoyl
Please check the ...	**Veuillez contrôler ...**	veryay kawngtroalay
battery brake fluid oil/water	**la batterie le liquide des freins l'huile/l'eau**	lah bahterree ler leekeed day frang lweel/loa
Would you check the tyre pressure?	**Pourriez-vous contrôler la pression des pneus?**	pooryay voo kawngtroalay lah prehssyawng day pnur
1.6 front, 1.8 rear.	**1,6 à l'avant, 1,8 à l'arrière.**	ang seess ah lahvahng, ang weet ah lahryehr
Please check the spare tyre, too.	**Vérifiez aussi la roue de secours.**	vayreefyay oassee lah roo der serkoor
Can you mend this puncture (fix this flat)?	**Pourriez-vous réparer ce pneu?**	pooryay voo raypahray ser pnur
Would you please change the ...?	**Pourriez-vous changer ...?**	pooryay voo shahngzhay
bulb fan belt	**l'ampoule la courroie du ventilateur**	lahngpool lah koorrwah dew vahngteelahturr

CAR HIRE, see page 20

spark(ing) plugs	les bougies	lay boozhee
tyre	le pneu	ler pnur
wipers	les essuie-glace	lay zehsswee glahss
Would you clean the windscreen (windshield)?	Pourriez-vous nettoyer le pare-brise?	pooryay voo nehtwahyay ler pahr breez

Asking the way — Street directions *Pour demander son chemin*

Can you tell me the way to ...?	Pourriez-vous m'indiquer la route de ...?	pooryay voo mangdeekay lah root der
How do I get to ...?	Comment-puis-je aller à ...?	kommahng pweezh ahlay ah
Are we on the right road for ...?	Sommes-nous bien sur la route pour ...?	som noo byang sewr lah root poor
How far is the next village?	A quelle distance se trouve le prochain village?	ah kehl deestahngss ser troov ler proshang veelahzh
How far is it to ... from here?	A quelle distance sommes-nous de ...?	ah kehl deestahngss som noo der
Is there a motorway (expressway)?	Y a-t-il une autoroute?	ee ahteel ewn oatoroot
How long does it take by car/on foot?	Combien de temps est-ce que cela prend en voiture/à pied?	kawngbyang der tahng ehss ker serlah prahng ahng vwahtewr/ah pyay
Can I drive to the centre of town?	Puis-je gagner le centre-ville en voiture?	pweezh gahñay ler sahngtr veel ahng vwahtewr
Can you tell me, where ...is?	Pourriez-vous me dire où se trouve ...?	pooryay voo mer deer oo ser troov
How can I find this place?	Comment puis-je trouver cet endroit?	kommahng pweezh troovay seh tahngdrwah
Where can I find this address?	Où puis-je trouver cette adresse?	oo pweezh troovay seht ahdrehss
Where's this?	Où est-ce?	oo ehss
Can you show me on the map where I am?	Pouvez-vous me montrer sur la carte où je suis?	poovay voo mer mawngtray sewr lah kahrt oo zher swee

Vous êtes sur la mauvaise route.	You're on the wrong road.
Allez tout droit.	Go straight ahead.
C'est là-bas à ...	It's down there on the ...
gauche/droite	left/right
en face de/derrière ...	opposite/behind ...
à côté de/au-delà de ...	next to/after ...
nord/sud	north/south
est/ouest	east/west
Allez jusqu'au premier/ deuxième carrefour.	Go to the first/second crossroads (intersection).
Tournez à gauche après les feux.	Turn left at the traffic lights.
Tournez à droite au prochain coin de rue.	Turn right at the next corner.
Prenez la route de ...	Take the road for ...
Vous devez revenir jusqu'à ...	You have to go back to ...
Suivez la direction ''Nice''.	Follow signs for Nice.

Parking *Stationnement*

In town centres, most street parking is metered. The blue zones require the *disque de stationnement* or parking disc (obtainable from petrol stations), which you set to show when you arrived and when you must leave.

Where can I park?	Où puis-je me garer?	oo pweezh mer gahray
Is there a car park nearby?	Y a-t-il un parking à proximité?	ee ahteel ang pahrkeeng ah proxeemeetay
May I park here?	Puis-je me garer ici?	pweezh mer gahray eessee
How long can I park here?	Combien de temps puis-je rester ici?	kawngbyang der tahng pweezh rehstay eessee
What's the charge per hour?	Quel est le tarif horaire?	kehl eh ler tahreef orehr
Do you have some change for the parking meter?	Avez-vous de la monnaie pour le parcomètre?	ahvay voo der lah monneh poor ler pahrkommehtr

Breakdown—Road assistance *Pannes – Assistance routière*

Where's the nearest garage?	**Où se trouve le garage le plus proche?**	oo ser troov ler gahrahzh ler plew prosh
Excuse me. My car has broken down.	**Excusez-moi. Ma voiture est en panne.**	ehxkewzay mwah. mah vwahtewr eh tahng pahn
May I use your phone?	**Puis-je me servir de votre téléphone?**	pweezh mer sehrveer der votr taylayfon
I've had a breakdown at ...	**Je suis tombé en panne à ...**	zher swee tawngbay ahng pahn ah
Can you send a mechanic?	**Pouvez-vous envoyer un mécanicien?**	poovay voo ahngvwahyay ang maykahneessyang
My car won't start.	**Je n'arrive pas à démarrer.**	zher nahreev pah ah daymahray
The battery is dead.	**La batterie est à plat.**	lah bahterree eh ah plah
I've run out of petrol (gasoline).	**Je suis en panne d'essence.**	zher swee ahng pahn dehssahngss
I have a flat tyre.	**J'ai un pneu à plat.**	zhay ang pnur ah plah
The engine is overheating.	**Le moteur chauffe.**	ler moturr shoaf
There is something wrong with ...	**J'ai un problème avec ...**	zhay ang problehm ahvehk
brakes	**les freins**	lay frang
carburetor	**le carburateur**	ler kahrbewrahturr
exhaust pipe	**le pot d'échappement**	ler poa dayshahpmahng
radiator	**le radiateur**	ler rahdyahturr
wheel	**une roue**	ewn roo
Can you send a breakdown van (tow truck)?	**Pouvez-vous envoyer une dépanneuse?**	poovay voo ahngvwahyay ewn daypahnurz
How long will you be?	**Combien de temps faut-il compter?**	kawngbyang der tahng foateel kawngtay

Accident—Police *Accident – Police*

Please call the police.	**Appelez la police, s'il vous plaît.**	ahperlay lah poleess seel voo pleh
There's been an accident. It's about 2 km. from ...	**Il y a eu un accident à environ 2 km de ...**	eel ee ah ew ang nahksseedahng ah ahngveerawng 2 keelomehtr der

Where is there a telephone?	**Où y a-t-il un téléphone?**	oo ee ahteel ang taylayfon
Call a doctor/an ambulance quickly.	**Appelez d'urgence un médecin/une ambulance.**	ahperlay dewrzhahngss ang maydsang/ewn ahngbewlahngss
There are people injured.	**Il y a des blessés.**	eel ee ah day blehssay
Here's my driving licence.	**Voici mon permis de conduire.**	vwahssee mawng pehrmee der kawngdweer
What's your name and address?	**Quels sont vos nom et adresse?**	kehl sawng voa nawng ay ahdrehss
What's your insurance company?	**Auprès de quelle compagnie êtes-vous assuré?**	oapreh der kehl kawngpahñee eht voo ahssewray

Road signs *Panneaux routiers*

ALLUMEZ VOS PHARES	Switch on headlights
ATTENTION ÉCOLE	Caution, school
ATTENTION TRAVAUX	Road works ahead (men working)
CÉDER LE PASSAGE	Give way (Yield)
CIRCULATION DIFFICILE	Slow traffic
CHAUSSÉE DÉFORMÉE	Poor road surface
CHUTES DE PIERRES	Falling rocks
DÉVIATION	Diversion/detour
FIN DE L'INTERDICTION DE ...	End of no ... zone
FORTE DÉCLIVITÉ	Steep hill
INTERDICTION DE DOUBLER	No overtaking (no passing)
NIDS DE POULE	Potholes
PASSAGE À NIVEAU	Level (railroad) crossing
PÉAGE	Toll
PISTE RÉSERVÉE AUX TRANSPORTS PUBLICS	Lane reserved for public transport
POIDS LOURDS	Heavy vehicles
RALENTIR	Slow down
RAPPEL	Reminder
RÉSERVÉ AUX PIÉTONS	Pedestrians only
SERREZ À DROITE	Keep right
SORTIE DE CAMIONS	Lorry (truck) exit
STATIONNEMENT AUTORISÉ	Parking allowed
STATIONNEMENT INTERDIT	No parking
VERGLAS	Icy road
VIRAGES	Bends/curves

Sightseeing

Where's the tourist office?	**Où se trouve le syndicat d'initiative (l'office du tourisme)?**	oo ser troov ler sangdeekah deeneessyahteev (loffeess dew tooreezm)
What are the main points of interest?	**Qu'y a-t-il de plus intéressant?**	kee ahteel der plew zangtayrehssahng
We're here for ...	**Nous sommes ici pour ...**	noo som zeessee poor
only a few hours	**quelques heures seulement**	kehlker zurr surlermahng
a day	**un jour**	ang zhoor
a week	**une semaine**	ewn sermehn
Can you recommend a sightseeing tour/ an excursion?	**Pourriez-vous me conseiller une visite guidée/une excursion?**	pooryay voo mer kawngssehyay ewn veezeet geeday/ewn ehxkewrsyawng
What's the point of departure?	**D'où part-on?**	doo pahrtawng
Will the bus pick us up at the hotel?	**Le bus nous prendra-t-il à l'hôtel?**	ler bewss noo prahngdrahteel ah loatehl
How much does the tour cost?	**A combien revient l'excursion?**	ah kawngbyang rervyang lehxkewrsyawng
What time does the tour start?	**A quelle heure commence l'excursion?**	ah kehl urr kommahngss lehxkewrsyawng
Is lunch included?	**Le déjeuner est-il compris?**	ler dayzhurnay ehteel kawngpree
What time do we get back?	**A quelle heure serons-nous de retour?**	ah kehl urr serrawng noo der rertoor
Do we have free time in ...?	**Aurons-nous un peu de temps libre à ...?**	oarawng noo ang pur der tahng leebr a
Is there an English-speaking guide?	**Y a-t-il un guide qui parle anglais?**	ee ahteel ang geed kee pahrl ahnggleh
I'd like to hire a private guide for ...	**Je voudrais retenir un guide pour ...**	zher voodreh rerterneer ang geed poor
half a day	**une demi-journée**	ewn dermee zhoornay
a full day	**toute une journée**	too tewn zhoornay

Where is/Where are the ...?	**Où se trouve/ Où se trouvent ...?**	oo ser troov/ oo ser troov
abbey	**l'abbaye**	lahbayee
art gallery	**la galerie d'art**	lah gahlerree dahr
artists' quarter	**le quartier des artistes**	ler kahrtyay day zahrteest
botanical gardens	**le jardin botanique**	ler zhahrdang bottahneek
building	**le bâtiment**	ler bahteemahng
business district	**le quartier des affaires**	ler kahrtyay day zahfehr
castle	**le château**	ler shahtoa
catacombs	**les catacombes**	lay kahtahkawngb
cathedral	**la cathédrale**	lah kahtaydrahl
cave	**la grotte**	lah grot
cemetery	**le cimetière**	ler seemertyehr
city centre	**le centre (de la ville)**	ler sahngtr (der lah veel)
chapel	**la chapelle**	lah shahpehl
church	**l'église**	laygleez
concert hall	**la salle de concert**	lah sahl der kawngssehr
convent	**le couvent**	ler koovahng
court house	**le palais de justice**	ler pahleh der zhewsteess
downtown area	**le centre (de la ville)**	ler sahngtr (der lah veel)
embankment	**le quai**	ler kay
exhibition	**l'exposition**	lehxpozeessyawng
factory	**l'usine**	lewzeen
fair	**la foire**	lah fwahr
flea market	**le marché aux puces**	ler mahrshay oa pewss
fortress	**la forteresse**	lah forterrehss
fountain	**la fontaine**	lah fawngtehn
gardens	**le jardin public**	ler zhahrdang pewbleek
harbour	**le port**	ler por
lake	**le lac**	ler lahk
library	**la bibliothèque**	lah beebleeyotehk
market	**le marché**	ler mahrshay
memorial	**le monument**	ler monewmahng
monastery	**le monastère**	ler monahstehr
monument	**le monument**	ler monewmahng
museum	**le musée**	ler mewzay
old town	**la vieille ville**	lah vyehy veel
opera house	**l'opéra**	lopayrah
palace	**le palais**	ler pahleh
park	**le parc**	ler pahrk
parliament building	**le Parlement**	ler pahrlermahng
planetarium	**le planétarium**	ler plahnaytahryom
royal palace	**le palais royal**	ler pahleh rwahyahl
ruins	**les ruines**	lay rween

shopping area	le quartier commerçant	ler kahrtyay kommehrssahng
square	la place	lah plahss
stadium	le stade	ler stahd
statue	la statue	lah stahtew
stock exchange	la bourse	lah boors
theatre	le théâtre	ler tayahtr
tomb	la tombe	lah tawngb
tower	la tour	lah toor
town hall	l'hôtel de ville	loatehl der veel
university	l'université	lewneevehrseetay
zoo	le jardin zoologique	ler zhahrdang zoalozheek

Admission   A l'entrée

Is ... open on Sundays?	Est-ce que ... est ouvert le dimanche?	ehss ker ... eh toovehr ler deemahngsh
When does it open?	A partir de quelle heure est-ce ouvert?	ah pahrteer der kehl urr ehss oovehr
When does it close?	Quelle est l'heure de fermeture?	kehl eh lurr der fermertewr
How much is the entrance fee?	Combien coûte l'entrée?	kawngbyang koot lahngtray
Is there any reduction for ...?	Y a-t-il une réduction pour ...?	ee ahteel ewn raydewksyawng poor
children	les enfants	lay zahngfahng
disabled	les handicapés	lay ahngdeekahpay
groups	les groupes	lay groop
pensioners	les retraités	lay rertrehtay
students	les étudiants	lay zaytewdyahng
Have you a guide-book (in English)?	Avez-vous un guide (en anglais)?	ahvay voo ang geed (ahng nahnggleh)
Can I buy a catalogue?	Puis-je acheter un catalogue?	pweezh ahshtay ang kahtahlog
Is it all right to take pictures?	Est-il permis de prendre des photos?	ehteel pehrmee der prahngdr day fotoa

ENTRÉE LIBRE	ADMISSION FREE
INTERDICTION DE PHOTOGRAPHIER	NO CAMERAS ALLOWED

Who—What—When? *Qui – Quoi – Quand?*

What's that building?	**Quel est ce bâtiment?**	kehl eh ser bahteemahng
Who was the ...?	**Qui était ...?**	kee ayteh
architect	**l'architecte**	lahrsheetehkt
artist	**l'artiste**	lahrteest
painter	**le peintre**	ler pangtr
sculptor	**le sculpteur**	ler skewlturr
Who built it?	**Qui l'a construit?**	kee lah kawngstrwee
When was it built?	**A quand remonte la construction?**	ah kahng rermawngt lah kawngstrewksyawng
Who painted that picture?	**Qui est l'auteur de ce tableau?**	kee eh loaturr der ser tahbloa
When did he live?	**A quelle époque vivait-il?**	ah kehl aypok veevehteel
Where's the house where ... lived?	**Où est la maison où vécut ...?**	oo eh lah mehzawng oo vaykew
We're interested in ...	**Nous nous intéressons ...**	noo noo zangtayrehssawng
antiques	**aux antiquités**	oa zahngteekeetay
archaeology	**à l'archéologie**	ah lahrkayolozhee
art	**à l'art**	ah lahr
botany	**à la botanique**	ah lah bottahneek
ceramics	**à la céramique**	ah lah sayrahmeek
coins	**aux monnaies**	oa monneh
fine arts	**aux beaux-arts**	oa boa zahr
furniture	**aux meubles**	oa murbl
geology	**à la géologie**	ah lah zhayolozhee
handicrafts	**à l'artisanat**	ah lahrteezahnah
history	**à l'histoire**	ah leestwahr
medicine	**à la médecine**	ah lah maydsseen
music	**à la musique**	ah lah mewzeek
natural history	**à l'histoire naturelle**	ah leestwahr nahtewrehl
ornithology	**à l'ornithologie**	ah lorneetolozhee
painting	**à la peinture**	ah lah pangtewr
pottery	**à la poterie**	ah lah potterree
religion	**à la religion**	ah lah rerleezhyawng
sculpture	**à la sculpture**	ah lah skewltewr
zoology	**à la zoologie**	ah lah zoalozhee
Where's the ... department?	**Où est le département de ...?**	oo eh ler daypahrtermahng der

It's ...	C'est ...	seh
amazing	étonnant	aytonnahng
awful	horrible	orreebl
beautiful	beau	boa
gloomy	sombre	sawngbr
impressive	impressionnant	angprehssyonnahng
interesting	intéressant	angtayrehssahng
magnificent	splendide	splahngdeed
overwhelming	imposant	angpoazahng
strange	étrange	aytrahngzh
superb	superbe	sewpehrb
terrifying	effrayant	ehfrayyahng
tremendous	formidable	formeedahbl
ugly	laid	leh

Religious services *Services religieux*

France is particularly rich in cathedrals and churches worth visiting, while Geneva in Switzerland was the cradle of Calvinism. Most places are open for the public to view, except of course when a service is in progress.

If you're interested in taking photographs, you should obtain permission first.

Is there a ... near here?	Y a-t-il près d'ici ...?	ee ahteel preh deessee
Catholic church	une église (catholique)	ewn aygleez (kahtoleek)
Protestant church	un temple (protestant)	ang tahngpl (protehstahng)
mosque	une mosquée	ewn moskay
synagogue	une synagogue	ewn seenahgog
At what time is ...?	A quelle heure commence ...?	ah kehl urr kommahngss
mass/the service	la messe/le culte	lah mehss/ler kewlt
Where can I find a ... who speaks English?	Où puis-je trouver un ... qui parle anglais?	oo pweezh troovay ang ... kee pahrl ahnggleh
priest/minister/rabbi	prêtre/pasteur/rabbin	prehtr/pahsturr/rahbang
I'd like to visit the church.	Je voudrais visiter l'église.	zher voodreh veezeetay laygleez

In the countryside *A la campagne*

Is there a scenic route to ...?	**Y a-t-il une route touristique pour ...?**	ee ahteel ewn root tooreesteek poor
How far is it to ...?	**A quelle distance est-on de ...?**	ah kehl deestahngss ehtawng der
Can we walk?	**Pouvons-nous y aller à pied?**	poovawng noo ee ahlay ah pyay
How high is that mountain?	**Quelle est l'altitude de cette montagne?**	kehl eh lahlteetewd der seht mawngtahñ
What's the name of that ...?	**Quel est le nom de ...?**	kehl eh ler nawng der
animal/bird	**cet animal/cet oiseau**	seht ahneemahl/seht wahzoa
flower/tree	**cette fleur/cet arbre**	seht flurr/seht ahrbr

Landmarks *Points de repère*

bridge	**le pont**	ler pawng
cliff	**la falaise**	lah fahlehz
farm	**la ferme**	lah fehrm
field	**le champ**	ler shahng
footpath	**le sentier**	ler sahngtyay
forest	**la forêt**	lah foreh
garden	**le jardin**	ler zhahrdang
hamlet	**le hameau**	ler ahmoa
hill	**la colline**	lah kolleen
house	**la maison**	lah mehzawng
lake	**le lac**	ler lahk
meadow	**le pré**	ler pray
mountain	**la montagne**	lah mawngtahñ
path	**le chemin**	ler shermang
peak	**le sommet**	ler sommeh
pond	**l'étang**	laytahng
river	**le fleuve/la rivière**	ler flurv/lah reevyehr
road	**la route**	lah root
sea	**la mer**	lah mehr
spring	**la source**	lah soorss
valley	**la vallée**	lah vahlay
village	**le village**	ler veelahzh
vineyard	**le vignoble**	ler veeñobl
wall	**le mur**	ler mewr
waterfall	**la chute d'eau**	lah shewt doa
wood	**le bois**	ler bwah

ASKING THE WAY, see page 76

Relaxing

Cinema (movies)—Theatre   *Cinéma – Théâtre*

You can find out what's playing from newspapers and bill-
boards. In Paris ask for the weekly entertainment guides
Pariscope and *l'Officiel des Spectacles*. In Brussels ask for
Le Bulletin. Most American and British films are dubbed.
However, some cinemas in Paris and Geneva show original
versions—usually with French subtitles.

What's showing at the cinema tonight?	**Qu'y a-t-il ce soir au cinéma?**	kee ahteel ser swahr oa seenaymah
What's playing at the ... Theatre?	**Que joue-t-on au théâtre ...?**	ker zhootawng oa tayahtr
What sort of play is it?	**De quel genre de pièce s'agit-il?**	der kehl zhahngr der pyehss sahzhee teel
Who's it by?	**Qui l'a écrite?**	kee lah aykreet
Can you recommend (a) ...?	**Pouvez-vous me conseiller ...?**	poovay voo mer kawngssehyay
good film	**un bon film**	ang bawng feelm
comedy	**une comédie**	ewn komaydee
musical	**une comédie musicale**	ewn komaydee mewseekahl
Where's that new film by ... being shown?	**Dans quel cinéma passe le nouveau film de ...?**	dahng kehl seenaymah pahss ler noovoa feelm der
Who's in it?	**Qui joue?**	kee zhoo
Who's playing the lead?	**Qui tient le rôle principal?**	kee tyang ler roal prangsseepahl
Who's the director?	**Qui en est le metteur en scène?**	kee ahng neh ler mehturr ahng sehn
At what theatre is that new play by ... being performed?	**Dans quel théâtre joue-t-on la nouvelle pièce de ...?**	dahng kehl tayahtr zhootawng lah noovehl pyehss der
Is there a sound-and-light show on some-where?	**Y a-t-il un spectacle son et lumière?**	ee ahteel ang spehktahkl sawng ay lewmyehr

What time does it begin?	**A quelle heure le spectacle commence-t-il?**	ah kehl urr ler spehktahkl kommahngss teel
Are there any seats for tonight?	**Y a-t-il des places pour ce soir?**	ee ahteel day plahss poor ser swahr
How much are the seats?	**Combien coûtent les places?**	kawngbyang koot lay plahss
I want to reserve 2 seats for the show on Friday evening.	**Je voudrais réserver 2 places pour le spectacle de vendredi soir.**	zher voodreh rayzehrvay 2 plahss poor ler spehktahkl der vahngdrerdee swahr
Can I have a ticket for the matinée on Tuesday?	**Je voudrais un billet pour la matinée de mardi.**	zher voodreh ang beeyeh poor lah mahteenay der mahrdee
I want a seat in the stalls (orchestra).	**Je voudrais une place au parterre.**	zher voodreh ewn plahss oa pahrtehr
Not too far back.	**Pas trop loin.**	pah troa lwang
Somewhere in the middle.	**Vers le milieu.**	vehr ler meelyur
How much are the seats in the circle (mezzanine)?	**Combien coûtent les places au balcon?**	kawngbyang koot lay plahss oa bahlkawng
May I please have a programme?	**Le programme, s'il vous plaît.**	ler programh seel voo pleh
Where's the cloakroom?	**Où est le vestiaire?**	oo eh ler vehstyehr

---

Je suis désolé(e), c'est complet.	I'm sorry, we're sold out.
Il ne reste que quelques places au balcon.	There are only a few seats left in the circle (mezzanine).
Votre billet, s'il vous plaît.	May I see your ticket?
Voici votre place.*	This is your seat.

---

* It's customary to tip usherettes (*l'ouvreuse*) in most French and Belgian theatres.

DAYS OF THE WEEK, see page 151

Opera—Ballet—Concert   *Opéra – Ballet – Concert*

Can you recommend a ...?	**Pouvez-vous me recommander ...?**	poovay voo mer rerkommahngday
ballet	**un ballet**	ang bahlleh
concert	**un concert**	ang kawngssehr
opera	**un opéra**	ang nopayrah
operetta	**une opérette**	ewn opayreht
Where's the opera house/the concert hall?	**Où se trouve l'Opéra/ la salle de concert?**	oo ser troov lopayrah/ lah sahl der kawngssehr
What's on at the opera tonight?	**Que joue-t-on ce soir à l'Opéra?**	ker zhootawng ser swahr ah lopayrah
Who's singing/ dancing?	**Qui chante/danse?**	kee shahngt/dahngss
What orchestra is playing?	**Quel est le nom de l'orchestre?**	kehl eh ler nawng der lorkehstr
What are they playing?	**Que jouera-t-on?**	ker zhoorah tawng
Who's the conductor/ soloist?	**Qui est le chef d'orchestre/le soliste?**	kee eh ler shehf dorkehstr/ ler soleest

Nightclubs   *Boîtes de nuit*

Can you recommend a good nightclub?	**Pouvez-vous m'indiquer une bonne boîte de nuit?**	poovay voo mangdeekay ewn bon bwaht der nwee
Is there a floor show?	**Est-ce qu'il y a un spectacle de cabaret?**	ehss keel ee ah ang spehktahkl der kahbahreh
What time does the show start?	**A quelle heure commence le spectacle?**	ah kehl urr kommahngss ler spehktahkl
Is evening dress required?	**La tenue de soirée est-elle exigée?**	lah ternew der swahray ehtehl ehxeezhay

Discos   *Discothèques*

Where can we go dancing?	**Où pouvons-nous danser?**	oo poovawng noo dahngssay
Is there a discotheque in town?	**Y a-t-il une discothèque en ville?**	ee ahteel ewn deeskotehk ahng veel
Would you like to dance?	**Voulez-vous danser?**	voolay voo dahngssay

Sports *Sports*

Football (soccer), tennis, boxing, wrestling and bicycle, car and horse racing are among popular spectator sports. If you like sailing, fishing, horseback riding, golf, tennis, hiking, cycling, swimming, golf or trap shooting, you'll find plenty of opportunity to satisfy your recreational bent.

Is there a football (soccer) match anywhere this Saturday?	Y a-t-il un match de football quelque part ce samedi?	ee ahteel ang "match" der "football" kehlker pahr ser sahmdee
Which teams are playing?	Quelles sont les équipes?	kehl sawng lay zaykeep
Can you get me a ticket?	Puis-je avoir un billet?	pweezh ahvwahr ang beeyeh

basketball	le basket-ball	ler "basket-ball"
boxing	la boxe	lah box
car racing	les courses d'autos	lay koors doato
cycling	le cyclisme	ler seekleesm
football (soccer)	le football	ler "football"
horse racing	les courses (de chevaux)	lay koors (der shervoa)
skiing	le ski	ler skee
swimming	la natation	lah nahtahssyawng
tennis	le tennis	ler tehnees
volleyball	le volley-ball	ler vollehboal

I'd like to see a boxing match.	Je voudrais voir un match de boxe.	zher voodreh vwahr ang "match" der box
What's the admission charge?	Combien coûte l'entrée?	kawngbyang koot lahngtray
Where's the nearest golf course?	Où se trouve le terrain de golf le plus proche?	oo ser troov ler tehrang der golf ler plew prosh
Where are the tennis courts?	Où se trouvent les courts de tennis?	oo ser troov lay koor der tehneess
What's the charge per ...?	Quel est le tarif par ...?	kehl eh ler tahreef pahr
day/round/hour	jour/partie/heure	zhoor/pahrtee/urr

Can I hire (rent) rackets?	Puis-je louer des raquettes?	pweezh looay day rahkeht
Where's the race course (track)?	Où est le champ de courses?	oo eh ler shahng der koors
Is there any good fishing around here?	Y a-t-il un bon endroit pour pêcher dans les environs?	ee ahteel ang bawng nahngdrwah poor pehshay dahng lay zahngveerawng
Do I need a permit?	Est-ce que j'ai besoin d'un permis?	ehss ker zhay berzwang dang pehrmee
Where can I get one?	Où puis-je m'en procurer un?	oo pweezh mahng prokewray ang
Can one swim in the lake/river?	Peut-on nager dans le lac/la rivière?	purtawng nahzhay dahng ler lahk/lah reevyehr
Is there a swimming pool here?	Y a-t-il une piscine?	ee ahteel ewn peesseen
Is it open-air or indoor?	Est-elle en plein air ou couverte?	ehtehl ahng plehn ehr oo koovehrt
Is it heated?	Est-elle chauffée?	ehtehl shoafay
What's the temperature of the water?	Quelle est la température de l'eau?	kehl eh la tahngpay-rahtewr der loa
Is there a sandy beach?	Y a-t-il une plage de sable?	ee ahteel ewn plahzh der sahbl

On the beach *A la plage*

Is it safe for swimming?	Peut-on nager sans danger?	purtawng nahzhay sahng dahngzhay
Is there a lifeguard?	Y a-t-il un gardien de plage?	ee ahteel ang gahrdyang der plahzh
Is it safe for children?	Est-ce sans danger pour les enfants?	ehss sahng dahngzhay poor lay zahngfahng
The sea is very calm.	La mer est très calme.	lah mehr eh treh kahlm
There are some big waves.	Il y a de grosses vagues.	eel ee ah der groass vahg
Are there any dangerous currents?	Y a-t-il des courants dangereux?	ee ahteel day koorahng dahngzherrur
What time is high tide/low tide?	A quelle heure est la marée haute/ basse?	ah kehl urr eh lah mahray oat/bahss

I want to hire a/an/some ...	Je voudrais louer ...	zher voodreh looay
bathing hut (cabana)	une cabine	ewn kahbeen
deck-chair	une chaise longue	ewn shehz lawngg
motorboat	un canot à moteur	ang kahnoa ah moturr
rowing-boat	une barque à rames	ewn bahrk ah rahm
sailboard	une planche à voile	ewn plahngsh ah vwahl
sailing-boat	un voilier	ang vwahlyay
skin-diving equipment	un équipement de plongée sous-marine	ang naykeepmahng der plawngzhay soomahreen
sunshade (umbrella)	un parasol	ang pahrahssol
surfboard	une planche de surf	ewn plahngsh der ''surf''
water-skis	des skis nautiques	day skee noateek

PLAGE PRIVÉE   PRIVATE BEACH
BAIGNADE INTERDITE   NO SWIMMING

Winter sports *Sports d'hiver*

Is there a skating rink near here?	Y a-t-il une patinoire près d'ici?	ee ahteel ewn pahteenwahr preh deessee
I'd like to ski.	Je voudrais faire du ski.	zher voodreh fehr dew skee
downhill/cross-country skiing	ski de piste/ski de fond	skee der peest/skee der fawng
Are there any ski runs for ...?	Y a-t-il des pistes pour ...?	ee ahteel day peest poor
beginners	débutants	daybewtahng
average skiers	skieurs moyens	skeeurr mwahyang
good skiers	bons skieurs	bawng skeeurr
Can I take skiing lessons?	Puis-je prendre des leçons de ski?	pweezh prahngdr day lerssawng der skee
Are there ski lifts?	Y a-t-il des téléskis?	ee ahteel day taylayskee
I want to hire ...	Je voudrais louer ...	zher voodreh looay
poles	des bâtons	day bahtawng
skates	des patins	day pahtang
ski boots	des chaussures de ski	day shoassewr der skee
skiing equipment	un équipement de ski	ang naykeepmahng der skee
skis	des skis	day skee

Making friends

Introductions *Présentations*

May I introduce ...?	**Puis-je vous présenter ...?**	pweezh voo prayzahngtay
John, this is ...	**Jean, voici ...**	zhahng vwahssee
My name is ...	**Je m'appelle ...**	zher mahpehl
Pleased to meet you.	**Enchanté(e).**	ahngshahngtay
What's your name?	**Comment vous appelez-vous?**	kommahng voo zahperlay voo
How are you?	**Comment allez-vous?**	kommahng tahlay voo
Fine, thanks. And you?	**Très bien, merci. Et vous?**	treh byang mehrsee. ay voo

Follow-up *Pour rompre la glace*

How long have you been here?	**Depuis combien de temps êtes-vous ici?**	derpwee kawngbyang der tahng eht voo zeessee
We've been here a week.	**Nous sommes ici depuis une semaine.**	noo som zeessee derpwee ewn sermehn
Is this your first visit?	**Est-ce la première fois que vous venez?**	ehss lah prermyehr fwah ker voo vernay
No, we came here last year.	**Non, nous sommes déjà venus l'an dernier.**	nawng noo som dayzhah vernew lahng dehrnyay
Are you enjoying your stay?	**Est-ce que vous vous plaisez ici?**	ehss ker voo voo plehzay eessee
Yes, I like it very much.	**Oui, je m'y plais beaucoup.**	wee zher mee pleh boakoo
I like the scenery a lot.	**Ce paysage me plaît beaucoup.**	ser payeezahzh mer pleh boakoo
Do you travel a lot?	**Est-ce que vous voyagez beaucoup?**	ehss ker voo vwahyahzhay boakoo
Where do you come from?	**D'où êtes-vous?**	doo eht voo
I'm from ...	**Je viens de ...**	zher vyang der
What nationality are you?	**Quelle est votre nationalité?**	kehl eh votr nahssyonahleetay

COUNTRIES, see page 146

I'm ...	Je suis de nationalité ...	zer swee der nahssyonahleetay
American	américaine	ahmayreekehn
British	britannique	breetahneek
Canadian	canadienne	kahnahdyehn
Irish	irlandaise	eerlahngdehz
Where are you staying?	Où logez-vous?	oo lozhay voo
Are you on your own?	Etes-vous seul(e)?	eht voo surl
I'm with my ...	Je suis avec ...	zher swee ahvehk
wife	ma femme	mah fahm
husband	mon mari	mawng mahree
family	ma famille	mah fahmeey
children	mes enfants	may zahngfahng
parents	mes parents	may pahrahng
boyfriend/girlfriend	mon ami/amie	mawng nahmee/nahmee

father/mother	le père/la mère	ler pehr/lah mehr
son/daughter	le fils/la fille	ler feess/lah feey
brother/sister	le frère/la sœur	ler frehr/lah surr
uncle/aunt	l'oncle/la tante	lawngkler/lah tahngt
nephew/niece	le neveu/la nièce	ler nurvur/lah nyehss
cousin	le cousin/la cousine	ler koozang/lah koozeen

Are you married/ single?	Etes-vous marié(e)/ célibataire?	eht voo mahryay/ sayleebahtehr
Do you have children?	Avez-vous des enfants?	ahvay voo day zahngfahng
What do you think of the country/people?	Comment trouvez-vous le pays/les gens?	kommahng troovay voo ler pehee/lay zhahng
What's your occupation?	Quelle est votre profession?	kehl eh votr profehssyawng
I'm a student.	Je suis étudiant(e).	zher swee zaytewdyahng(t)
What are you studying?	Qu'étudiez-vous?	kaytewdyay voo
I'm here on a business trip.	Je suis en voyage d'affaires.	zher swee zahng vwahyahzh dahfehr
Do you play cards/ chess?	Jouez-vous aux cartes/aux échecs?	zhooay voo oa kahrt/ oa zayshehk

The weather *Le temps*

What a lovely day!	**Quelle belle journée!**	kehl behl zhoornay
What awful weather!	**Quel sale temps!**	kehl sahl tahng
Isn't it cold/ hot today?	**Qu'il fait froid/ Quelle chaleur!**	keel feh frwah/kehl shahlurr
Is it usually as warm as this?	**Fait-il toujours aussi chaud?**	fehteel toozhoor oassee shoa
Do you think it's going to ... tomorrow?	**Pensez-vous qu'il ... demain?**	pahngsay voo keel ... dermang
be a nice day	**fera beau**	ferrah boa
rain	**pleuvra**	plurvrah
snow	**neigera**	nehzherrah
What is the weather forecast?	**Quelles sont les prévisions météo?**	kehl sawng lay prayveezyawng maytayoa

cloud	**le nuage**	ler newahzh
fog	**le brouillard**	ler brooyahr
frost	**le gel**	ler zhehl
ice	**la glace**	lah glahss
lightning	**l'éclair**	layklehr
moon	**la lune**	lah lewn
rain	**la pluie**	lah plwee
sky	**le ciel**	ler syehl
snow	**la neige**	lah nehzh
star	**l'étoile**	laytwahl
sun	**le soleil**	ler solehy
thunder	**le tonnerre**	ler tonnehr
thunderstorm	**l'orage**	lorahzh
wind	**le vent**	ler vahng

Invitations *Invitations*

Would you like to have dinner with us on ...?	**Voudriez-vous dîner avec nous ...?**	voodreeyay voo deenay ahvehk noo
May I invite you for lunch?	**Puis-je vous inviter à déjeuner?**	pweezh voo zangveetay ah dayzhurnay

DAYS OF THE WEEK, see page 151

Can you come over for a drink this evening?	Pouvez-vous venir prendre un verre chez moi ce soir?	poovay voo verneer prahngdr ang vehr shay mwah ser swahr
There's a party. Are you coming?	Il y a une réception. Viendrez-vous?	eel ee ah ewn rayssehp-syawng. vyangdray voo
That's very kind of you.	C'est très aimable.	seh treh zehmahbl
Great. I'd love to come.	Je viendrai avec plaisir.	zher vyangdray ahvehk plehzeer
What time shall we come?	A quelle heure faut-il venir?	ah kehl urr foateel verneer
May I bring a friend/ a girlfriend?	Puis-je amener un ami/une amie?	pweezh ahmernay ang nahmee/ewn ahmee
I'm afraid we've got to leave now.	Nous devons partir maintenant.	noo dervawng pahrteer mangternahng
Next time you must come to visit us.	La prochaine fois, il faudra que vous veniez chez nous.	lah proshehn fwah eel foadrah ker voo vernyay shay noo
Thanks for the evening. It was great.	Merci pour la soirée. C'était formidable.	mehrsee poor lah swahray. sayteh formeedahbl

Dating *Rendez-vous*

Do you mind if I smoke?	Est-ce que ça vous dérange que je fume?	ehss ker sah voo dayrahngzh ker zher fewm
Would you like a cigarette?	Voulez-vous une cigarette?	voolay voo ewn seegahreht
Do you have a light, please?	Avez-vous du feu, s'il vous plaît?	ahvay voo dew fur seel voo pleh
Why are you laughing?	Pourquoi riez-vous?	poorkwah reeyay voo
Is my French that bad?	Mon français est-il si mauvais?	mawng frahngsseh ehteel see moaveh
Do you mind if I sit down here?	Me permettez-vous de m'asseoir ici?	mer pehrmehtay voo der mahssswahr eessee
Can I get you a drink?	Puis-je vous offrir un verre?	pweezh voo zoffreer ang vehr
Are you waiting for someone?	Attendez-vous quelqu'un?	ahtahngday voo kehlkang

Are you free this evening?	Etes-vous libre ce soir?	eht voo leebr ser swahr
Would you like to go out with me tonight?	Voulez-vous sortir avec moi ce soir?	voolay voo sorteer ahvehk mwah ser swahr
Would you like to go dancing?	Aimeriez-vous aller danser?	ehmerryay voo ahlay dahngssay
I know a good discotheque.	Je connais une bonne discothèque.	zher konneh ewn bon deeskotehk
Shall we go to the cinema (movies)?	Nous pourrions aller au cinéma.	noo pooryawng ahlay oa seenaymah
Would you like to go for a drive?	Aimeriez-vous faire un tour en voiture?	ehmerryay voo fehr ang toor ahng vwahtewr
Where shall we meet?	Où nous retrouverons-nous?	oo noo rertrooverrawng noo
I'll pick you up at your hotel.	Je viendrai vous prendre à votre hôtel.	zher vyangdray voo prahngdr ah votr oatehl
I'll call for you at 8.	Je viendrai vous chercher à 8 heures.	zher vyangdray voo shehrshay ah 8 urr
May I take you home?	Puis-je vous raccompagner?	pweezh voo rahkawngpahñay
Can I see you again tomorrow?	Puis-je vous revoir demain?	pweezh voo rervwahr dermang
What's your telephone number?	Quel est votre numéro de téléphone?	kehl eh votr newmayroa der taylayfon

... and you might answer:

I'd love to, thank you.	Avec plaisir, merci.	ahvehk plehzeer mehrsee
Thank you, but I'm busy.	Merci, mais je suis pris(e).	mehrsee meh zher swee pree(z)
No, I'm not interested, thank you.	Non, cela ne m'intéresse pas.	nawng serlah ner mangtayrehss pah
Leave me alone, please!	Laissez-moi tranquille!	lehssay mwah trahngkeel
Thank you, it's been a wonderful evening.	Merci, j'ai passé une merveilleuse soirée.	mehrsee zhay pahssay ewn mehrvehyurz swahray
I've enjoyed myself.	Je me suis bien amusé(e).	zher mer swee byang nahmewzay

Shopping guide

This shopping guide is designed to help you find what you want with ease, accuracy and speed. It features:

1. a list of all major shops, stores and services (p. 98)
2. some general expressions required when shopping to allow you to be specific and selective (p. 100)
3. full details of the shops and services most likely to concern you. Here you'll find advice, alphabetical lists of items and conversion charts listed under the headings below.

LAUNDRY, see page 29/HAIRDRESSER'S, see page 30

Shops, stores and services *Magasins et services*

Shops usually open at around 9 a.m. and close anytime between 5.30 and 7 p.m. (until 6 in Belgium and until 6.30 in Switzerland). Most businesses close for an hour or two at noon—except department stores. Some shops are open on Sundays and holidays in France. They generally close Saturdays at 5 p.m. in Switzerland. Shopkeepers take a day off during the week—usually Monday.

Where's the nearest ...?	Où est ... le/la plus proche?	oo eh ... ler/lah plew prosh
antique shop	l'antiquaire	lahngteekehr
art gallery	la galerie d'art	lah gahlerree dahr
baker's	la boulangerie	lah boolahngzherree
bank	la banque	lah bahngk
barber's	le coiffeur	ler kwahfurr
beauty salon	l'institut de beauté	langsteetew der boatay
bookshop	la librairie	lah leebrehree
butcher's	la boucherie	lah boosherree
cake shop	la pâtisserie	lah pahteesserree
camera shop	le magasin de photos	ler mahgahzang der fotoa
chemist's	la pharmacie	lah fahrmahssee
confectioner's	la confiserie	lah kawngfeezerree
dairy	la laiterie	lah lehterree
delicatessen	la charcuterie/ le traiteur	lah shahrkewterree/ ler trehturr
dentist	le dentiste	ler dahngteest
department store	le grand magasin	ler grahng mahgahzang
drugstore	la pharmacie	lah fahrmahssee
dry cleaner's	la teinturerie	lah tangtewrerree
electrician	l'électricien	laylehktreessyang
fishmonger's	la poissonnerie	lah pwahssonnerree
flower shop	le fleuriste	ler flurreest
furrier's	le fourreur	ler foorrurr
greengrocer's	le primeur	ler preemurr
grocery	l'épicerie/le magasin d'alimentation	laypeesserree/ler mahgahzang dahleemahngtah-ssyawng
hairdresser's (ladies/men)	le coiffeur (pour dames/messieurs)	ler kwahfurr (poor dahm/mehssyur)
hardware store	la quincaillerie	lah kangkahyerree
health food shop	le magasin de diététique	ler mahgahzang der dyaytayteek

hospital	l'hôpital	loapeetahl
ironmonger's	la quincaillerie	lah kangkahyerree
jeweller's	la bijouterie	lah beezhooterree
launderette	la laverie automatique	lah lahverree oatomahteek
library	la bibliothèque	lah beebleeyotehk
laundry	la blanchisserie	lah blahngsheesserree
market	le marché	ler mahrshay
newsagent's	le marchand de journaux	ler mahrshahng der zhoornoa
newsstand	le kiosque à journaux	ler kyosk ah zhoornoa
optician	l'opticien	lopteessyang
pastry shop	la pâtisserie	lah pahteesserree
photographer	le photographe	ler fotograhf
police station	le poste de police	ler post der poleess
post office	le bureau de poste	ler bewroa der post
shoemaker's (repairs)	la cordonnerie	lah kordonnerree
shoe shop	le magasin de chaussures	ler mahgahzang der shoassewr
shopping centre	le centre commercial	ler sahngtr kommehrsyahl
souvenir shop	le magasin de souvenirs	ler mahgahzang der sooverneer
sporting goods shop	le magasin d'articles de sport	ler mahgahzang dahrteekl der spor
stationer's	la papeterie	lah pahpehterree
supermarket	le supermarché	ler sewpehrmahrshay
tailor's	le tailleur	ler tahyurr
telegraph office	le bureau du télégraphe	ler bewroa dew taylaygrahf
tobacconist's	le bureau de tabac	ler bewroa der tahbah
toy shop	le magasin de jouets	ler mahgahzang der zhooeh
travel agency	l'agence de voyages	lahzhahngss der vwahyahzh
vegetable store	le primeur	ler preemurr
veterinarian	le vétérinaire	ler vaytayreenehr
watchmaker's	l'horlogerie	lorlozherree
wine merchant	le marchand de vin	ler mahrshahng der vang

ENTRÉE	ENTRANCE
SORTIE	EXIT
SORTIE DE SECOURS	EMERGENCY EXIT

General expressions *Expressions générales*

Where? *Où?*

Where's there a good ...?	Où y a-t-il un bon/ une bonne ...?	oo ee ahteel ang bawng/ ewn bon
Where can I find a ...?	Où puis-je trouver ...?	oo pweezh troovay
Where's the main shopping area?	Où se trouve le quartier commerçant?	oo ser troov ler kahrtyay kommehrssahng
Is it far from here?	Est-ce loin d'ici?	ehss lwang deessee
How do I get there?	Comment puis-je m'y rendre?	kommahng pweezh mee rahngdr

```
SOLDES    SALE
```

Service *Service*

Can you help me?	Pourriez-vous m'aider?	pooryay voo mehday
I'm just looking.	Je ne fais que regarder.	zher ner feh ker rergahrday
I want ...	Je désire ...	zher dayzeer
Can you show me some ...?	Pourriez-vous me montrer ...?	pooryay voo mer mawngtray
Do you have any ...?	Avez-vous ...?	ahvay voo
Where's the ... department?	Où se trouve le rayon ...?	oo ser troov ler rehyawng
Where is the lift (elevator)/escalator?	Où est l'ascenseur/ l'escalier mécanique?	oo eh lahssahngssurr/ lehskahlyay maykahneek
Where do I pay?	Où est la caisse?	oo eh lah kehss

That one *Celui-là*

Can you show me ...?	Pouvez-vous me montrer ...?	poovay voo mer mawngtray
this/that	ceci/cela	serssee/serlah
the one in the window/in the display case	celui qui est en vitrine/ à l'étalage	serlwee kee eh ahng veetreen/ah laytahlahzh

Defining the article *Description de l'article*

I'd like a ... one.	**Je désire un ...**	zher dayzeer ang
big	**grand**	grahng
cheap	**bon marché**	bawng mahrshay
dark	**foncé**	fawngssay
good	**bon**	bawng
heavy	**lourd**	loor
large	**grand**	grahng
light (weight)	**léger**	layzhay
light (colour)	**clair**	klehr
oval	**ovale**	ovahl
rectangular	**rectangulaire**	rehktahnggewlehr
round	**rond**	rawng
small	**petit**	pertee
square	**carré**	kahray
sturdy	**solide**	soleed
I don't want anything too expensive.	**Je ne voudrais pas quelque chose de trop cher.**	zher ner voodreh pah kehlker shoaz der troa shehr

Preference *Préférences*

Can you show me some more?	**Pouvez-vous m'en montrer d'autres?**	poovay voo mahng mawngtray doatr
Haven't you anything ...?	**N'auriez-vous pas quelque chose de ...?**	noaryay voo pah kehlker shoaz der
cheaper/better	**meilleur marché/ mieux**	mehyurr mahrshay/myur
larger/smaller	**plus grand/plus petit**	plew grahng/plew pertee

How much? *Combien?*

How much is this?	**Combien coûte ceci?**	kawngbyang koot serssee
How much are they?	**Combien coûtent-ils?**	kawngbyang koot teel
I don't understand.	**Je ne comprends pas.**	zher ner kawngprahng pah
Please write it down.	**Pourriez-vous l'écrire, s'il vous plaît?**	pooryay voo laykreer seel voo pleh
I don't want to spend more than ... francs.	**Je ne veux pas dépenser plus de ... francs.**	zher ner vur pah daypahngssay plew der ... frahng

COLOURS, see page 113

Decision *Décision*

It's not quite what I want.	Ce n'est pas exactement ce que je veux.	ser neh pah zehxahkter-mahng ser ker zher vur
No, I don't like it.	Non, cela ne me plaît pas.	nawng serlah ner mer pleh pah
I'll take it.	Je le prends.	zher ler prahng

Ordering *Commande*

| Can you order it for me? | Pourriez-vous me le commander? | pooray voo mer ler kommahngday |
| How long will it take? | Combien de temps cela prendra-t-il? | kawngbyang der tahng serlah prahngdrah teel |

Delivery *Livraison*

I'll take it with me.	Je l'emporte.	zher lahngport
Deliver it to the ... Hotel.	Veuillez le livrer à l'Hôtel ...	vuryay ler leevray ah loatehl
Please send it to this address.	Veuillez l'envoyer à cette adresse.	vuryay lahngvwahyay ah seht ahdrehss
Will I have any difficulty with the customs?	Aurai-je des difficultés avec la douane?	oarehzh day deefeekewltay ahvehk lah dwahn

Paying *Paiement*

How much is it?	Combien vous dois-je?	kawngbyang voo dwahzh
Can I pay by traveller's cheque?	Puis-je payer en chèques de voyage?	pweezh pehyay ahng shehk der vwahyahzh
Do you accept dollars/pounds?	Acceptez-vous les dollars/livres?	ahksehptay voo lay dollar/leevr
Do you accept credit cards?	Acceptez-vous les cartes de crédit?	ahksehptay voo lay kahrt der kraydee
Do I have to pay the VAT (sales tax)?	Dois-je payer la T.V.A.?	dwahzh pehyay lah tay vay ah
Haven't you made a mistake in the bill?	N'y a-t-il pas une erreur dans la facture?	nee ahteel pah zewn ehrurr dahng lah fahktewr

Anything else? *Autre chose?*

No, thanks, that's all.	**Non merci, ce sera tout.**	nawng mehrsee ser serrah too
Yes, I want ...	**Oui, je voudrais ...**	wee zher voodreh
Show me ...	**Veuillez me montrer ...**	vuryay mer mawngtray
May I have a bag, please?	**Puis-je avoir un sac, s'il vous plaît?**	pweezh ahvwahr ang sahk seel voo pleh

Dissatisfied? *Mécontent?*

Can you please exchange this?	**Pourriez-vous échanger ceci?**	pooray voo ayshahngzhay serssee
I want to return this.	**Je voudrais vous rendre ceci.**	zher voodreh voo rahngdr serssee
I'd like a refund. Here's the receipt.	**Je voudrais me faire rembourser. Voici la quittance.**	zher voodreh mer fehr rahngboorsay. vwahssee lah keetahngss

---

Puis-je vous être utile?	Can I help you?
Que désirez-vous?	What would you like?
Quelle ... désirez-vous?	What ... would you like?
couleur/forme qualité/quantité	colour/shape quality/quantity
Je suis désolé(e), nous n'en avons pas.	I'm sorry, we haven't any.
Notre stock est épuisé.	We're out of stock.
Pouvons-nous le commander?	Shall we order it for you?
Désirez-vous l'emporter ou faut-il vous l'envoyer?	Will you take it with you or shall we send it?
Autre chose?	Anything else?
Cela fera ... francs, s'il vous plaît.	That's ... francs, please.
La caisse se trouve là-bas.	The cashier's over there.

Bookshop—Stationer's   *Librairie – Papeterie*

In France, bookshops and stationers' are usually separate shops, though the latter will often sell paperbacks. Newspapers and magazines are sold at newsstands.

Where's the nearest …?	**Où est … le/la plus proche?**	oo eh … ler/lah plew prosh
bookshop	**la librairie**	lah leebrehree
stationer's	**la papeterie**	lah pahpehterree
newsstand	**le kiosque à journaux**	ler kyosk ah zhoornoa
Where can I buy an English-language newspaper?	**Où puis-je acheter un journal en anglais?**	oo pweezh ahshertay ang zhoornahl ahng nahnggleh
Where's the guide-book section?	**Où sont les guides de voyage?**	oo sawng lay geed der vwahyahzh
Where do you keep the English books?	**Où se trouvent les livres en anglais?**	oo ser troov lay leevr ahng nahnggleh
Have you any of …'s books in English?	**Avez-vous des livres de … en anglais?**	ahvay voo day leevr der … ahng nahnggleh
Do you have second-hand books?	**Avez-vous des livres d'occasion?**	ahvay voo day leevr dokahzyawng
I want to buy a/an/ some …	**Je voudrais acheter …**	zher voodreh ahshertay
address book	**un carnet d'adresses**	ang kahrneh dahdrehss
ball-point pen	**un stylo à bille**	ang steeloa ah beey
book	**un livre**	ang leevr
calendar	**un calendrier**	ang kahlahngdreeyay
carbon paper	**du papier carbone**	dew pahpyay kahrbon
cellophane tape	**du ruban adhésif**	dew rewbahng ahdayzeef
crayons	**des crayons de couleur**	day krehyawng der koolurr
dictionary French-English pocket	**un dictionnaire français-anglais de poche**	ang deeksyonnehr frahngsseh ahnggleh der posh
drawing paper	**du papier à dessin**	dew pahpyay ah dehssang
drawing pins	**des punaises**	day pewnehz
envelopes	**des enveloppes**	day zahngverlop
eraser	**une gomme**	ewn gom
exercise book	**un cahier**	ang kahyay
felt-tip pen	**un crayon feutre**	ang krehyawng furtr

fountain pen	un stylo	ang steeloa
glue	de la colle	der lah kol
grammar book	une grammaire	ewn grahmehr
guidebook	un guide	ang geed
ink	de l'encre	der lahngkr
black/red/blue	noire/rouge/bleue	nwahr/roozh/blur
(adhesive) labels	des étiquettes (autocollantes)	day zayteekeht (oatokollahngt)
magazine	une revue	ewn rervew
map	une carte (géographique)	ewn kahrt (zhayoagrahfeek)
map of the town	un plan de ville	ang plahng der veel
road map of ...	une carte routière de ...	ewn kahrt rootyehr der
mechanical pencil	un porte-mine	ang port meen
newspaper	un journal	ang zhoornahl
American/English	américain/anglais	amayreekang/ahnggleh
notebook	un bloc-notes	ang blok not
note paper	du papier à lettres	dew pahpyay ah lehtr
paintbox	une boîte de couleurs	ewn bwaht der koolurr
paper	du papier	dew pahpyay
paperback	un livre de poche	ang leevr der posh
paperclips	des trombones	day trawngbon
paper napkins	des serviettes en papier	day sehrvyeht ahng pahpyay
paste	de la colle	der lah kol
pen	une plume	ewn plewm
pencil	un crayon	ang krehyawng
pencil sharpener	un taille-crayon	ang tahy krehyawng
playing cards	des cartes à jouer	day kahrt ah zhooay
pocket calculator	une calculatrice de poche	ewn kahlkewlahtreess der posh
postcard	une carte postale	ewn kahrt postahl
propelling pencil	un porte-mine	ang port meen
refill (for a pen)	une recharge (pour stylo)	ewn rershahrzh (poor steeloa)
rubber	une gomme	ewn gom
ruler	une règle	ewn rehgl
staples	des agrafes	day zahgrahf
string	de la ficelle	der lah feessehl
thumbtacks	des punaises	day pewnehz
tissue paper	du papier de soie	dew pahpyay der swah
typewriter ribbon	un ruban de machine à écrire	ang rewbahng der mahsheen ah aykreer
typing paper	du papier à machine	dew pahpyay ah mahsheen
writing pad	un bloc	ang blok

Camping equipment *Matériel de camping*

I'd like a/an/some ...	Je voudrais ...	zher voodreh
bottle-opener	un ouvre-bouteilles	ahng noovr bootehy
bucket	un seau	ahng soa
butane gas	du butane	dew bewtahn
campbed	un lit de camp	ang lee der kahng
can opener	un ouvre-boîtes	ang noovr bwaht
candles	des bougies	day boozhee
(folding) chair	une chaise (pliante)	ewn shehz (pleeyahngt)
charcoal	du charbon de bois	dew shahrbawng der bwah
clothes pegs	des pinces à linge	day pangss ah langzh
compass	une boussole	ewn boossol
cool box	une glacière	ewn glahssyehr
corkscrew	un tire-bouchon	ang teer booshawng
crockery	de la vaisselle	der lah vehssehl
cutlery	des couverts	day koovehr
deck-chair	une chaise longue	ewn shehz lawngg
dishwashing detergent	du produit (à) vaisselle	dew prodwee (ah) vehssehl
first-aid kit	une trousse de premiers secours	ewn trooss der prermyay serkoor
fishing tackle	un attirail de pêche	ang nahteerahy der pehsh
flashlight	une lampe de poche	ewn lahngp der posh
food box	une boîte à conservation	ewn bwaht ah kawng-ssehrrvahssyawng
frying-pan	une poêle	ewn pwahl
groundsheet	un tapis de sol	ang tahpee der sol
hammer	un marteau	ang mahrtoa
hammock	un hamac	ang ahmahk
haversack	une musette	ewn mewzeht
ice pack	une cartouche réfrigérante	ewn kahrtoosh rayfree-zhayrahngt
kerosene	du pétrole	dew paytrol
knapsack	un sac à dos	ang sahk ah doa
lamp	une lampe	ewn lahngp
lantern	une lanterne	ewn lahngtehrn
matches	des allumettes	day zahlewmeht
mattress	un matelas	ang mahterlah
methylated spirits	de l'alcool à brûler	der lahlkol ah brewlay
mosquito net	une moustiquaire	ewn moosteekehr
pail	un seau	ang soa
paper napkins	des serviettes en papier	day sehrvyeht ahng pahpyay
paraffin	du pétrole	dew paytrol
penknife	un canif	ang kahneef

CAMPING, see page 32

picnic basket	un panier à pique-nique	ang pahnyay ah peekneek
plastic bag	un sac en plastique	ang sahk ahng plahsteek
rope	de la corde	der lah kord
rucksack	un sac de montagne	ang sahk der mawngtañ
saucepan	une casserole	ewn kahsserrol
scissors	des ciseaux	day seezoa
screwdriver	un tournevis	ang toornerveess
sleeping bag	une sac de couchage	ang sahk der kooshahzh
stew pot	une marmite	ewn mahrmeet
(folding) table	une table (pliante)	ewn tahbl (pleeyahngt)
tent	une tente	ewn tahngt
tent pegs	des piquets de tente	day peekeh der tahngt
tent pole	un montant de tente	ang mawngtahng der tahngt
tinfoil	du papier d'aluminium	dew pahpyay dahlewmeenyom
tin opener	un ouvre-boîtes	ang noovr bwaht
tongs	une pince	ewn pangss
torch	une lampe de poche	ewn lahngp der posh
vacuum flask	un thermos	ang tehrmoass
washing powder	de la lessive	der lah lehsseev
water flask	une gourde	ewn goord
wood alcohol	de l'alcool à brûler	der lahlkol ah brewlay

Crockery *Vaisselle*

cups	des tasses	day tahss
mugs	des grosses tasses	day gross tahss
plates	des assiettes	day zahssyeht
saucers	des soucoupes	day sookoop
tumblers	des gobelets	day goberleh

Cutlery *Couverts*

forks	des fourchettes	day foorsheht
knives	des couteaux	day kootoa
dessert knives	des couteaux à dessert	day kootoa ah dehssehr
spoons	des cuillères	day kweeyehr
teaspoons	des cuillères à café	day kweeyehr ah kahfay
(made of) plastic	(en) plastique	ahng plahsteek
(made of) stainless steel	(en) inox	(ahng) eenox

Chemist's (drugstore) *Pharmacie*

You will recognize a chemist's by the sign outside—a green cross, which is lit at night. In the window you'll see a notice telling you where the nearest all-night chemist's is. Go to a *parfumerie* (pahrfewmerree) for perfume and cosmetics. Otherwise, other toilet and household articles can be bought from a *droguerie* (drogerree).

This section is divided into two parts:

1. Pharmaceutical—medicine, first-aid, etc.
2. Toiletry—toilet articles, cosmetics

General *Généralités*

Where's the nearest (all-night) chemist's?	**Où se trouve la pharmacie (de nuit) la plus proche?**	oo ser troov lah fahrmahssee der nwee lah plew prosh
What time does the chemist's open/ close?	**A quelle heure ouvre/ ferme la pharmacie?**	ah kehl urr oovr/fehrm lah fahrmahssee

1—Pharmaceutical *Médicaments, premiers soins, etc.*

I want something for ...	**Je voudrais quelque chose contre ...**	zher voodreh kehlker shoaz kawngtr
a cold/a cough	le rhume/la toux	ler rewm/lah too
hay fever	le rhume des foins	ler rewm day fwang
insect bites	les piqûres d'insectes	lay peekewr dangsehkt
a hangover	la gueule de bois	lah gurl der bwah
sunburn	les coups de soleil	lay koo der solehy
travel sickness	le mal du voyage	ler mahl dew vwahyahzh
an upset stomach	les indigestions	lay zangdeezhehstyawng
Can I make up this prescription for me?	**Pourriez-vous me préparer cette ordonnance?**	pooryay voo mer praypahray seht ordonnahngss
Can I get it without a prescription?	**Puis-je l'obtenir sans ordonnance?**	pweezh lobterneer sahng zordonnahngss
Shall I wait?	**Dois-je attendre?**	dwahzh ahtahngdr

DOCTOR, see page 137

Guide des achats

Can I have a/an/ some ...?	Puis-je avoir ...?	pweezh ahvwahr
analgesic	un analgésique	ang nahnahlzhayzeek
antiseptic cream	de la pommade antiseptique	der lah pommahd ahngteessehpteek
aspirin	de l'aspirine	der lahspeereen
bandage	un bandage	ang bahngdahzh
elastic bandage	bandage élastique	bahngdahzh aylahsteek
Band-Aids	du sparadrap	dew spahrahdrah
contraceptives	des contraceptifs	day kawngtrahssehpteef
corn plasters	des emplâtres pour les cors	day zahngplahtr poor lay kor
cotton wool (absorbent cotton)	du coton hydrophile	dew kotawng eedrofeel
cough drops	des pastilles contre la toux	day pahsteey kawngtr lah too
disinfectant	un désinfectant	ang dayzangfehktahng
ear drops	des gouttes pour les oreilles	day goot poor lay zorehy
Elastoplast	du sparadrap	dew spahrahdrah
eye drops	des gouttes oculaires	day goot okewlehr
gauze	de la gaze	der lah gahz
insect repellent/ spray	de la crème anti-insecte/une bombe insecticide	der lah krehm ahngtee-angssehkt/ewn bawngb angssehkteesseed
iodine	de la teinture d'iode	der lah tangtewr dyod
laxative	un laxatif	ang lahxahteef
mouthwash	un gargarisme	ang gahrgahreezm
nose drops	des gouttes nasales	day goot nahzahl
sanitary towels (napkins)	des serviettes hygiéniques	day sehrvyeht eezhyayneek
sleeping pills	un somnifère	ang somneefehr
suppositories	des suppositoires	day sewpoazeetwahr
... tablets	des comprimés ...	day kawngpreemay
tampons	des tampons hygiéniques	day tahngpawng eezhyayneek
thermometer	un thermomètre	ang tehrmomehtr
throat lozenges	des pastilles pour la gorge	day pahsteey poor lah gorzh
tranquillizers	un tranquillisant	ang trahngkeeleezahng
vitamin pills	des vitamines	day veetahmeen

POISON	POISON
POUR USAGE EXTERNE	FOR EXTERNAL USE ONLY

2—Toiletry *Articles de toilette*

I'd like a/an/some …	Je voudrais …	zher voodreh
after-shave lotion	de la lotion après rasage	der lah lossyawng ahpreh rahzahzh
astringent	un astringent	ang nahstrangzhahng
bath essence	du bain de mousse	dew bang der mooss
bath salts	des sels de bain	day sehl der bang
cream	une crème	ewn krehm
cleansing cream	une crème démaquillante	ewn krehm daymahkeeyahngt
foundation cream	du fond de teint	dew fawng der tang
moisturizing cream	une crème hydratante	ewn krehm eedrahtahngt
night cream	une crème de nuit	ewn krehm der nwee
cuticle remover	un produit pour enlever les cuticules	ahng prodwee poor ahng-lervay lay kewteekewl
deodorant	un déodorant	ang dayodorahng
emery board	une lime à ongles	ewn leem ah awnggl
eye liner	un eye-liner	ang "eye liner"
eye pencil	un crayon pour les yeux	ang krehyawng poor lay zyur
eye shadow	du fard à paupières	dew fahr ah poapyehr
face powder	de la poudre	der lah poodr
foot cream	de la crème pour les pieds	der lah krehm poor lay pyay
hand cream	de la crème pour les mains	der lah krehm poor lay mang
lipsalve	du beurre de cacao	dew burr der kahkahoa
lipstick	du rouge à lèvres	dew roozh ah lehvr
make-up remover pads	des disques démaquillants	day deesk daymahkeeyahng
nail brush	une brosse à ongles	ewn bross ah awnggl
nail clippers	un coupe-ongles	ang koop awnggl
nail file	une lime à ongles	ewn leem ah awnggl
nail polish	du vernis à ongles	dew vehrnee ah awnggl
nail polish remover	du dissolvant	dew deessolvahng
nail scissors	des ciseaux à ongles	day seezoa ah awnggl
perfume	du parfum	dew pahrfang
powder	de la poudre	der lah poodr
powder puff	une houppette	ewn oopeht
razor	un rasoir	ang rahzwahr
razor blades	des lames de rasoir	day lahm der rahzwahr
rouge	du fard à joues	dew fahr ah zhoo
safety pins	des épingles de sûreté	day zaypanggl der sewrtay

shaving brush	un blaireau	ang blehroa
shaving cream	de la crème à raser	der lah krehm ah rahzay
soap	du savon	dew sahvawng
sponge	une éponge	ewn aypawngzh
sun-tan cream	de la crème solaire	der lah krehm solehr
sun-tan oil	de l'huile solaire	der lweel solehr
talcum powder	du talc	dew tahlk
tissues	des mouchoirs en papier	day mooshwahr ahng pahpay
toilet paper	du papier hygiénique	dew pahpyay eezhyayneek
toilet water	de l'eau de toilette	der loa der twahleht
toothbrush	une brosse à dents	ewn bross ah dahng
toothpaste	du dentifrice	dew dahngteefreess
towel	une serviette	ewn sehrvyeht
tweezers	une pince à épiler	ewn pangss ah aypeelay

For your hair *Pour vos cheveux*

bobby pins	des pinces à cheveux	day shahngpwang shervur
colour shampoo	un shampooing colorant	ang shahngpwang kolorahng
comb	un peigne	ang pehñ
curlers	des bigoudis	day beegoodee
dry shampoo	un shampooing sec	ang shahngpwang sehk
dye	une teinture	ewn tangtewr
hairbrush	une brosse à cheveux	ewn bross ah shervur
hairgrips	des pinces à cheveux	day pangss ah shervur
hair lotion	une lotion capillaire	ewn lossyawng kahpeelehr
hairpins	des épingles à cheveux	day zaypanggl ah shervur
hair spray	de la laque	der lah lahk
setting lotion	un fixatif	ang feexahteef
shampoo	du shampooing	dew shahngpwang
for dry/greasy (oily) hair	pour cheveux secs/gras	poor shervur sehk/grah
tint	une coloration	ewn kolorahssyawng
wig	une perruque	ewn pehrewk

For the baby *Pour votre bébé*

baby food	des aliments pour bébés	day zahleemahng poor baybay
dummy (pacifier)	une tétine	ewn tayteen
feeding bottle	un biberon	ang beebuhrrawng
nappies (diapers)	des couches	day koosh

Clothing *Habillement*

If you want to buy something specific, prepare yourself in advance. Look at the list of clothing on page 116. Get some idea of the colour, material and size you want. They're all listed on the next few pages.

General *Généralités*

I'd like ...	**Je voudrais ...**	zher voodreh
I want ... for a 10-year-old boy/girl.	**Je voudrais ... pour un garçon/une fillette de 10 ans.**	zher voodreh ... poor ang gahrsawng/ewn feeyeht der 10 ahng
I want something like this.	**Je voudrais quelque chose dans ce genre.**	zher voodreh kehlker shoaz dahng ser zhahngr
I like the one in the window.	**Celui qui est en vitrine me plaît.**	serlwee kee eh tahng veetreen mer pleh
How much is that per metre?	**Combien coûte le mètre?**	kawngbyang koot ler mehtr

1 centimetre (cm.)	= 0.39 in.	1 inch =	2.54 cm.
1 metre (m.)	= 39.37 in.	1 foot =	30.5 cm.
10 metres	= 32.81 ft.	1 yard =	0.91 m.

Colour *Couleur*

I want something in ...	**Je voudrais quelque chose en ...**	zher voodreh kehlker shoaz ahng
I want a darker/lighter shade.	**Je voudrais un ton plus foncé/plus clair.**	zher voodreh ang tawng plew fawngssay/plew klehr
I want something to match this.	**Je voudrais quelque chose d'assorti à cela.**	zher voodreh kehlker shoaz dahssortee ah serlah
I don't like the colour.	**Je n'aime pas cette couleur.**	zher nehm pah seht koolurr

beige	**beige**	behzh
black	**noir**	nwahr
blue	**bleu**	blur
brown	**brun**	brang
fawn	**fauve**	foav
golden	**doré**	doray
green	**vert**	vehr
grey	**gris**	gree
mauve	**mauve**	moav
orange	**orange**	orahngzh
pink	**rose**	roaz
purple	**violet**	vyoleh
red	**rouge**	roozh
scarlet	**écarlate**	aykahrlaht
silver	**argenté**	ahrzhahngtay
turquoise	**turquoise**	tewrkwahz
white	**blanc**	blahng
yellow	**jaune**	zhoan
light ...	... **clair**	... klehr
dark ...	... **foncé**	... fawngssay

uni	**à rayures**	**à pois**	**à carreaux**	**fantaisie**
(ewnee)	(ah rehyewr)	(ah pwah)	(ah kahroa)	(fahngtayzee)

Material *Tissus*

Do you have anything in ...?	**Avez-vous quelque chose en ...?**	ahvay voo kehlker shoaz ahng
Is that ...?	**Est-ce ...?**	ehss
handmade	**fait à la main**	feh ah lah mang
imported	**importé**	angportay
made here	**de fabrication locale**	der fahbreekahssyawng lokahl
I want something thinner.	**Je voudrais quelque chose de plus mince.**	zher voodreh kehlker shoaz der plew mangss
Do you have any better quality?	**N'auriez-vous pas une meilleure qualité?**	noaray voo pah zewn mehyurr kahleetay

What's it made of?	En quoi est-ce?	ahng kwah ehss

cambric	batiste	bahteest
camel-hair	poil de chameau	pwahl der shahmoa
chiffon	mousseline	moosserleen
corduroy	velours côtelé	verloor koaterlay
cotton	coton	kotawng
crepe	crêpe	krehp
denim	toile de coton	twahl der kotawng
felt	feutre	furtr
flannel	flanelle	flahnehl
gabardine	gabardine	gahbahrdeen
lace	dentelle	dahngtehl
leather	cuir	kweer
linen	lin	lang
poplin	popeline	popperleen
satin	satin	sahtang
silk	soie	swah
suede	daim	dang
terrycloth	tissu-éponge	teessew aypawngzh
velvet	velours	verloor
velveteen	velours de coton	verloor der kotawng
wool	laine	lehn
worsted	peigné	pehñay

Is it ...?	Est-ce ...?	ehss
pure cotton/wool	pur coton/pure laine	pewr kotawng/pewr lehn
synthetic	synthétique	sangtayteek
colour fast	grand teint	grahng tang
wrinkle resistant	infroissable	angfrwahssahbl

Is it hand washable/ machine washable?	Peut-on le laver à la main/ à la machine?	purtawng ler lahvay ah lah mang/ ah lah mahsheen

Will it shrink?	Est-ce que cela rétrécit au lavage?	ehss ker serlah raytrayssee oa lahvahzh

Size *Taille*

I take size 38.	Je porte du 38.	zher port dew 38
Could you measure me?	Pouvez-vous prendre mes mesures?	poovay voo prahngdr may merzewr
I don't know the French sizes.	Je ne connais pas les tailles françaises.	zher ner konneh pah lay tahy frahngssehz

Sizes can vary somewhat from one manufacturer to another, so be sure to try on shoes and clothing before you buy.

Women *Dames*

	Dresses/Suits					
American	8	10	12	14	16	18
British	10	12	14	16	18	20
Continental	36	38	40	42	44	46

	Stockings							Shoes			
American } British	8	8½	9	9½	10	10½		6	7	8	9
								4½	5½	6½	7½
Continental	0	1	2	3	4	5		37	38	40	41

Men *Messieurs*

	Suits/Overcoats							Shirts			
American } British	36	38	40	42	44	46		15	16	17	18
Continental	46	48	50	52	54	56		38	41	43	45

	Shoes								
American } British	5	6	7	8	8½		9	9½	10	11
Continental	38	39	41	42	43		43	44	44	45

A good fit?   *Un essayage?*

Can I try it on?	**Puis-je l'essayer?**	pweezh lehssehyay
Where's the fitting room?	**Où est la cabine d'essayage?**	oo eh lah kahbeen dehssehyahzh
Is there a mirror?	**Y a-t-il un miroir?**	ee ahteel ang meerwahr
It fits very well.	**Cela va très bien.**	serlah vah treh byang
It doesn't fit.	**Cela ne me va pas.**	serlah ner mer vah pah

NUMBERS, see page 147

It's too ...	C'est trop ...	seh troa
short/long	court/long	koor/lawng
tight/loose	étroit/large	aytrwah/lahrzh
How long will it take to alter?	Combien de temps faut-il compter pour la retouche?	kawngbyang der tahng foateel kawngtay poor lah rertoosh

Clothes and accessories   *Vêtements et accessoires*

I would like a/an some ...	Je voudrais ...	zher voodreh
anorak	un anorak	ang nahnorahk
bathing cap	un bonnet de bain	ang bonneh der bang
bathing suit	un costume de bain	ang kostewm der bang
bathrobe	un peignoir (de bain)	ang pehnwahr (der bang)
blouse	un chemisier	ang shermeezyay
bow tie	un nœud papillon	ang nur pahpeeyawng
bra	un soutien-gorge	ang sootyang gorzh
braces	des bretelles	day brertehl
briefs	un slip	ang sleep
cap	une casquette	ewn kahskeht
cardigan	un cardigan	ang kahrdeegahng
coat	un manteau	ang mahngtoa
dress	une robe	ewn rob
dressing gown	un peignoir	ang pehnwahr
evening dress (woman's)	une robe du soir	ewn rob dew swahr
girdle	une gaine	ewn gehn
gloves	des gants	day gahng
handbag	un sac à main	ang sahk ah mang
handkerchief	un mouchoir	ang mooshwahr
hat	un chapeau	ang shahpoa
jacket (man's)	un veston	ang vehstawng
jacket (woman's)	une jaquette	ewn zhahkeht
jeans	des jeans	day "jeans"
jersey	un tricot	ang treekoa
jumper (Br.)	un chandail	ang shahngdahy
nightdress	une chemise de nuit	ewn shermeez der nwee
overalls	une salopette	ewn sahlopeht
pair of ...	une paire de ...	ewn pehr der
panties	un slip	ang sleep
pants (Am.)	un pantalon	ang pahngtahlawng
panty girdle	une gaine-culotte	ewn gehn kewlot
panty hose	un collant	ang kollahng

pullover	**un pull(over)**	ang pewl(ovehr)
roll-neck (turtle-neck)	**à col roulé**	ah kol roolay
round-neck	**à col rond**	ah kol rawng
V-neck	**à col en V**	ah kol ahng vay
with long/short sleeves	**avec manches longues/courtes**	ahvehk mahngsh lawngg/koort
without sleeves	**sans manches**	sahng mahngsh
pyjamas	**un pyjama**	ang peezhahmah
raincoat	**un imperméable**	ang nangpehrmayahbl
scarf	**un foulard**	ang foolahr
shirt	**une chemise**	ewn shermeez
shorts	**un short**	ang short
skirt	**une jupe**	ewn zhewp
slip	**un jupon**	ang zhewpawng
socks	**des chaussettes**	day shoasseht
sports jacket	**une veste de sport**	ewn vehst der spor
stockings	**des bas**	day bah
suit (man's)	**un complet**	ang kawngpleh
suit (woman's)	**un tailleur**	ang tahyurr
suspenders (Am.)	**des bretelles**	day brertehl
sweater	**un chandail**	ang shahngdahy
sweatshirt	**un sweatshirt**	ang ''sweatshirt''
swimming trunks	**un maillot de bain**	ang mahyoa der bang
swimsuit	**un costume de bain**	ang kostewm der bang
T-shirt	**un teeshirt**	ang teeshirt
tie	**une cravate**	ewn krahvaht
tights	**un collant**	ang kollahng
top coat	**un pardessus**	ang pahrderssew
tracksuit	**un survêtement**	ang sewrvehtermahng
trousers	**un pantalon**	ang pahngtahlawng
umbrella	**un parapluie**	ang pahrahplwee
underpants	**un caleçon/slip**	ang kahlssawng/sleep
undershirt	**un maillot de corps**	ang mahyoa der kor
vest (Am.)	**un gilet**	ang zheeleh
vest (Br.)	**un maillot de corps**	ang mahyoa der kor
waistcoat	**un gilet**	ang zheeleh

belt	**une ceinture**	ewn sangtewr
buckle	**une boucle**	ewn bookl
button	**un bouton**	ang bootawng
pocket	**une poche**	ewn posh
press stud (snap fastener)	**un bouton-pression**	ang bootawng prehssyawng
zip (zipper)	**une fermeture-éclair**	ewn fehrmertewr ayklehr

Shoes *Chaussures*

I'd like a pair of ...	**Je voudrais une paire de ...**	zher voodreh ewn pehr der
boots	**bottes**	bot
moccasins	**mocassins**	mokahssang
plimsolls (sneakers)	**tennis**	tehneess
sandals	**sandales**	sahngdahl
shoes	**chaussures**	shoassewr
flat	**à talons plats**	ah tahlawng plah
with a heel	**à talons hauts**	ah tahlawng oa
slippers	**pantoufles**	pahngtoofl
These are too ...	**Ceux-ci sont trop ...**	sursee sawng troa
narrow/wide	**étroits/larges**	aytrwah/lahrzh
large/small	**grands/petits**	grahng/pertee
Do you have a larger/smaller size?	**Avez-vous une pointure plus grande/plus petite?**	ahvay voo zewn pwangtewr plew grahngd/plew perteet
Do you have the same in black?	**Avez-vous les mêmes en noir?**	ahvay voo lay mehm ang nwahr
cloth	**en toile**	ang twahl
leather	**en cuir**	ang kweer
rubber	**en caoutchouc**	ang kahootshoo
suede	**en daim**	ang dang
Is it genuine leather?	**Est-ce du cuir véritable?**	ehss dew kweer vayreetahbl
I need some shoe polish/shoelaces.	**Je voudrais du cirage/des lacets.**	zher voodreh dew seerahzh/day lahsseh

Shoes worn out? Here's the key to getting them fixed again:

Can you repair these shoes?	**Pouvez-vous réparer ces chaussures?**	poovay voo raypahray say shoassewr
Can you stitch this?	**Pouvez-vous coudre ceci?**	poovay voo koodr serssee
I want new soles and heels.	**Je voudrais un ressemelage complet.**	zher voodreh ang rersser-merlahzh kawngpleh
When will they be ready?	**Quand seront-elles prêtes?**	kahng serrawng tehl preht

COLOURS, see page 113

Electrical appliances *Appareils électriques*

220-volt, 50-cycle A.C. is used almost everywhere in France, Switzerland and Belgium.

What's the voltage?	**Quel est le voltage?**	kehl eh ler voltahzh
Do you have a battery for this?	**Avez-vous une pile pour ceci?**	ahvay voo ewn peel poor serssee
This is broken. Can you repair it?	**Ceci est cassé. Pouvez-vous le réparer?**	serssee eh kahssay. poovay voo ler raypahray
Can you show me how it works?	**Pourriez-vous me montrer comment cela fonctionne?**	pooryay voo mer mawngtray kommahng serlah fawngksyon
I'd like (to hire) a video cassette.	**Je voudrais (louer) une vidéocassette.**	zher voodreh (looay) ewn veedayoakahsseht
I'd like a/an/some ...	**Je voudrais ...**	zher voodreh
adaptor	**une prise de raccordement**	ewn preez der rahkordermang
amplifier	**un amplificateur**	ang nahngpleefeekahturr
bulb	**une ampoule**	ewn ahngpool
clock-radio	**un radio-réveil**	ang rahdyoa rayvehy
electric toothbrush	**une brosse à dents électrique**	ewn bross ah dahng aylehktreek
extension lead (cord)	**un prolongateur**	ang prolawnggahturr
hair dryer	**un sèche-cheveux**	ang sehsh shervur
headphones	**un casque à écouteurs**	ang kahsk ah aykooturr
(travelling) iron	**un fer à repasser (de voyage)**	ang fehr ah rerpahssay (der vwahyahzh)
lamp	**une lampe**	ewn lahngp
plug	**une fiche**	ewn feesh
portable ...	**... portatif**	... portahteef
radio	**un poste de radio**	ang post der rahdyoa
car radio	**un autoradio**	ang noatorahdyoa
record player	**un tourne-disque**	ang toorner deesk
shaver	**un rasoir électrique**	ang rahzwahr aylehktreek
speakers	**des haut-parleurs**	day oa pahrlurr
(cassette) tape recorder	**un magnétophone (à cassettes)**	ang mahñaytofon (ah kahsseht)
(colour) television	**un téléviseur (en couleur)**	ang taylayveezurr (ang koolurr)
transformer	**un transformateur**	ang trahngsformahturr
video-recorder	**un magnétoscope**	ang mahñaytoskop

Grocery   *Magasin d'alimentation*

I'd like some bread, please.	**Je voudrais du pain, s'il vous plaît.**	zher voodreh dew pang seel voo pleh
What sort of cheese do you have?	**Quelle sorte de fromage avez-vous?**	kehl sort der fromahzh ahvay voo
A piece of ...	**Un morceau de ...**	ang morsoa der
that one	celui-là	serlwee lah
the one on the shelf	celui sur l'étagère	serlwee sewr laytahzhehr
I'll have one of those, please.	**Je prendrai un de ceux-là, s'il vous plaît.**	zher prahngdray ang der sur lah seel voo pleh
May I help myself?	**Puis-je me servir?**	pweezh mer sehrveer
I'd like ...	**Je voudrais ...**	zher voodreh
a kilo of apples	un kilo de pommes	ang keeloa der pom
half a kilo of tomatoes	un demi-kilo/une livre de tomates	ang dermee keeloa/ewn leevr der tomaht
100 grams of butter	100 grammes de beurre	sahng grahm der burr
a litre of milk	un litre de lait	ang leetr der leh
half a dozen eggs	une demi-douzaine d'œufs	ewn dermee doozehn dur
4 slices of ham	4 tranches de jambon	4 trahngsh der zhahngbawng
a packet of tea	un paquet de thé	ang pahkeh der tay
a jar of jam	un pot de confiture	ang poa der kawngfeetewr
a tin (can) of peaches	une boîte de pêches	ewn bwaht der pehsh
a tube of mustard	un tube de moutarde	ang tewb der mootahrd
a box of chocolates	une boîte de chocolats	ewn bwaht der shokolah

---

1 kilogram or kilo (kg.) = 1000 grams (g.)

100 g. = 3.5 oz.	½ kg. = 1.1 lb.
200 g. = 7.0 oz.	1 kg. = 2.2 lb.

1 oz. =   28.35 g.
1 lb. = 453.60 g.

---

1 litre (l.) = 0.88 imp. qt. or 1.06 U.S. qt.

1 imp. qt. = 1.14 l.	1 U.S. qt. = 0.95 l.
1 imp. gal. = 4.55 l.	1 U.S. gal. = 3.8 l.

FOOD, see also page 63

Jeweller's—Watchmaker's *Bijouterie – Horlogerie*

Could I please see that?	**Pourrais-je voir ceci, s'il vous plaît?**	poorehzh vwahr serssee seel voo pleh
Do you have anything in gold?	**Avez-vous quelque chose en or?**	ahvay voo kehlker shoaz ahng nor
How many carats is this?	**Combien de carats y a-t-il?**	kawngbyang der kahrah ee ahteel
Is this real silver?	**Est-ce de l'argent véritable?**	ehss der lahrzhahng vayreetahbl
Can you repair this watch?	**Pouvez-vous réparer cette montre?**	poovay voo raypahray seht mawngtr
I'd like a/an/some ...	**Je voudrais ...**	zher voodreh
alarm clock	**un réveil**	ang rayvehy
bangle	**un bracelet**	ang brahsserleh
battery	**une pile**	ewn peel
bracelet	**un bracelet**	ang brahsserleh
chain bracelet	**une gourmette**	ewn goormeht
charm bracelet	**un bracelet à breloques**	ang brahsserleh ah brerlok
brooch	**une broche**	ewn brosh
chain	**une chaînette**	ewn shehneht
charm	**une breloque**	ewn brerlok
cigarette case	**un étui à cigarettes**	ang naytwee ah seegahreht
cigarette lighter	**un briquet**	ang breekeh
clip	**un clip**	ang kleep
clock	**une pendule**	ewn pahngdewl
cross	**une croix**	ewn krwah
cuckoo clock	**un coucou**	ang kookoo
cuff links	**des boutons de manchettes**	day bootawng der mahngsheht
cutlery	**des couverts**	day koovehr
earrings	**des boucles d'oreilles**	day bookl dorehy
gem	**une pierre précieuse**	ewn pyehr prayssyurz
jewel box	**un coffret à bijoux**	ang kofreh ah beezhoo
mechanical pencil	**un porte-mine**	ang port meen
music box	**une boîte à musique**	ewn bwaht ah mewzeek
necklace	**un collier**	ang kollyay
pendant	**un pendentif**	ang pahngdahngteef
pin	**une épingle**	ewn aypanggl
pocket watch	**une montre de gousset**	ewn mawngtr der goosseh

powder compact	**un poudrier**	ang poodreeyay
propelling pencil	**un porte-mine**	ang port meen
ring	**une bague**	ewn bahg
engagement ring	**une bague de fiançailles**	ewn bahg der fyahngssahy
signet ring	**une chevalière**	ewn shervahlyehr
wedding ring	**une alliance**	ewn ahlyahngss
rosary	**un chapelet**	ang shaperleh
silverware	**de l'argenterie**	der lahrzhahngterree
tie clip	**une pince à cravate**	ewn pangss ah krahvaht
tie pin	**une épingle à cravate**	ewn aypanggl ah krahvaht
watch	**une montre**	ewn mawngtr
automatic	**automatique**	oatomahteek
digital	**digitale**	deezheetahl
quartz	**à quartz**	ah kwahrtss
with a second hand	**avec trotteuse**	ahvehk trotturz
watchstrap	**un bracelet de montre**	ang brahsserleh der mawngtr
wristwatch	**une montre-bracelet**	ewn mawngtr brahsserleh

amber	**ambre**	ahngbr
amethyst	**améthyste**	ahmayteest
chromium	**chrome**	kroam
copper	**cuivre**	kweevr
coral	**corail**	korahy
crystal	**cristal**	kreestahl
cut glass	**cristal taillé**	kreestahl tahyay
diamond	**diamant**	dyahmahng
emerald	**émeraude**	aymerroad
enamel	**émail**	aymahy
gold	**or**	or
gold plate	**plaqué or**	plahkay or
ivory	**ivoire**	eevwahr
jade	**jade**	zhahd
onyx	**onyx**	oneeks
pearl	**perle**	pehrl
pewter	**étain**	aytang
platinum	**platine**	plahteen
ruby	**rubis**	rewbee
sapphire	**saphir**	sahfeer
silver	**argent**	ahrzhahng
silver plate	**plaqué argent**	plahkay ahrzhahng
stainless steel	**inox**	eenox
topaz	**topaze**	topahz
turquoise	**turquoise**	tewrkwahz

Optician *Opticien*

I've broken my glasses.	**J'ai cassé mes lunettes.**	zhay kahssay may lewneht
Can you repair them for me?	**Pouvez-vous me les réparer?**	poovay voo mer lay raypahray
When will they be ready?	**Quand seront-elles prêtes?**	kahng serrawng tehl preht
Can you change the lenses?	**Pouvez-vous changer les verres?**	poovay voo shahngzhay lay vehr
I want tinted lenses.	**Je voudrais des verres teintés.**	zher voodreh day vehr tangtay
The frame is broken.	**La monture est cassée.**	lah mawngtewr eh kahssay
I'd like a spectacle case.	**Je voudrais un étui à lunettes.**	zher voodreh ang naytwee ah lewneht
I'd like to have my eyesight checked.	**Je voudrais faire contrôler ma vue.**	zher voodreh fehr kawngtroalay mah vew
I'm short-sighted/long-sighted.	**Je suis myope/presbyte.**	zher swee myop/prehsbeet
I want some contact lenses.	**Je voudrais des verres de contact.**	zher voodreh day vehr der kawngtahkt
I've lost one of my contact lenses.	**J'ai perdu un verre de contact.**	zhay pehrdew ang vehr der kawngtahkt
Could you give me another one?	**Pouvez-vous m'en donner un autre?**	poovay voo mahng donnay ang noatr
I have hard/soft lenses.	**J'ai des verres de contact durs/souples.**	zhay day vehr der kawngtahkt dewr/soopl
Have you any contact-lens liquid?	**Avez-vous un liquide pour verres de contact?**	ahvay voo ang leekeed poor vehr der kawngtahkt
I'd like to buy a pair of sunglasses.	**Je voudrais acheter une paire de lunettes de soleil.**	zher voodreh ahshtay ewn pehr der lewneht der solehy
May I look in a mirror?	**Puis-je me voir dans un miroir?**	pweezh mer vwahr dahng zang meerwahr
I'd like to buy a pair of binoculars.	**Je voudrais acheter des jumelles.**	zher voodreh ahshtay day zhewmehl

Photography *Photographie*

I want a(n) ... camera.	**Je voudrais un appareil de photo ...**	zher voodreh ang nahpahrehy der fotoa
automatic	**automatique**	oatomahteek
inexpensive	**bon marché**	bawng mahrshay
simple	**simple**	sangpl
Show me some cine (movie) cameras, please.	**Veuillez me montrer des caméras, s'il vous plaît.**	vuryay mer mawngtray day kahmayrah seel voo pleh
I'd like to have some passport photos taken.	**Je voudrais me faire faire des photos d'identité.**	zher voodreh mer fehr fehr day fotoa deetahngteetay

Film *Film*

I'd like a film for this camera.	**Je voudrais un film pour cet appareil.**	zher voodreh ang feelm poor seht ahpahrehy
black and white	**en noir et blanc**	ang nwahr ay blahng
colour	**en couleurs**	ang koolurr
colour negative	**pour négatifs couleurs**	poor naygahteef koolurr
colour slide	**pour diapositives**	poor dyahpoazeeteev
cartridge	**un chargeur**	ang shahrzhurr
roll film	**une bobine**	ewn bobeen
video cassette	**une vidéocassette**	ewn veedayoakahsseht
24/36 exposures	**vingt-quatre/ trente-six poses**	vangt kahtr/trahngt see poaz
this size	**ce format**	ser formah
this ASA/DIN number	**ce chiffre ASA/DIN**	ser sheefr ahzah/deen
artificial light type	**pour lumière artificielle**	poor lewmyehr ahrteefeessyehl
daylight type	**pour lumière du jour**	poor lewmyehr dew zhoor
fast (high-speed)	**ultrarapide**	ewltrahrahpeed
fine grain	**à grain fin**	ah grang fang

Processing *Développement*

| How much do you charge for developing? | **Combien coûte le développement?** | kawngbyang koot ler dayvlopmahng |

I want ... prints of each negative.	Je voudrais ... copies de chaque négatif.	zher voodreh ... koppee der shahk naygahteef
with a mat finish	sur papier mat	sewr pahpyay maht
with a glossy finish	sur papier brillant	sewr pahpyay breeyahng
Will you please enlarge this?	Veuillez agrandir ceci, s'il vous plaît.	vuryay ahgrahngdeer serssee seel voo pleh
When will the photos be ready?	Quand les photos seront-elles prêtes?	kahng lay fotoa serrawng tehl preht

Accessories and repairs *Accessoires et réparations*

I want a/an/some ...	Je voudrais ...	zher voodreh
battery	une pile	ewn peel
cable release	un déclencheur	ang dayklahngshurr
camera case	un étui (à appareil photo)	ang naytwee (ah ahpahrehy fotoa)
(electronic) flash	un flash (électronique)	ang "flash" (aylehktroneek)
filter	un filtre	ang feeltr
for black and white	pour noir et blanc	poor nwahr ay blahng
for colour	pour la couleur	poor lah koolurr
lens	un objectif	ang nobzhehkteef
telephoto lens	un téléobjectif	ang taylayobzhehkteef
wide-angle lens	un grand-angulaire	ang grahng tahngewlehr
lens cap	un capuchon (d'objectif)	ang kahpewshawng (dobzhehkteef)
Can you repair this camera?	Pouvez-vous réparer cet appareil?	poovay voo raypahray seht ahpahrehy
The film is jammed.	Le film est bloqué.	ler feelm eh blokay
There's something wrong with the ...	Il y a quelque chose qui ne va pas avec ...	eel ee ah kehlker shoaz kee ner vah pah ahvehk
exposure counter	le compte-poses	ler kawngt poaz
film winder	le levier d'avancement	ler lervyay dahvahngssmahng
flash attachment	la glissière du flash	lah gleessyehr dew "flash"
lens	l'objectif	lobzhehkteef
light meter	la cellule photo-électrique	lah sehllewl foto-aylehktreek
rangefinder	le télémètre	ler taylaymehtr
shutter	l'obturateur	lobtewrahturr

NUMBERS, see page 147

Tobacconist's *Bureau de tabac*

Tobacco is a state monopoly in France. You recognize licensed tobacconist's—cafés, bars and many newsstands—by the conspicuous red cone. In Belgium and Switzerland you can also buy cigarettes in restaurants, supermarkets, etc.

A packet of cigarettes, please.	**Un paquet de cigarettes, s'il vous plaît.**	ang pahkeh der seegahreht seel voo pleh
Do you have any American/English cigarettes?	**Avez-vous des cigarettes américaines/anglaises?**	ahvay voo day seegahreht ahmayreekehn/ahngglehz
I'd like a carton.	**J'en voudrais une cartouche.**	zhahng voodreh ewn kahrtoosh
Give me a/some ..., please.	**Donnez-moi ..., s'il vous plaît.**	donnay mwah ... seel voo pleh
candy	**des bonbons**	day bawngbawng
chewing gum	**du chewing-gum**	dew "chewing gum"
chewing tobacco	**du tabac à chiquer**	dew tahbah ah sheekay
chocolate	**du chocolat**	dew shokolah
cigarette case	**un étui à cigarettes**	ang naytwee ah seegahreht
cigarette holder	**un fume-cigarette**	ang fewm seegahreht
cigarettes	**des cigarettes**	day seegahreht
filter-tipped/	**avec filtre/**	ahvehk feeltr/
without filter	**sans filtre**	sahng feeltr
light/dark tobacco	**du tabac blond/brun**	dew tahbah blawng/brang
mild/strong	**légères/fortes**	layzhehr/fort
menthol	**mentholées**	mahngtolay
king-size	**long format**	lawng formah
cigars	**des cigares**	day seegahr
lighter	**un briquet**	ang breekeh
lighter fluid/gas	**de l'essence/du gaz à briquet**	der lehssahngss/dew gahz ah breekeh
matches	**des allumettes**	day zahlewmeht
pipe	**une pipe**	ewn peep
pipe cleaners	**des nettoie-pipes**	day nehtwah peep
pipe tobacco	**du tabac pour pipe**	dew tahbah poor peep
pipe tool	**un cure-pipe**	ang kewr peep
postcard	**une carte postale**	ewn kahrt postahl
snuff	**du tabac à priser**	dew tahbah ah preezay
stamps	**des timbres**	day tangbr
sweets	**des bonbons**	day bawngbawng
wick	**une mèche**	ewn mehsh

Miscellaneous *Divers*

Souvenirs *Souvenirs*

Here are some suggestions for articles which you might like
to bring back as a souvenir or a gift. Some regions of France
produce articles which you may be specially interested in,
e.g., lace in Brittany, Normandy and Auvergne, porcelain
in Limoges and Sèvres, pottery in Brittany, Alsace and
Provence.

crystal	**le cristal**	ler kreestahl
cutlery	**la coutellerie**	lah kootehlerree
lace	**les dentelles**	lay dahngtehl
perfume	**le parfum**	ler pahrfang
porcelain	**la porcelaine**	lah porserlehn
pottery	**la poterie**	lah poterree
women's top fashion	**la haute couture**	lah oat kootewr

Lace, crystal and porcelain are also good buys in Belgium.
In addition, you might consider buying there:

copperware	**les objets en cuivre**	lay zobzheh ahng kweevr
diamonds	**les diamants**	lay dyahmahng
tapestry	**la tapisserie**	lah tahpeesserree

Some typical products of Switzerland are:

chocolate	**le chocolat**	ler shokolah
cuckoo clock	**le coucou**	ler kookoo
fondue forks	**les fourchettes à fondue**	lay foorsheht ah fawngdew
fondue pot	**le caquelon**	ler kahkerlawng
watch	**la montre**	lah mawngtr

Records — Cassettes *Disques – Cassettes*

Do you have any records by ...?	**Avez-vous des disques de ...?**	ahvay voo day deesk der
I'd like a ...	**Je voudrais ...**	zher voodreh
cassette	**une cassette**	ewn kahsseht
video cassette	**une vidéocassette**	ewn veedayoakahsseht
compact disc	**un disque compact**	ang deesk kawngpahkt

L.P. (33 rpm)	**33 T. (Tours)**	trahngt trwah (toor)
E.P. (45 rpm)	**Super 45 T.**	sewpehr kahrahngt sangk toor
single	**45 T. Simple**	kahrahngt sangk toor sangpl

Have you any songs by ...?	**Avez-vous des chansons de ...?**	ahvay voo day shahng-ssawng der
Can I listen to this record?	**Puis-je écouter ce disque?**	pweezh aykootay ser deesk
chamber music	**la musique de chambre**	lah mewzeek der shahngbr
classical music	**la musique classique**	lah mewzeek klahsseek
folk music	**la musique folklorique**	lah mewzeek folkloreek
instrumental music	**la musique instrumentale**	lah mewzeek angstrewmahngtahl
jazz	**le jazz**	ler jazz
light music	**la musique légère**	lah mewzeek layzhehr
orchestral music	**la musique symphonique**	lah mewzeek sangfoneek
pop music	**la musique pop**	lah mewzeek pop

Toys *Jouets*

I'd like a toy/game ...	**Je voudrais un jouet/ jeu ...**	zher voodreh ang zhooeh/ zhur
for a boy	**pour un garçon**	poor ang gahrssawng
for a 5-year-old girl	**pour une fillette de 5 ans**	poor ewn feeyeht der 5 ahng
(beach) ball	**un ballon (de plage)**	ang bahlawng (der plahzh)
bucket and spade (pail and shovel)	**un seau et une pelle**	ang soa ay ewn pehl
building blocks (bricks)	**un jeu de construction**	ang zhur der kawngstrewksyawng
card game	**un jeu de cartes**	ang zhur der kahrt
chess set	**un jeu d'échecs**	ang zhur dayshehk
doll	**une poupée**	ewn poopay
electronic game	**un jeu électronique**	ang zhur aylehktroneek
flippers	**des palmes**	day pahlm
roller skates	**des patins à roulettes**	day pahtang ah rooleht
snorkel	**un tuba**	ang tewbah

Your money: banks—currency

In all European French-speaking countries, the basic unit of currency is the *franc* (frahng), divided into 100 *centimes* (sahngteem). However, these various francs have different value. *Franc* is abbreviated to *Fr* or *F*.

In France, there are coins of 5, 10, 20 and 50 centimes and of 1, 2, 5 and 10 francs. Banknotes come in denominations of 20, 50, 100, 200 and 500 francs.

In Switzerland there are coins of 5, 10, 20 and 50 centimes and of 1, 2 and 5 francs. There are banknotes of 10, 20, 50, 100, 500 and 1,000 francs.

Belgium has coins of 50 centimes and of 1, 5, 20 and 50 francs; there are banknotes of 50, 100, 500, 1,000 and 5,000 francs.

Though hours can vary, banks are generally open from 8.30 or 9 a.m. to noon and from 1.30 or 2 to 4.30 or 5 p.m., Monday to Friday. Main branches often remain open during the lunch hours. In all three countries, you will find currency exchange offices *(bureaux de change)* which are often open outside regular banking hours.

Credit cards may be used in an increasing number of hotels, restaurants, shops, etc. Signs are posted indicating which cards are accepted.

Traveller's cheques are accepted by hotels, travel agents and many shops, although the exchange rate is invariably better at a bank. Don't forget to take your passport when going to cash a traveller's cheque. Eurocheques are also accepted.

Where's the nearest bank?	**Où est la banque la plus proche?**	oo eh lah bahngk lah plew prosh
Where's the nearest currency exchange office?	**Où est le bureau de change le plus proche?**	oo eh ler bewroa der shahngzh ler plew prosh

At the bank *A la banque*

I want to change some dollars/pounds.	**Je voudrais changer des dollars/livres.**	zher voodreh shahngzhay day dollahr/leevr
I want to cash a traveller's cheque.	**Je désire toucher ce chèque de voyage.**	zher dayzeer tooshay ser shehk der vwahyahzh
What's the exchange rate?	**Quel est le cours du change?**	kehl eh ler koor dew shahngzh
How much commission do you charge?	**Quelle commission prenez-vous?**	kehl kommeessyawng prernay voo
Can you cash a personal cheque?	**Puis-je toucher un chèque à ordre?**	pweezh tooshay ang shehk ah ordr
Can you telex my bank in London?	**Pouvez-vous envoyer un télex à ma banque à Londres?**	poovay voo ahngvwahyay ang taylehx ah mah bahngk ah lawngdr
I have a/an/some ...	**Je possède ...**	zher possehd
bank card	**une carte d'identité bancaire**	ewn kahrt deedahngteetay bahngkehr
credit card	**une carte de crédit**	ewn kahrt der kraydee
Eurocheques	**des eurocheques**	day zurroshehk
introduction from ...	**une introduction de ...**	ewn angtrodewksyawng der
letter of credit	**une lettre de crédit**	ewn lehtr der kraydee
I'm expecting some money from New York. Has it arrived?	**J'attends de l'argent de New York. Est-il déjà arrivé?**	zhahtahng der lahrzhahng der New York. ehteel dayzhah ahreevay
Please give me ... notes (bills) and some small change.	**Donnez-moi ... billets et de la monnaie, s'il vous plait.**	donnay mwah ... beeyeh ay der lah monneh seel voo pleh
Give me ... large notes and the rest in small notes.	**Donnez-moi ... grosses coupures, et le reste en petites coupures.**	donnay mwah ... groass koopewr ay ler rehst ahng perteet koopewr

Deposit—Withdrawal *Dépôts – Retraits*

I want to credit this to my account.	**Je voudrais déposer ceci sur mon compte.**	zher voodreh daypoazay serssee sewr mawng kawngt
I want to ...	**Je désire ...**	zher dayzeer
open an account	**ouvrir un compte**	oovreer ang kawngt
withdraw ... francs	**retirer ... francs**	rerteeray ... frahng

NUMBERS, see page 147

| I want to credit this to Mr...'s account. | **Je voudrais créditer de cette somme le compte de M. ...** | zher voodreh kraydeetay der seht som ler kawngt der mersyur |
| Where should I sign? | **Où dois-je signer?** | oo dwahzh seeñay |

Business terms · *Termes d'affaires*

My name is ...	**Je m'appelle ...**	zher mahpehl
Here's my card.	**Voici ma carte.**	vwahssee mah kahrt
I have an appointment with ...	**J'ai rendez-vous avec ...**	zhay rahngday voo ahvehk
Can you give me an estimate of the cost?	**Pouvez-vous me donner une estimation du coût?**	poovay voo mer donnay ewn ehsteemahssyawng dew koo
What's the rate of inflation?	**Quel est le taux d'inflation?**	kehl eh ler toa dangflahssyawng
Can you provide me with an interpreter/ a secretary?	**Pourriez-vous me procurer un interprète/une secrétaire?**	pooryay voo mer prokewray ang nangtehrpreht/ewn serkraytehr
Where can I make photocopies?	**Où puis-je faire des photocopies?**	oo pweezh fehr day fotokopee

amount	**la somme**	lah som
balance	**la position**	lah poazeessyawng
capital	**le capital**	ler kahpeetahl
cheque book	**le carnet de chèques**	ler kahrneh der shehk
contract	**le contrat**	ler kawngtrah
expenses	**les frais**	lay freh
interest	**l'intérêt**	langtayreh
investment	**l'investissement**	langvehsteessmahng
invoice	**la facture**	lah fahktewr
loss	**la perte**	lah pehrt
mortgage	**l'hypothèque**	leepotehk
payment	**le paiement**	ler pehmahng
percentage	**le pourcentage**	ler poorssahngtahzh
profit	**le bénéfice**	ler baynayfeess
purchase	**l'achat**	lahshah
sale	**la vente**	lah vahngt
share	**l'action**	lahksyawng
transfer	**le transfert**	ler trahngsfehr
value	**la valeur**	lah vahlurr

At the post office

Post offices in France bear the sign *Postes et Télécommunications* or *P&T,* and are generally open from 8 a.m. to noon and from 2 to 6.30 p.m. Swiss post offices are recognized by a *PTT* sign and are open from 7.30 a.m. to noon and from 1.45 to 6.30 p.m. In Belgium, post offices are marked *Postes/Posterijen.* Main ones are open from 9 a.m. to 6 p.m. Note that telephone and telegraph services in Belgium are separated from the post office. In all three countries, post offices are open only in the morning on Saturdays.

In France you can buy stamps either at the post office or a tobacco shop. Letter boxes (mailboxes) are painted yellow in France and Switzerland and red in Belgium.

Where's the nearest post office?	**Où se trouve le bureau de poste le plus proche?**	oo ser troov ler bewroa der post ler plew prosh
What time does the post office open/close?	**A quelle heure ouvre/ferme la poste?**	ah kehl urr oovr/fehrm lah post
A stamp for this letter/postcard, please.	**Un timbre pour cette lettre/carte postale, s'il vous plaît.**	ang tangbr poor seht lehtr/kahrt postahl seel voo pleh
I want ... ...-centime stamps.	**Je voudrais ... timbres à ... centimes.**	zher voodreh ... tangbr ah ... sahngteem
What's the postage for a letter to London?	**Quel est le tarif d'une lettre pour Londres?**	kehl eh ler tahreef dewn lehtr poor lawngdr
What's the postage for a postcard to Los Angeles?	**Quel est le tarif d'une carte postale pour Los Angeles?**	kehl eh ler tahreef dewn kahrt postahl poor Los Angeles
Where's the letter box (mailbox)?	**Où se trouve la boîte aux lettres?**	oo ser troov lah bwaht oa lehtr
I want to send this parcel.	**Je voudrais expédier ce colis.**	zher voodreh ehxpaydyay ser kolee

A la poste

I want to send this by ...	**Je voudrais envoyer ceci ...**	zher voodreh ahngvwahyay serssee
airmail	**par avion**	pahr ahvyawng
express (special delivery)	**par exprès**	pahr ehxprehss
registered mail	**recommandé**	rerkommahngday
At which counter can I cash an international money order?	**A quel guichet puis-je toucher un mandat international?**	ah kehl geesheh pweezh tooshay ang mahngdah angtehrnahssyonahl
Where's the poste restante (general delivery)?	**Où se trouve la poste restante?**	oo ser troov lah post rehstahngt
Is there any mail for me? My name is ...	**Y a-t-il du courrier pour moi? Je m'appelle ...**	ee ahteel dew kooryay poor mwah. zher mahpehl

TIMBRES	STAMPS
COLIS	PARCELS
MANDATS	MONEY ORDERS

Telegrams *Télégrammes*

In France and Switzerland cables and telegrams are dispatched by the post office. In Belgium you must got to a separate *Téléphone/Télégraphe* office.

I want to send a telegram/telex.	**Je voudrais envoyer un télégramme/télex.**	zher voodreh ahngvwahyay ang taylaygrahm/taylehx
May I please have a form?	**Puis-je avoir une formule, s'il vous plaît?**	pweezh ahvwahr ewn formewl seel voo pleh
How much is it per word?	**Quel est le tarif par mot?**	kehl eh ler tahreef pahr moa
How long will a cable to Boston take?	**Combien de temps met un télégramme pour arriver à Boston?**	kawngbyang der tahng meh ang taylaygrahm poor ahreevay ah Boston
How much will this telex cost?	**Combien coûtera ce télex?**	kawngbyang kooterrah ser taylehx

Telephoning *Pour téléphoner*

The telephone system in France, Belgium and Switzerland is virtually entirely automatic. International or long-distance calls can be made from phone boxes, but if you need assistance in placing the call, go to the post office (in Belgium, to the *Téléphone/Télégraphe* office) or ask at your hotel. In France there are two types of payphones. One takes a range of coins, the other is card operated. Telecards are sold at post offices, railway ticket counters and shops recognized by a "Télécarte" sign, and are available for 40 or 120 charge units.

Telephone numbers are given in pairs in French so that 12 34 56 would be expressed in French, twelve, thirty-four, fifty-six.

Where's the telephone?	**Où se trouve le téléphone?**	oo ser troov ler taylayfon
Where's the nearest telephone booth?	**Où se trouve la cabine téléphonique la plus proche?**	oo ser troov lah kahbeen taylayfoneek lah plew prosh
May I use your phone?	**Puis-je utiliser votre téléphone?**	pweezh ewteeleezay votr taylayfon
Do you have a telephone directory for Lyons?	**Avez-vous un annuaire téléphonique de Lyon?**	ahvay voo ang nahnewehr taylayfoneek der lyawng
What's the dialling (area) code for ...?	**Quel est l'indicatif de ...?**	kehl eh langdeekahteef der
How do I get the international operator?	**Comment obtient-on le service international?**	kommahng obtyang tawng ler sehrveess angtehrnahssyonahl

Operator *Opératrice*

Good morning, I want Geneva 23 45 67.	**Bonjour, je voudrais le 23 45 67 à Genève.**	bawngzhoor zher voodreh ler 23 45 67 ah zhernehv
Can you help me get this number?	**Pouvez-vous m'aider à obtenir ce numéro?**	poovay voo mehday ah obterneer ser newmayroa

NUMBERS, see page 147

| I want to place a personal (person-to-person) call. | **Je voudrais une communication avec préavis.** | zher voodreh ewn kommewneekahssyawng ahvehk prayahvee |
| I want to reverse the charges. | **Je voudrais téléphoner en P.C.V.** | zher voodreh taylayfonay ahng pay say vay |

Speaking *Au téléphone*

Hello. This is ... speaking.	**Allô. C'est ... à l'appareil.**	ahloa. seh ... ah lahpahrehy
I want to speak to ...	**Je désire parler à ...**	zher dayzeer pahrlay ah
I want extension ...	**Je voudrais l'interne ...**	zher voodreh langtehrn
Speak louder/more slowly, please.	**Veuillez parler plus fort/lentement.**	vuryay pahrlay plew for/lahngtmahng

Bad luck *Pas de chance*

Would you please try again later?	**Pourriez-vous rappeler un peu plus tard, s'il vous plaît?**	pooryay voo rahperlay ang pur plew tahr seel voo pleh
Operator, you gave me the wrong number.	**Mademoiselle, vous m'avez donné un faux numéro.**	mahdmwahzehl voo mahvay donnay ang foa newmayroa
Operator, we were cut off.	**Mademoiselle, nous avons été coupés.**	mahdmwahzehl noo zahvawng zaytay koopay

Telephone alphabet *Code d'épellation*

A	**Anatole**	ahnahtol	N	**Nicolas**	neekolah
B	**Berthe**	behrt	O	**Oscar**	oskahr
C	**Célestin**	saylehstang	P	**Pierre**	pyehr
D	**Désiré**	dayzeeray	Q	**Quintal**	kangtahl
E	**Eugène**	urzhehn	R	**Raoul**	rahool
F	**François**	frahngsswah	S	**Suzanne**	sewzahn
G	**Gaston**	gahstawng	T	**Thérèse**	tayrehz
H	**Henri**	ahngree	U	**Ursule**	ewrsewl
I	**Irma**	eermah	V	**Victor**	veektor
J	**Joseph**	zhozehf	W	**William**	veelyahm
K	**Kléber**	klaybehr	X	**Xavier**	ksahvyay
L	**Louis**	looee	Y	**Yvonne**	eevon
M	**Marcel**	mahrssehl	Z	**Zoé**	zoay

Not there *La personne n'est pas là ...*

When will he/she be back?	**Quand sera-t-il/elle de retour?**	kahng serrah teel/tehl der rertoor
Will you tell him/her I called? My name is ...	**Veuillez lui dire que j'ai appelé. Je m'appelle ...**	vuryay lwee deer ker zhay ahperlay. zher mahpehl
Would you ask him/her to call me?	**Pourriez-vous lui demander de me rappeler?**	pooryay voo lwee dermahngday der mer rahperlay
Would you please take a message?	**Pourriez-vous prendre un message, s'il vous plaît?**	pooryay voo prahngdr ang mehssahzh seel voo pleh

Charges *Taxes*

What was the cost of that call?	**Quel est le prix de la communication?**	kehl eh ler pree der lah kommewneekahssyawng
I want to pay for the call.	**Je voudrais payer la communication.**	zher voodreh pehyay lah kommewneekahssyawng

---

Il y a un appel (téléphonique) pour vous.	There's a telephone call for you.
Quel numéro demandez-vous?	What number are you calling?
Ce n'est pas libre.	The line's engaged.
Il n'y a personne.	There's no answer.
Vous vous êtes trompé(e) de numéro.	You've got the wrong number.
Le téléphone est en dérangement.	The phone is out of order.
Un moment!	Just a moment.
Ne quittez pas!	Hold on, please.
Il/Elle est absent(e) pour le moment.	He's/She's out at the moment.

Doctor

To be at ease, make sure your health insurance policy covers any illness or accident while on holiday. If not, ask your insurance representative, automobile association or travel agent for details of special health insurance.

General *Généralités*

Can you get me a doctor?	Pouvez-vous m'appeler un médecin?	poovay voo mahperlay ang maydssang
Is there a doctor here?	Y a-t-il un médecin ici?	ee ahteel ang maydssang eessee
I need a doctor, quickly.	J'ai besoin d'un médecin, vite.	zhay berzwang dang maydssang veet
Where can I find a doctor who speaks English?	Où puis-je trouver un médecin qui parle anglais?	oo pweezh troovay ang maydssang kee pahrl ahnggleh
Where's the surgery (doctor's office)?	Où est le cabinet de consultation?	oo eh ler kahbeeneh der kawngssewltahssyawng
What are the surgery (office) hours?	Quelles sont les heures de consultation?	kehl sawng lay zurr der kawngssewltahssyawng
Could the doctor come to see me here?	Le médecin pourrait-il venir me voir?	ler maydssang pooreh teel verneer mer vwahr
What time can the doctor come?	A quelle heure peut-il venir?	ah kehl urr purteel verneer
Can you recommend a/an ...?	Pouvez-vous m'indiquer ...?	poovay voo mangdeekay
general practitioner	un généraliste	ang zhaynayrahleest
children's doctor	un pédiatre	ang paydyahtr
eye specialist	un oculiste	ang nokewleest
gynaecologist	un gynécologue	ang zheenaykolog
Can I have an appointment ...?	Puis-je avoir un rendez-vous ...?	pweezh ahwahr ang rahngday voo
tomorrow	pour demain	poor dermang
as soon as possible	dès que possible	deh ker posseebl

CHEMIST'S, see page 108

Parts of the body *Parties du corps*

appendix	l'appendice	lahpangdeess
arm	le bras	ler brah
artery	l'artère	lahrtehr
back	le dos	ler doa
bladder	la vessie	lah vehssee
bone	l'os	loss
bowels	les intestins	lay zangtehstang
breast	le sein	ler sang
chest	la poitrine	lah pwahtreen
ear	l'oreille	lorehy
eye(s)	l'œil (les yeux)	lery (lay zyur)
face	le visage	ler veezahzh
finger	le doigt	ler dwah
foot	le pied	ler pyay
gland	la glande	lah glahngd
hand	la main	lah mang
head	la tête	lah teht
heart	le cœur	ler kurr
jaw	la mâchoire	lah mahshwahr
joint	l'articulation	lahrteekewlahssyawng
kidney	le rein	ler rang
knee	le genou	ler zhernoo
leg	la jambe	lah zhahngb
lip	la lèvre	lah lehvr
liver	le foie	ler fwah
lung	le poumon	ler poomawng
mouth	la bouche	lah boosh
muscle	le muscle	ler mewskl
neck	le cou	ler koo
nerve	le nerf	ler nehr
nervous system	le système nerveux	ler seestehm nehrvur
nose	le nez	ler nay
rib	la côte	lah koat
shoulder	l'épaule	laypoal
skin	la peau	lah poa
spine	la colonne vertébrale	lah kolon vehrtaybrahl
stomach	l'estomac	lehstomah
tendon	le tendon	ler tahngdawng
thigh	la cuisse	lah kweess
throat	la gorge	lah gorzh
thumb	le pouce	ler pooss
toe	l'orteil	lortehy
tongue	la langue	lah lahngg
tonsils	les amygdales	lay zahmeedahl
vein	la veine	lah vehn

Accident—Injury   *Accidents – Blessures*

There has been an accident.	**Il est arrivé un accident.**	eel eh tahreevay ang nahkseedahng
My child has had a fall.	**Mon enfant a fait une chute.**	mawng nahngfahng ah feh ewn shewt
He/She has hurt his/her head.	**Il/Elle s'est blessé(e) à la tête.**	eel/ehl seh blehssay ah lah teht
He's/She's unconscious.	**Il/Elle s'est évanoui(e).**	eel/ehl seh tayvahnooee
He's/She's bleeding (heavily).	**Il/Elle saigne (abondamment).**	eel/ehl sehñ (ahbawngdahmmahng)
He's/She's (seriously) injured.	**Il/Elle s'est (grièvement) blessé(e).**	eel/ehl seh (gryehvmahng) blehssay
His/Her arm is broken.	**Il/Elle s'est cassé le bras.**	eel/ehl seh kahssay ler brah
His/Her ankle is swollen.	**Sa cheville est enflée.**	sah sherveey eh tahngflay
I've been stung.	**Quelque chose m'a piqué.**	kehlker shoaz mah peekay
I've got something in my eye.	**J'ai reçu quelque chose dans l'œil.**	zhay rerssew kehlker shoaz dahng lery
I've got a/an ...	**J'ai ...**	zhay
blister	**une ampoule**	ewn ahngpool
boil	**un furoncle**	ang fewrawngkl
bruise	**une contusion**	ewn kawngtewzyawng
burn	**une brûlure**	ewn brewlewr
cut	**une coupure**	ewn koopewr
graze	**une éraflure**	ewn ayrahflewr
insect bite	**une piqûre d'insecte**	ewn peekewr dangssehkt
lump	**une bosse**	ewn boss
rash	**une éruption**	ewn ayrewpsyawng
sting	**une piqûre**	ewn peekewr
swelling	**une enflure**	ewn ahngflewr
wound	**une blessure**	ewn blehssewr
Could you have a look at it?	**Pourriez-vous l'examiner?**	pooryay voo lehxahmeenay
I can't move my ...	**Je ne peux pas bouger le/la/les ...**	zher ner pur pah boozhay ler/lah/lay ...
It hurts.	**Cela me fait mal.**	serlah mer feh mahl

Où avez-vous mal?	Where does it hurt?
Quel genre de douleur éprouvez-vous?	What kind of pain is it?
sourde/aiguë/lancinante persistante/intermittente	dull/sharp/throbbing constant/on and off
C'est ...	It's ...
cassé/foulé déboîté/déchiré	broken/sprained dislocated/torn
Il faut vous faire une radio.	I want you to have an X-ray taken.
Il faudra vous mettre un plâtre.	You'll get a plaster.
C'est infecté.	It's infected.
Etes-vous vacciné(e) contre le tétanos?	Have you been vaccinated against tetanus?
Je vais vous donner un antiseptique/calmant.	I'll give you an antiseptic/ a painkiller.

Illness *Maladies*

I'm not feeling well.	Je ne me sens pas bien.	zher ner mer sahng pah byang
I'm ill.	Je suis malade.	zher swee mahlahd
I feel ...	J'ai ...	zhay
dizzy	des vertiges	day vehrteezh
nauseous	des nausées	day noazay
shivery	des frissons	day freessawng
I've got a fever.	J'ai de la fièvre.	zhay der lah fyehvr
My temperature is 38 degrees.	J'ai 38 de fièvre.	zhay 38 de fyehvr
I've been vomiting.	J'ai eu des vomissements.	zhay ew day voameessmahng
I'm constipated/ I've got diarrhoea.	Je suis constipé(e)/ J'ai la diarrhée.	zher swee kawngsteepay/ zhay la dyahray
My ... hurt(s).	J'ai mal à ...	zhay mahl ah

I've got (a/an) ...	J'ai ...	zhay
asthma	de l'asthme	der lahsm
backache	mal aux reins	mahl oa rang
cold	un rhume	ang rewm
cough	la toux	lah too
cramps	des crampes	day krahngp
earache	mal aux oreilles	mahl oa zorehy
hay fever	le rhume des foins	ler rewm day fwang
headache	mal à la tête	zhay mahl ah lah teht
indigestion	une indigestion	ewn angdeezhehstyawng
nosebleed	des saignements de nez	day sehñmahng der nay
palpitations	des palpitations	day pahlpeetahssyawng
rheumatism	des rhumatismes	day rewmahteezm
sore throat	mal à la gorge	mahl ah lah gorzh
stiff neck	un torticolis	ang torteekolee
stomach ache	mal à l'estomac	mahl ah lehstomah
sunstroke	une insolation	ewn angsolahssyawng
I have difficulties breathing.	J'ai de la peine à respirer.	zhay der lah pehn ah rehspeeray
I have a pain in my chest.	Je ressens une douleur dans la poitrine.	zher rersahng ewn doolurr dahng lah pwahtreen
I had a heart attack ... years ago.	J'ai eu une crise cardiaque il y a ... ans.	zhay ew ewn kreez kahrdyahk eel ee a ... ahng
My blood pressure is too high/too low.	Ma tension est trop élevée/basse.	mah tahngssyawng eh troa paylervay/bahss
I'm allergic to ...	Je suis allergique à ...	zher swee zahlehrzheek ah
I'm a diabetic.	Je suis diabétique.	zher swee dyahbayteek

Women's section *Typiquement féminin ...*

I have period pains.	J'ai des règles douloureuses.	zhay day rehgl dooloorurz
I have a vaginal infection.	J'ai une infection vaginale.	zhay ewn angfehksyawng vahzheenahl
I'm on the pill.	Je prends la pilule.	zher prahng lah peelewl
I haven't had my period for 2 months.	Je n'ai pas eu mes règles depuis 2 mois.	zher nay pah ew may rehgl derpwee 2 mwah
I'm (3 months) pregnant.	Je suis enceinte (de 3 mois).	zher swee zahngssangt (der 3 mwah)

Depuis combien de temps éprouvez-vous ces troubles?	How long have you been feeling like this?
Est-ce la première fois que vous en souffrez?	Is this the first time you've had this?
Je vais prendre votre température/tension.	I'll take your temperature/blood pressure.
Relevez votre manche.	Roll up your sleeve, please.
Déshabillez-vous (jusqu'à la ceinture), s'il vous plaît.	Please undress (down to the waist).
Etendez-vous là, s'il vous plaît.	Please lie down over here.
Ouvrez la bouche.	Open your mouth.
Respirez à fond.	Breathe deeply.
Toussez, s'il vous plaît.	Cough, please.
Où avez-vous mal?	Where do you feel the pain?
Vous avez ...	You've got (a/an) ...
l'appendicite	appendicitis
une cystite	cystitis
une gastrite	gastritis
la grippe	flu
une inflammation de ...	inflammation of ...
une intoxication alimentaire	food poisoning
la jaunisse	jaundice
une maladie vénérienne	venereal disease
une pneumonie	pneumonia
la rougeole	measles
Je vais vous faire une piqûre.	I'll give you an injection.
Je voudrais un prélèvement de votre sang/de vos selles/de votre urine.	I want a specimen of your blood/stools/urine.
Vous devrez garder le lit ... jours.	You must stay in bed for ... days.
Vous devriez consulter un spécialiste.	I want you to see a specialist.
Je désire que vous alliez à l'hôpital vous faire faire un bilan (de santé).	I want you to go to the hospital for a general check-up.

Prescription—Treatment   *Ordonnance – Traitement*

This is my usual medicine.	**Voici mon médicament habituel.**	vwahssee mawng maydee-kahmahng ahbeetewehl
Can you give me a prescription for this?	**Pouvez-vous me donner une ordonnance pour cela?**	poovay voo mer donnay ewn ordonnahngss poor serlah
Can you prescribe a/an/some ...?	**Pourriez-vous me prescrire ...?**	pooryay voo mer prehskreer
antidepressant	**un remontant**	ang rermawngtahng
sleeping pills	**un somnifère**	ang somneefehr
tranquillizer	**un tranquillisant**	ang trahngkeeleezahng
I'm allergic to antibiotics/penicillin.	**Je suis allergique aux antibiotiques/ à la pénicilline.**	zher swee zahlehrzheek oa zahngteebyoteek/ ah lah payneesseeleen
I don't want anything too strong.	**Je ne veux pas quelque chose de trop fort.**	zher ner vur pah kehlker shoaz der troa for
How many times a day should I take it?	**Combien de fois par jour faut-il le prendre?**	kawngbyang der fwah pahr zhoor foateel ler prahngdr
Must I swallow them whole?	**Dois-je les avaler?**	dwahzh lay zahvahlay

---

Quel traitement suivez-vous?	What treatment are you having?
Quel médicament prenez-vous?	What medicine are you taking?
En injection ou par voie orale?	Injection or oral?
Prenez ... cuillères à café de ce médicament ...	Take ... teaspoons of this medicine ...
Prenez une pilule avec un verre d'eau ...	Take one pill with a glass of water ...
toutes les ... heures	every ... hours
... fois par jour	... times a day
avant/après les repas	before/after each meal
le matin/le soir	in the morning/at night
en cas de douleurs	in case of pain
pendant ... jours	for ... days

CHEMISTS'S, see p. 108

Fee *Honoraires*

How much do I owe you?	**Combien vous dois-je?**	kawngbyang voo dwahzh
May I have a receipt for my health insurance?	**Puis-je avoir une quittance pour mon assurance maladie?**	pweezh ahvwahr ewn keettahngss poor mawng nahssewrahngss mahlahdee
Can I have a medical certificate?	**Puis-je avoir un certificat médical?**	pweezh ahvwahr ang sehrteefeekah maydeekahl
Would you fill in this health insurance form, please?	**Ayez l'obligeance de remplir cette feuille maladie.**	ehyay lobleezhahngss der rahngpleer seht fury mahlahdee

Hospital *Hôpital*

What are the visiting hours?	**Quelles sont les heures de visite?**	kehl sawng lay zurr der veezeet
When can I get up?	**Quand pourrai-je me lever?**	kahng poorehzh mer lervay
When will the doctor come?	**Quand le médecin doit-il passer?**	kahng ler maydssang dwahteel pahssay
I'm in pain.	**J'ai mal.**	zhay mahl
I can't eat/sleep.	**Je ne peux pas manger/dormir.**	zher ner pur pah mahngzhay/dormeer
Can I have a pain-killer/some sleeping pills?	**Puis-je avoir un calmant/somnifère?**	pweezh ahwahr ang kahlmahng/somneefehr
Where is the bell?	**Où est la sonnette?**	oo eh lah sonneht

nurse	**l'infirmière**	langfeermyehr
patient	**le patient/la patiente**	ler pahssyahng/ lah pahssyahngt
anaesthetic	**l'anesthésique**	lahnehstayzeek
blood transfusion	**la transfusion (sanguine)**	lah trahngsfewzyawng (sahnggeen)
injection	**la piqûre**	lah peekewr
operation	**l'opération**	lopayrahssyawng
bed	**le lit**	ler lee
bedpan	**le bassin**	ler bahssang
thermometer	**le thermomètre**	ler tehrmomehtr

Dentist *Dentiste*

Can you recommend a good dentist?	**Pouvez-vous m'indiquer un bon dentiste?**	poovay voo mangdeekay ang bawng dahngteest
Can I make an (urgent) appointment to see Dr...?	**Puis-je prendre un rendez-vous (urgent) avec le docteur ...?**	pweezh prahngdr ang rahngday voo (ewrzhahng) ahvehk ler dokturr
Can't you possibly make it earlier than that?	**Ne pourriez-vous pas me prendre plus tôt?**	ner pooray voo pah mer prahngdr plew toa
I have a broken tooth.	**Je me suis cassé une dent.**	zher mer swee kahssay ewn dahng
I have a toothache.	**J'ai mal aux dents.**	zhay mahl oa dahng
I have an abscess.	**J'ai un abcès.**	zhay ang nahbseh
This tooth hurts.	**Cette dent me fait mal.**	seht dahng mer feh mahl
at the top	**en haut**	ahng oa
at the bottom	**en bas**	ahng bah
in the front	**devant**	dervahng
at the back	**au fond**	oa fawng
Can you fix it temporarily?	**Pouvez-vous faire un traitement provisoire?**	poovay voo fehr ang trehtmahng proveezwahr
I don't want it extracted.	**Je ne voudrais pas me la faire arracher.**	zher ner voodreh pah mer lah fehr ahrahshay
Could you give me an anaesthetic?	**Pouvez-vous faire une anesthésie locale?**	poovay voo fehr ewn ahnehstayzee lokahl
I've lost a filling.	**J'ai perdu un plombage.**	zhay pehrdew ang plawngbahzh
The gum ...	**La gencive ...**	lah zhahngsseev
is very sore is bleeding	**est très douloureuse saigne**	eh treh dooloorurz sehñ
I've broken this denture.	**J'ai cassé mon dentier.**	zhay kahssay mawng dahngtyay
Can you repair this denture?	**Pouvez-vous réparer ce dentier?**	poovay voo raypahray ser dahngtyay
When will it be ready?	**Quand sera-t-il prêt?**	kahng serrah teel preh

Reference section

Where do you come from? *D'où venez-vous?*

Africa	l'Afrique	lahfreek
Asia	l'Asie	lahzee
Australia	l'Australie	loastrahlee
Europe	l'Europe	lurrop
North America	l'Amérique du Nord	lahmayreek dew nor
South America	l'Amérique du Sud	lahmayreek dew sewd
Algeria	l'Algérie	lahlzhayree
Austria	l'Autriche	loatreesh
Belgium	la Belgique	lah behlzheek
Canada	le Canada	ler kahnahdah
China	la Chine	lah sheen
Denmark	le Danemark	ler dahnmahrk
England	l'Angleterre	lahngglertehr
Finland	la Finlande	lah fanglahngd
France	la France	lah frahngss
Germany	l'Allemagne	lahlmahñ
Great Britain	la Grande-Bretagne	lah grahngd brertañ
Greece	la Grèce	lah grehss
India	l'Inde	langd
Ireland	l'Irlande	leerlahngd
Israel	Israël	eesrahehl
Italy	l'Italie	leetahlee
Japan	le Japon	ler zhahpawng
Luxembourg	le Luxembourg	ler lewxahngboor
Morocco	le Maroc	ler mahrok
Netherlands	les Pays-Bas	lay peheebah
New Zealand	la Nouvelle-Zélande	lah noovehl zaylahngd
Norway	la Norvège	lah norvehzh
Portugal	le Portugal	ler portewgahl
Scotland	l'Ecosse	laykoss
South Africa	l'Afrique du Sud	lahfreek dew sewd
Soviet Union	l'Union soviétique	lewnyawng sovyayteek
Spain	l'Espagne	lehspañ
Sweden	la Suède	lah swehd
Switzerland	la Suisse	lah sweess
Tunisia	la Tunisie	lah tewneezee
Turkey	la Turquie	lah tewrkee
United States	les Etats-Unis	lay zaytah zewnee
Wales	le Pays de Galles	ler pehee der gahl
Yugoslavia	la Yougoslavie	lah yoogoslahvee

Numbers *Nombres*

0	**zéro**	zayroa
1	**un, une**	ang ewn
2	**deux**	dur
3	**trois**	trwah
4	**quatre**	kahtr
5	**cinq**	sangk
6	**six**	seess
7	**sept**	seht
8	**huit**	weet
9	**neuf**	nurf
10	**dix**	deess
11	**onze**	awngz
12	**douze**	dooz
13	**treize**	trehz
14	**quatorze**	kahtorz
15	**quinze**	kangz
16	**seize**	sehz
17	**dix-sept**	deess seht
18	**dix-huit**	deez weet
19	**dix-neuf**	deez nurf
20	**vingt**	vang
21	**vingt et un**	vang tay ang
22	**vingt-deux**	vangt dur
23	**vingt-trois**	vangt trwah
24	**vingt-quatre**	vangt kahtr
25	**vingt-cinq**	vangt sangk
26	**vingt-six**	vangt seess
27	**vingt-sept**	vangt seht
28	**vingt-huit**	vangt weet
29	**vingt-neuf**	vangt nurf
30	**trente**	trahngt
31	**trente et un**	trahngt ay ang
32	**trente-deux**	trahngt dur
33	**trente-trois**	trahngt trwah
40	**quarante**	kahrahngt
41	**quarante et un**	kahrahngt ay ang
42	**quarante-deux**	kahrahngt dur
43	**quarante-trois**	kahrahngt trwah
50	**cinquante**	sangkahngt
51	**cinquante et un**	sangkahngt ay ang
52	**cinquante-deux**	sangkahngt dur
53	**cinquante-trois**	sangkahngt trwah
60	**soixante**	swahssahngt
61	**soixante et un**	swahssahngt ay ang
62	**soixante-deux**	swahssahngt dur

63	**soixante-trois**	swahssahngt trwah
70*	**soixante-dix**	swahssahngt deess
71	**soixante et onze**	swahssahngt ay awngz
72	**soixante-douze**	swahssahngt dooz
73	**soixante-treize**	swahssahngt trehz
80*	**quatre-vingts**	kahtrer vang
81	**quatre-vingt-un**	kahtrer vang ang
82	**quatre-vingt-deux**	kahtrer vang dur
83	**quatre-vingt-trois**	kahtrer vang trwah
90*	**quatre-vingt-dix**	kahtrer vang deess
91	**quatre-vingt-onze**	kahtrer vang awngz
92	**quatre-vingt-douze**	kahtrer vang dooz
93	**quatre-vingt-treize**	kahtrer vang trehz
100	**cent**	sahng
101	**cent un**	sahng ang
102	**cent deux**	sahng dur
110	**cent dix**	sahng deess
120	**cent vingt**	sahng vang
130	**cent trente**	sahng trahngt
140	**cent quarante**	sahng kahrahngt
150	**cent cinquante**	sahng sangkahngt
160	**cent soixante**	sahng swahssahngt
170	**cent soixante-dix**	sahng swahssahngt deess
180	**cent quatre-vingts**	sahng kahtrer vang
190	**cent quatre-vingt-dix**	sahng kahtrer vang deess
200	**deux cents**	dur sahng
300	**trois cents**	trwah sahng
400	**quatre cents**	kahtrer sahng
500	**cinq cents**	sang sahng
600	**six cents**	seess sahng
700	**sept cents**	seht sahng
800	**huit cents**	wee sahng
900	**neuf cents**	nurf sahng
1000	**mille**	meel
1100	**mille cent**	meel sahng
1200	**mille deux cents**	meel dur sahng
2000	**deux mille**	dur meel
5000	**cinq mille**	sang meel
10,000	**dix mille**	dee meel
50,000	**cinquante mille**	sangkahngt meel
100,000	**cent mille**	sahng meel
1,000,000	**un million**	ang meelyawng
1,000,000,000	**un milliard**	ang meelyahr

---

* In certain areas, particularly in Belgium and Switzerland, older forms are still in use:
70 = **septante** (sehptahngt), 80 = **huitante** (weetahngt), 90 = **nonante** (nonahngt).

first	**premier (1er)**	prermyay
second	**deuxième (2e)**	durzyehm
third	**troisième (3e)**	trwahzyehm
fourth	**quatrième**	kahtreeyehm
fifth	**cinquième**	sangkyehm
sixth	**sixième**	seezyehm
seventh	**septième**	sehtyehm
eighth	**huitième**	weetyehm
ninth	**neuvième**	nurvyehm
tenth	**dixième**	deezyehm

once/twice	**une fois/deux fois**	ewn fwah/dur fwah
three times	**trois fois**	trwah fwah

a half	**une moitié**	ewn mwahtyay
half a …	**un/une demi-**	ang/ewn dermee
half of …	**la moitié de …**	lah mwahtyay der
half (adj.)	**demi**	dermee
a quarter/one third	**un quart/un tiers**	ang kahr/ang tyehr
a pair of	**une paire de**	ewn pehr der
a dozen	**une douzaine**	ewn doozehn

one per cent	**un pour cent**	ang poor sahng
3.4%	**3,4%**	trwah veergewl kahtr poor sahng

1981	**mille neuf cent quatre-vingt-un**	meel nurf sahng kahtr vang ang
1992	**mille neuf cent quatre-vingt-douze**	meel nurf sahng kahtr vang dooz
2003	**deux mille trois**	dur meel trwah

Year and age *Année et âge*

year	**l'an/l'année**	lahng/lahnay
leap year	**l'année bissextile**	lahnay beessehxteel
decade	**la décennie**	lah dayssehnee
century	**le siècle**	ler syehkl

this year	**cette année**	seht ahnay
last year	**l'année dernière**	lahnay dehrnyehr
next year	**l'année prochaine**	lahnay proshehn
each year	**chaque année**	shahk ahnay

2 years ago	**il y a 2 ans**	eel ee ah 2 zahng
in one year	**dans un an**	dahng zang nahng
in the eighties	**dans les années quatre-vingts**	dahng lay zahnay kahtr vang
the 16th century	**le seizième siècle**	ler sehzyehm syehkl
in the 20th century	**au vingtième siècle**	oa vangtyehm syehkl

How old are you?	**Quel âge avez-vous?**	kehl ahzh ahvay voo
I'm 30 years old.	**J'ai trente ans.**	zhay trahngt ahng
He/She was born in 1960.	**Il/Elle est né(e) en mille neuf cent soixante.**	eel/ehl eh nay ahng meel nurf sahng swahssahngt
What is his/her age?	**Quel âge a-t-il/elle?**	kehl ahzh ahteel/ehl
Children under 16 are not admitted.	**Les enfants de moins de seize ans ne sont pas admis.**	lay zahngfahng der mwang der sehz ahng ner sawng pah zahdmee

Seasons *Saisons*

spring/summer	**le printemps/l'été**	ler prangtahng/laytay
autumn/winter	**l'automne/l'hiver**	loaton/leevehr
in spring	**au printemps**	oa prangtahng
during the summer	**pendant l'été**	pahngdahng laytay
in autumn	**en automne**	ahng noaton
during the winter	**pendant l'hiver**	pahngdahng leevehr
high season	**haute saison**	oat sehzawng
low season	**basse saison**	bahss sehzawng

Months *Mois*

January	**janvier***	zhahngvyay
February	**février**	fayvreeyay
March	**mars**	mahrs
April	**avril**	ahvreel
May	**mai**	may
June	**juin**	zhwang
July	**juillet**	zhweeyeh
August	**août**	oot
September	**septembre**	sehptahngbr
October	**octobre**	oktobr
November	**novembre**	novahngbr
December	**décembre**	dayssahngbr
in September	**en septembre**	ahng sehptahngbr
since October	**depuis octobre**	derpwee oktobr
the beginning of January	**le début (de) janvier**	ler daybew (der) zhahngvyay
the middle of February	**la mi-février**	lah mee fayvreeyay
the end of March	**la fin (de) mars**	lah fang (der) mahrs

* The names of months aren't capitalized in French.

Days and Date *Jours et date*

What day is it today?	**Quel jour sommes-nous?**	kehl zhoor som noo
Sunday	**dimanche***	deemahngsh
Monday	**lundi**	langdee
Tuesday	**mardi**	mahrdee
Wednesday	**mercredi**	mehrkrerdee
Thursday	**jeudi**	zhurdee
Friday	**vendredi**	vahngdrerdee
Saturday	**samedi**	sahmdee
It's ...	**Nous sommes ...**	noo som
July 1	**le 1er juillet**	ler prermyay zhweeyeh
March 10	**le 10 mars**	ler dee mahrs
in the morning	**le matin**	ler mahtang
during the day	**pendant la journée**	pahngdahng lah zhoornay
in the afternoon	**l'après-midi**	lahpreh meedee
in the evening	**le soir**	ler swahr
at night	**la nuit**	lah nwee
the day before yesterday	**avant-hier**	ahvahng tyehr
yesterday	**hier**	yehr
today	**aujourd'hui**	oazhoordwee
tomorrow	**demain**	dermang
the day after tomorrow	**après-demain**	ahpreh dermang
the day before	**la veille**	lah vehy
the next day	**le lendemain**	ler lahngdermang
two days ago	**il y a deux jours**	eel ee ah dur zhoor
in three days' time	**dans trois jours**	dahng trwah zhoor
last week	**la semaine passée**	lah sermehn pahssay
next week	**la semaine prochaine**	lah sermehn proshehn
for a fortnight (two weeks)	**pendant quinze jours**	pahngdahng kangz zhoor
birthday	**l'anniversaire**	lahneevehrsehr
day off	**le jour de congé**	ler zhoor der kawngzhay
holiday	**le jour férié**	ler zhoor fayryay
holidays/vacation	**les vacances**	lay vahkahngss
week	**la semaine**	lah sermehn
weekend	**le week-end**	ler "weekend"
working day	**le jour ouvrable**	ler zhoor oovrahbl

---

* The names of days aren't capitalized in French.

Public holidays *Jours fériés*

While there may be additional regional holidays, only national holidays in France (F), Belgium (B) and Switzerland (CH) are cited below.

			F	CH	B
January 1	**Nouvel An**	New Year's Day	F	CH*	B
January 2				CH*	
May 1	**Fête du Travail**	Labour Day	F		B
May 8	**Fête de la Libération**	Victory Day (1945)	F		
July 14	**Fête Nationale**	Bastille Day	F		
July 21	**Fête Nationale**	National Day			B
August 1	**Fête Nationale**	National Day		CH*	
August 15	**Assomption**	Assumption Day	F		B
November 1	**Toussaint**	All Saints Day	F		B
November 11	**Armistice**	Armistice Day	F		B
December 25	**Noël**	Christmas	F	CH	B
December 26	**Saint-Etienne**	St. Stephen's Day		CH*	
Movable dates:	**Vendredi-Saint**	Good Friday	F	CH*	
	Lundi de Pâques	Easter Monday	F	CH*	B
	Ascension	Ascension	F	CH	B
	Lundi de Pentecôte	Whit Monday	F	CH	B

* Most cantons.

Merry Christmas!	**Joyeux Noël!**	zhwahyur noehl
Happy New Year!	**Bonne année!**	bon ahnay
Happy Easter!	**Joyeuses Pâques!**	zhwahyurz pahk
Happy birthday!	**Bon anniversaire!**	bawng nahneevehrsehr
Best wishes!	**Mes/Nos meilleurs vœux!**	may/noa mehyurr vur
Congratulations!	**Félicitations!**	fayleesseetahssyawng
Good luck/ All the best!	**Bonne chance!**	bon shahngss
Have a good trip!	**Bon voyage!**	bawng vwahyahzh
Have a good holiday!	**Bonnes vacances!**	bon vahkahngss
Best regards from ...	**Meilleures salutations de ...**	mehyurr sahlewtahssyawng der
My regards to ...	**Mes amitiés à ...**	may zahmeetyay ah

What time is it? *Quelle heure est-il?*

Excuse me. Can you tell me the time?	**Pardon. Pouvez-vous m'indiquer l'heure?**	pahrdawng. poovay voo mangdeekay lurr
It's ...	**Il est ...**	eel eh
five past one	**une heure cinq***	ewn urr sangk
ten past two	**deux heures dix**	dur zurr deess
a quarter past three	**trois heures un quart**	trwah zurr ang kahr
twenty past four	**quatre heures vingt**	kahtr urr vang
twenty-five past five	**cinq heures vingt-cinq**	sangk urr vangt sangk
half past six	**six heures et demie**	see zurr ay dermee
twenty-five to seven	**sept heures moins vingt-cinq**	seht urr mwang vangt sangk
twenty to eight	**huit heures moins vingt**	weet urr mwang vang
a quarter to nine	**neuf heures moins un quart**	nurv urr mwang zang kahr
ten to ten	**dix heures moins dix**	dee zurr mwang deess
five to eleven	**onze heures moins cinq**	awnz urr mwang sangk
twelve o'clock (noon/midnight)	**douze heures (midi/minuit)**	dooz urr (meedee/meenwee)
in the morning	**du matin**	dew mahtang
in the afternoon	**de l'après-midi**	der lahpreh meedee
in the evening	**du soir**	dew swahr
The train leaves at ...	**Le train part à ...**	ler trang pahr ah
13.04 (1.04 p.m.)	**treize heures quatre***	trehz urr kahtr
0.40 (0.40 a.m.)	**zéro heure quarante**	zayroa urr kahrahngt
in five minutes	**dans cinq minutes**	dahng sank meenewt
in a quarter of an hour	**dans un quart d'heure**	dahng zang kahr durr
half an hour ago	**il y a une demi-heure**	eel ee ah ewn dermee urr
about two hours	**environ deux heures**	ahngveerawng dur zurr
more than 10 minutes	**plus de dix minutes**	plew der dee meenewt
less than 30 seconds	**moins de trente secondes**	mwang der trahngt sergawngd
The clock is fast/slow.	**L'horloge avance/a du retard.**	lorlozh ahvahngss/ah dew rertahr

---

* In ordinary conversation, time is expressed as shown here. However, official time uses a 24-hour clock which means that after noon hours are counted from 13 to 24.

Common abbreviations   *Abréviations courantes*

apr. J.-C.	après Jésus-Christ	A.D.
av. J.-C.	avant Jésus-Christ	B.C.
bd, boul.	boulevard	boulevard
c.-à-d.	c'est-à-dire	that is to say, i.e.
c/c	compte courant	current account
CCP	compte de chèques postaux	postal account
CEE	Communauté Economique Européenne	European Economic Community
CFF	Chemins de Fer Fédéraux	Swiss Federal Railways
ch	chevaux-vapeur	horsepower
Cie, Co.	Compagnie	Co.
CRS	Compagnies Républicaines de Sécurité	French order and riot police
CV	chevaux-vapeur	horsepower
E.U.	Etats-Unis	U.S.A.
exp.	expéditeur	sender
h	heure	hour, o'clock
hab.	habitants	inhabitants, population
M./MM.	Monsieur/Messieurs	Mr./Messrs.
Mlle	Mademoiselle	Miss
Mme	Madame	Mrs.
ONU	Organisation des Nations Unies	United Nations Organization
PDG	président-directeur général	chairman (president) of the board
p.ex.	par exemple	for instance, e.g.
p.p.	port payé	postage paid
RATP	Régie Autonome des Transports Parisiens	Paris transport authority
RN	route nationale	national road
s/	sur	on
SA	société anonyme	Ltd., Inc.
S.à.R.L.	société à responsabilité limitée	limited liability company
SI	Syndicat d'Initiative	tourist office (France)
SNCB	Société Nationale des Chemins de Fer Belges	Belgian National Railways
SNCF	Société Nationale des Chemins de Fer Français	French National Railways
s.v.p.	s'il vous plaît	please
T.T.C.	Toutes taxes comprises	all taxes included
T.V.A.	Taxe à la Valeur Ajoutée	VAT, value-added tax

Signs and notices *Ecriteaux*

A louer	For hire/For rent/To let
Ascenseur	Lift (elevator)
Attention	Caution
Attention au chien	Beware of the dog
A vendre	For sale
Caisse	Cash desk
Chaud	Hot
Chemin privé	Private road
Chiens interdits	Dogs not allowed
Complet	Full/No vacancies
Dames	Ladies
Danger (de mort)	Danger (of death)
Défense de . . .	. . . forbidden
Défense d'entrer sous peine d'amende	Trespassers will be prosecuted
Défense de fumer	No smoking
Entrée	Entrance
Entrée interdite	No entrance
Entrée libre	Admission free
Entrez sans frapper	Enter without knocking
Fermé	Closed
Fermez la porte	Close the door
Froid	Cold
Fumeurs	Smoking allowed
Haute tension	High voltage
Hommes	Men
Hors service	Out of order
Libre	Vacant
Messieurs	Gentlemen
Ne pas déranger	Do not disturb
Ne pas toucher, s.v.p.	Do not touch
Occupé	Occupied
Ouvert de . . . à . . .	Open from . . . to . . .
Peinture fraîche	Wet paint
Piste cyclable	Cycle path
Poussez	Push
Privé	Private
Renseignements	Information
Réservé	Reserved
Soldes	Sale
Sonnez, s'il vous plaît	Please ring
Sortie	Exit
Sortie de secours	Emergency exit
Tirez	Pull

Emergency *Urgences*

Call the police	**Appelez la police**	ahperlay lah poleess
DANGER	**DANGER**	dahngzhay
FIRE	**AU FEU**	oa fur
Gas	**Gaz**	gahz
Get a doctor	**Appelez un médecin**	ahperlay ang maydssang
Go away	**Allez-vous-en**	ahlay voo zahng
HELP	**AU SECOURS**	oa serkoor
Get help quickly	**A l'aide, vite**	ah lehd veet
I'm ill	**Je suis malade**	zher swee mahlahd
I'm lost	**Je me suis perdu(e)**	zher mer swee pehrdew
Leave me alone	**Laissez-moi tranquille**	lehssay mwah trahngkeel
LOOK OUT	**ATTENTION**	ahtahngssyawng
POLICE	**POLICE**	poleess
Quick	**Vite**	veet
STOP	**ARRÊTEZ**	ahrehtay
Stop that man/ woman	**Arrêtez cet homme/ cette femme**	ahrehtay seht om/ seht fahm
STOP THIEF	**AU VOLEUR**	oa volurr

Emergency telephone numbers *Numéros d'urgence*

	Belgium	France	Switzerland
Fire	900	18	118
Ambulance	900	17	117
Police	901	17	117

Lost! *En cas de perte ou de vol*

Where's the ...?	**Où est ...?**	oo eh
lost property (lost and found) office?	**le bureau des objets trouvés**	ler bewroa day zobzheh troovay
police station	**le poste de police**	ler post der poleess
I want to report a theft.	**Je voudrais déclarer un vol.**	zher voodreh dayklahray ang vol
My ... has been stolen.	**On m'a volé ...**	awng mah volay
I've lost my ...	**J'ai perdu ...**	zhay pehrdew
handbag	**mon sac à main**	mawng sahk ah mang
passport	**mon passeport**	mawng pahsspor
wallet	**mon portefeuille**	mawng portfury

CAR ACCIDENTS, see page 78

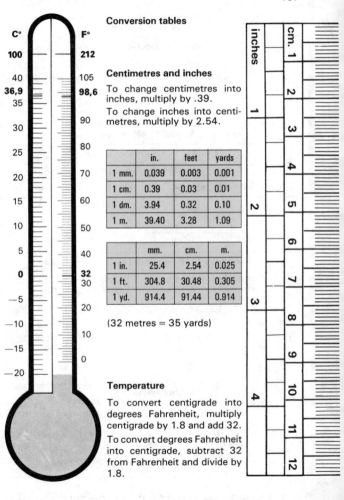

Conversion tables

Centimetres and inches

To change centimetres into inches, multiply by .39.
To change inches into centimetres, multiply by 2.54.

	in.	feet	yards
1 mm.	0.039	0.003	0.001
1 cm.	0.39	0.03	0.01
1 dm.	3.94	0.32	0.10
1 m.	39.40	3.28	1.09

	mm.	cm.	m.
1 in.	25.4	2.54	0.025
1 ft.	304.8	30.48	0.305
1 yd.	914.4	91.44	0.914

(32 metres = 35 yards)

Temperature

To convert centigrade into degrees Fahrenheit, multiply centigrade by 1.8 and add 32.

To convert degrees Fahrenheit into centigrade, subtract 32 from Fahrenheit and divide by 1.8.

REFERENCE SECTION

Renseignements divers

Kilometres into miles

1 kilometre (km.) = 0.62 miles

km.	10	20	30	40	50	60	70	80	90	100	110	120	130
miles	6	12	19	25	31	37	44	50	56	62	68	75	81

Miles into kilometres

1 mile = 1.609 kilometres (km.)

miles	10	20	30	40	50	60	70	80	90	100
km.	16	32	48	64	80	97	113	129	145	161

Fluid measures

1 litre (l.) = 0.88 imp. quart or 1.06 U.S. quart

1 imp. quart = 1.14 l.	1 U.S. quart = 0.95 l.
1 imp. gallon = 4.55 l.	1 U.S. gallon = 3.8 l.

litres	5	10	15	20	25	30	35	40	45	50
imp. gal.	1.1	2.2	3.3	4.4	5.5	6.6	7.7	8.8	9.9	11.0
U.S. gal.	1.3	2.6	3.9	5.2	6.5	7.8	9.1	10.4	11.7	13.0

Weights and measures

1 kilogram or kilo (kg.) = 1000 grams (g.)

100 g. = 3.5 oz.	½ kg. = 1.1 lb.
200 g. = 7.0 oz.	1 kg. = 2.2 lb.

1 oz. = 28.35 g.
1 lb. = 453.60 g.

CLOTHING SIZES, see page 115/YARDS AND INCHES, see page 112

Basic Grammar

Articles   *Articles*

All nouns in French are either masculine or feminine.

1. Definite article (the):

masc. *le* **train**   the train   fem. *la* **voiture**   the car

Le and **la** are contracted to **l'** when followed by a vowel or a silent **h***.

l'avion   the plane   **l'hôtel**   the hotel

Plural (masc. and fem.):

les **trains**   *les* **voitures**   *les* **avions**

2. Indefinite article (a/an):

masc. *un* **timbre**   a stamp   fem. *une* **lettre**   a letter

Plural (masc. and fem.):

des **timbres**   stamps   *des* **lettres**   letters

3. Some/any (partitive)

Expressed by **de, du, de la, de l', des** as follows:

masc. **du** (= **de** + **le**)   **de l'** when followed by a
fem. **de la**   vowel or a silent **h***

Plural (masc. and fem.): **des** (= **de** + **les**)

du **sel**   some salt   *de la* **moutarde**   some mustard
de l' **ail**   some garlic   *des* **oranges**   some oranges

In negatives sentences, **de** is generally used.

Il n'y a pas *de* **taxis.**   There aren't any taxis.
Je n'ai pas *d'* **argent.**   I haven't any money.

Note the concentration **d'** before a vowel.

---

* In French the letter *h* at the beginning of a word is not pronounced. However, in several words the *h* is what is called "aspirate", i.e., no liaison is made with the word preceding it. E.g., *le héros*.

Nouns *Noms*

1. As already noted, nouns are either masculine or feminine. There are no short cuts for determining gender (though, note that most nouns ending in **-e, -té, -tion** are feminine). So always learn a noun together with its accompanying article.

2. The plural of the majority of nouns is formed by adding **s** to the singular. (The final **s** is not pronounced.)

3. To show possession, use the preposition **de** (of).

la **fin** *de* la **semaine**	the end of the week
le **début** *du* **mois**	the beginning of the month
le **patron** *de* l'**hôtel**	the owner of the hotel
les **valises** *des* **voyageurs**	the traveller's luggage
la **chambre** *de* **Robert**	Robert's room

Adjectives *Adjectifs*

1. Adjectives agree with the noun in gender and number. Most of them form the feminine by adding **e** to the masculine (unless the word already ends in **e**). For the plural, add **s**.

a. **un grand magasin**	a big shop	**des grands magasins**
b. **une auto anglaise**	an English car	**des autos anglaises**

2. As can be seen from the above, adjectives can come (a) before the noun or (b) after the noun. Since it is basically a question of sound and idiom, rules are difficult to formulate briefly; but adjectives more often follow nouns.

3. **Demonstrative adjectives:**

this/that	**ce** *(masc.)*
	cet *(masc. before a vowel or silent **h**)*
	cette *(fem.)*
these/those	**ces** *(masc. and fem.)*

4. **Possessive adjectives:** These agree in number and gender with *the noun they modify,* i.e., with the thing possessed and not the possessor.

	masc.	fem.	plur.
my	**mon**	**ma**	**mes**
your	**ton**	**ta**	**tes**
his/her/its	**son**	**sa**	**ses**
our	**notre**	**notre**	**nos**
your	**votre**	**votre**	**vos**
their	**leur**	**leur**	**leurs**

Thus, depending on the context:

son **fils**	can mean *his* son or *her* son
sa **chambre**	can mean *his* room or *her* room
ses **vêtements**	can mean *his* clothes or *her* clothes

Personal pronouns *Pronoms personnels*

	Subject	Direct object	Indirect object	After a preposition
I	**je**	**me**	**me**	**moi**
you	**tu**	**te**	**te**	**toi**
he/it (masc.)	**il**	**le**	**lui**	**lui**
she/it (fem.)	**elle**	**la**	**lui**	**elle**
we	**nous**	**nous**	**nous**	**nous**
you	**vous**	**vous**	**vous**	**vous**
they (masc.)	**ils**	**les**	**leur**	**eux**
they (fem.)	**elles**	**les**	**leur**	**elles**

Note: There are two forms for "you" in French: **tu** is used when talking to relatives, close friends and children (and between young people); **vous** is used in all other cases, and is also the plural form of **tu.**

Prepositions *Prépositions*

There is a list of prepositions on page 15. Be careful with **à** (to, at) and **de** (of, from).

à + le = au	**de + le = du**
à + les = aux	**de + les = des**

Adverbs *Adverbes*

Adverbs are generally formed by adding **-ment** to the feminine form of the adjective.

masc.:	fem.:	adverb:
lent (slow)	**lente**	**lentement**
sérieux (serious)	**sérieuse**	**sérieusement**

Verbs *Verbes*

Here we are concerned only with the infinitive and the present tense.

Learn these two **auxiliary verbs:**

être (to be)	**avoir** (to have)
je suis *(I am)*	**j'ai** *(I have)*
tu es *(you are)*	**tu as** *(you have)*
il/elle est *(he, she, it is)*	**il/elle a** *(he, she, it has)*
nous sommes *(we are)*	**nous avons** *(we have)*
vous êtes *(you are)*	**vous avez** *(you have)*
ils/elles sont *(they are)*	**ils/elles ont** *(they have)*

Il y a is equivalent to "there is/there are":

Il y a une lettre pour vous.	There's a letter for you.
Il y a trois colis pour elle.	There are three parcels for her.
Y a-t-il du courrier pour moi?	Is there any post for me?
Il n'y pas de lettres pour vous.	There are no letters for you.

Regular verbs follow one of three patterns (conjugations) depending on the ending of the infinitive.

Infinitive	1 ends in **-er**	2 ends in **-ir**	3 ends in **-re**
	parler (to speak)	**finir** (to finish)	**attendre** (to wait)
je	parle	finis	attends*
tu	parles	finis	attends
il/elle	parle	finit	attend
nous	parlons	finissons	attendons
vous	parlez	finissez	attendez
ils/elles	parlent	finissent	attendent
Imperative	parlez	finissez	attendez

*j'attends: je is contracted before the following vowel

Irregular verbs: As in all languages, these have to be learned. Here are four you'll find useful.

Infinitive	**pouvoir** (to be able)	**aller** (to go)	**voir** (to see)	**faire** (to do/make)
je	**peux**	**vais**	**vois**	**fais**
tu	**peux**	**vas**	**vois**	**fais**
il/elle	**peut**	**va**	**voit**	**fait**
nous	**pouvons**	**allons**	**voyons**	**faisons**
vous	**pouvez**	**allez**	**voyez**	**faites**
ils/elles	**peuvent**	**vont**	**voient**	**font**
Imperative	–	**allez**	**voyez**	**faites**

Negatives *Négations*

Negatives are generally formed by putting **ne** before the verb and **pas** after it (**ne** is contracted to **n'** before a following vowel or a silent **h**).

Je parle français.	I speak French.
Je *ne* parle *pas* français.	I don't speak French.
Elle est riche.	She is rich.
Elle *n'*est *pas* riche.	She isn't rich.

Questions *Questions*

Questions may be formed in one of two ways:

1. by inverting the subject and the verb (putting the verb first, the subject second):

Est-elle riche?	Is she rich?
Avez-vous des enfants?	Have you any children?
Parle-t-il français?*	Does he speak French?

2. by using the expression "**est-ce que**" + the affirmative word order.

Est-ce que vous parlez français? Do you speak French?

---

* **t** is inserted between the two vowels

Dictionary
and alphabetical index

English–French

f feminine	m masculine	pl plural

a un, une 159
abbey abbaye f 81
abbreviation abréviation f 154
able, to be pouvoir 163
about *(approximately)* environ 153
above au-dessus (de) 15, 63
abscess abcès m 145
absent absent(e) 136
absorbent cotton coton hydrophile m 109
accept, to accepter 62, 102
accessories accessoires m/pl 116, 125
accident accident m 78, 139
accommodation logement m 22
account compte m 130, 131
ache douleur f 141
adaptor prise de raccordement f 119
address adresse f 21, 31, 76, 79, 102
address book carnet d'adresses m 104
adhesive autocollant(e) 105
admission entrée f 82, 89, 155
admitted admis(e) 150
Africa Afrique f 146
after après 15; au-delà de 77
afternoon après-midi m 151, 153
after-shave lotion lotion après rasage f 110
age âge m 149, 150
ago il y a 149, 151
air conditioner climatiseur m 28
air conditioning climatisation f 23
airmail par avion 133
airplane avion m 65
airport aéroport f 16, 21, 65
alarm clock réveil m 121

alcoholic alcoolisé 59
Algeria Algérie f 146
allergic allergique 141, 143
allow, to autoriser 79
almond amande f 54
alphabet alphabet m 9
also aussi 15
alter, to *(garment)* retoucher 116
amazing étonnant 84
amber ambre m 122
ambulance ambulance f 79
American américain(e) 93, 105, 126
American plan pension complète f 24
amethyst améthyste f 122
amount montant m 62; somme f 131
amplifier amplificateur m 119
anaesthetic anesthésique m 144, 145
analgesic analgésique m 109
anchovy anchois m 44
and et 15
animal animal m 85
aniseed anis m 50
ankle cheville f 139
anorak anorak m 116
answer réponse f 136
antibiotic antibiotique m 143
antidepressant remontant m 143
antiques antiquités f/pl 83
antique shop antiquaire m 98
antiseptic antiseptique 109
antiseptic antiseptique m 140
any de, de la, du (pl des) 15
anyone quelqu'un 12
anything quelque chose 17, 25, 113
anywhere quelque part 89
aperitif apéritif m 56

DICTIONARY

appendicitis appendicite f 142
appendix appendice m 138
appetizer hors-d'œuvre m 41
apple pomme f 54, 63
apple juice jus de pomme m 60
appliance appareil m 119
appointment rendez-vous m 30, 131, 137, 145
apricot abricot m 54
April avril m 150
archaeology archéologie f 83
architect architecte m 83
area code indicatif m 134
arm bras m 138, 139
arrival arrivée f 16, 65
arrive, to arriver 65, 68, 130
art art m 83
art gallery galerie d'art f 81, 98
artichoke artichaut m 49
artificial artificiel(le) 124
artist artiste m/f 83
ashtray cendrier m 27, 36
Asia Asie f 146
ask, to demander 25, 61, 136
asparagus asperge f 49
aspirin aspirine f 109
assorted varié(e) 41
asthma asthme m 141
at à 15
at least au moins 24
at once immédiatement 31
August août m 150
aunt tante f 93
Australia Australie f 146
automatic automatique 20, 122, 124
autumn automne m 150
available disponible 40
average moyen(ne) 91
awful horrible 84

B

baby bébé m 24, 111
baby food aliments pour bébés m/pl 111
babysitter garde d'enfants f 27
back dos m 138
backache mal de reins m 141
bacon bacon m 38; lard m 46
bacon and eggs œufs au bacon m/pl 38
bad mauvais(e) 14, 95
bag sac m 18, 103

baggage bagages m/pl 18, 26, 31, 71
baggage cart chariot à bagages m 18, 71
baggage check consigne f 67, 71
baggage locker consigne automatique f 18, 67, 71
baked au four 45, 47
baker's boulangerie f 98
balance (account) position f 131
balcony balcon m 23
ball (inflated) ballon m 128
ballet ballet m 88
ball-point pen stylo à bille m 104
banana banane f 54, 63
bandage bandage m 109
Band-Aid sparadrap m 109
bangle bracelet m 121
bangs frange f 30
bank (finance) banque f 98, 129
bank card carte d'identité bancaire f 130
banknote billet m 130; coupure m 130
bar bar m 33, 67; (chocolate) plaque f 64
barber's coiffeur m 30, 98
bass (fish) bar m 44
bath (hotel) salle de bains f 23, 25, 27
bath essence bain de mousse m 110
bathing cap bonnet de bain m 116
bathing hut cabine f 91
bathing suit costume de bain m 116
bathrobe peignoir (de bain) m 116
bathroom salle de bains f 27
bath salts sels de bain m/pl 110
bath towel serviette de bain f 27
battery pile f 119, 121, 125; (car) batterie f 75, 78
bay leaf laurier m 50
be, to être 161; se trouver 11
beach plage f 90
beach ball ballon de plage m 128
bean haricot m 49
beard barbe f 31
beautiful beau, belle 14, 84
beauty salon salon de beauté m 30; institut de beauté m 98
bed lit m 24, 144
bed and breakfast chambre avec petit déjeuner m 24
bedpan bassin m 144
beef bœuf m 46
beer bière f 56, 63
beet(root) betterave f 49

Dictionnaire

before *(place)* devant 15; *(time)* avant 15, 151
begin, to commencer 80, 87, 88
beginner débutant(e) *m/f* 91
beginning début *m* 150
behind derrière 15, 77
beige beige 113
Belgian belge 18
Belgium Belgique *f* 146
bell *(electric)* sonnette *f* 144
bellboy chasseur *m* 26
below au-dessous (de) 15
belt ceinture *f* 117
bend *(road)* virage *m* 79
berth couchette *f* 69, 70, 71
best meilleur(e) 152
better meilleur(e) 14, 113; mieux 25, 101
between entre 15
bicycle bicyclette *f* 74
big grand(e) 14, 101
bilberry myrtille *f* 54
bill note *f* 31; addition *f* 62; facture *f* 102; *(banknote)* billet *m* 130; coupure *m* 130
billion *(Am.)* milliard *m* 148
binoculars jumelles *f/pl* 123
bird oiseau *m* 85
birth naissance *f* 25
birthday anniversaire *m* 151, 152
biscuit *(Br.)* biscuit *m* 63
bitter amer, amère 61
black noir(e) 113
blackberry mûre *f* 54
blackcurrant cassis *m* 54
bladder vessie *f* 138
blade lame *f* 110
blanket couverture *f* 27
bleach décoloration *f* 30
bleed, to saigner 139, 145
blind *(window)* store *m* 29
blister ampoule *f* 139
block, to boucher 28
blood sang *m* 142
blood pressure tension *f* 141
blood transfusion transfusion (sanguine) *f* 144
blouse chemisier *m* 116
blow-dry brushing *m* 30
blue bleu(e) 113
blueberry myrtille *f* 54
boar *(wild)* sanglier *m* 48; *(young)* marcassin *m* 48
boarding house pension *f* 19, 22
boat bateau *m* 74

bobby pin pince à cheveux *f* 111
body corps *m* 138
boil furoncle *m* 139
boiled bouilli(e) 47
boiled egg œuf à la coque *m* 38
bone os *m* 138
book livre *m* 12, 104
book, to réserver 69
booking office bureau de réservation *m* 19, 67
booklet carnet *m* 72
bookshop librairie *f* 98, 104
boot botte *f* 118
born né(e) 150
botanical gardens jardin botanique *m* 81
botany botanique *f* 83
bottle bouteille *f* 17, 59
bottle-opener ouvre-bouteilles *m* 106
bottom bas *m* 145
bowels intestins *m/pl* 138
bow tie nœud papillon *m* 116
box boîte *f* 120
boxing boxe *f* 89
boy garçon *m* 112, 128
boyfriend ami *m* 93
bra soutien-gorge *m* 116
bracelet bracelet *m* 121
braces *(suspenders)* bretelles *f/pl* 116
braised braisé 47
brake frein *m* 78
brandy cognac *m* 60
bread pain *m* 36, 38, 64
break, to casser 29, 119, 123, 145; se casser 139, 145
break down, to être en panne 78
breakdown panne *f* 78
breakdown van dépanneuse *f* 78
breakfast petit déjeuner *m* 24, 34, 38
breast sein *m* 138
breathe, to respirer 141
bridge pont *m* 85
briefs slip *m* 116
brill barbue *f* 44
bring, to apporter 13
bring down, to descendre 31
British britannique 93
broken cassé(e) 29, 119, 140
brooch broche *f* 121
brother frère *m* 93
brown brun(e) 113
bruise contusion *f* 139
brush brosse *f* 111

Brussels sprouts choux de Bruxelles m/pl 49
bucket seau m 106, 128
buckle boucle f 117
build, to construire 83
building bâtiment m 81, 83
bulb ampoule f 28, 75, 119
burn brûlure f 139
bus bus m 18, 19, 65, 72, 73
business affaires f/pl 16, 131
business trip voyage d'affaires m 93
bus stop arrêt de bus m 72, 73
busy occupé(e) 96
butane gas butane m 32, 106
butcher's boucherie f 98
butter beurre m 36, 38, 64
button bouton m 29, 117
buy, to acheter 82, 104

C

cabana cabine f 91
cabbage chou m 49
cabin cabine f 74
cable télégramme m 133
cable car télécabine f 74
cable release déclencheur m 125
caffein-free décaféiné 38, 60
cake gâteau m 55, 64
calculator calculatrice f 105
calendar calendrier m 104
call (phone) appel m 135; communication f 136
call, to appeler 11, 78, 136, 156
call back, to rappeler 136
calm calme 90
cambric batiste m 114
camel-hair poil de chameau m 114
camera appareil de photo m 124, 125
camera case étui à appareil photo m 125
camera shop magasin de photos m 98
camp, to camper 32
campbed lit de camp m 106
camping camping m 32
camping equipment matériel de camping m 106
camp site camping m 32
can (of peaches) boîte f 120
can (to be able) pouvoir 12, 163
Canada Canada m 146
Canadian canadien(ne) 93
cancel, to annuler 65
candle bougie f 106

candy bonbon m 126
can opener ouvre-boîtes m 106
cap casquette f 116
caper câpre f 50
capital (finance) capital m 131
car voiture f 19, 20, 75, 76, 78
carat carat m 121
caravan caravane f 32
caraway cumin m 50, 64
carbon paper papier carbone m 104
carbonated gazeux(euse) 60
carburetor carburateur m 78
card carte f 93, 131
card game jeu de cartes m 128
cardigan cardigan m 116
car hire location de voitures f 20
carp carpe f 44
car park parking m 77
car racing courses d'autos m/pl 89
car radio autoradio m 119
car rental location de voitures f 20
carrot carotte f 49
carry, to porter 21
cart chariot m 18
carton (of cigarettes) cartouche (de cigarettes) f 17
cartridge (camera) chargeur m 124
case (instance) cas m 143; (cigarettes etc) étui m 121, 123, 125
cash, to toucher 130, 133
cash desk caisse f 155
cashier caissier m 103
cassette cassette f 119, 127
castle château m 81
catacomb catacombe f 81
catalogue catalogue m 82
cathedral cathédrale f 81
Catholic catholique 84
cauliflower chou-fleur m 49
caution attention f 79, 155
cave grotte f 81
cellophane tape ruban adhésif m 104
cemetery cimetière m 81
centimetre centimètre m 112
centre centre m 19, 21, 76, 81
century siècle m 149
ceramics céramique f 83
cereal céréales f/pl 38
certificate certificat m 144
chain (jewellery) chaînette f 121
chain bracelet gourmette f 121
chair chaise f 106
chamber music musique de chambre f 128

change *(money)* monnaie *f* 62, 77, 130
change, to changer 61, 65, 68, 73, 75, 123; *(money)* 18, 130
chapel chapelle *f* 1
charcoal charbon de bois *m* 106
charge tarif *m* 20, 32, 77, 89; note *f* 28; taxe *f* 136
charge, to faire payer 24; *(commission)* prendre 130
charm *(trinket)* breloque *f* 121
charm bracelet bracelet à breloques *m* 121
cheap bon marché 14, 24, 25, 101
check chèque *m* 130; *(restaurant)* addition *f* 62
check, to contrôler 75, 123; vérifier 75; *(luggage)* faire enregistrer 71
check book carnet de chèques *m* 131
check in, to *(airport)* enregistrer 65
check out, to partir 31
checkup *(medical)* bilan de santé *m* 142
cheers! à votre santé! 56
cheese fromage *m* 53, 64
chemist's pharmacie *f* 98, 108
cheque chèque *m* 130
cheque book carnet de chèques *m* 131
cherry cerise *f* 54
chervil cerfeuil *m* 50
chess échecs *m/pl* 93
chess set jeu d'échecs *m* 128
chest poitrine *f* 138, 141
chestnut marron *m* 54
chewing gum chewing-gum *m* 126
chewing tobacco tabac à chiquer *m* 126
chicken poulet *m* 48, 63
chicken breast suprême de volaille *m* 49
chicory endive *f* 49; *(Am.)* chicorée *f* 49
chiffon mousseline *f* 114
child enfant *m/f* 24, 61, 82, 93, 139, 150
children's doctor pédiatre *m/f* 137
China Chine *f* 146
chips (pommes) frites *f/pl* 51, 63; *(Am.)* chips *m/pl* 51, 64
chives ciboulette *f* 50
chocolate chocolat *m* 120, 126, 127; *(hot)* chocolat chaud *m* 38, 60
chocolate bar plaque de chocolat *f* 64
choice choix *m* 40

chop côtelette *f* 46
Christmas Noël *m* 152
chromium chrome *m* 122
church église *f* 81, 84; *(Protestant)* temple *m* 84
cigar cigare *m* 126
cigarette cigarette *f* 17, 95, 126
cigarette case étui à cigarettes *m* 121, 126
cigarette holder fume-cigarette *m* 126
cigarette lighter briquet *m* 121
cine camera caméra *f* 124
cinema cinéma *m* 86, 96
cinnamon cannelle *f* 50
circle *(theatre)* balcon *m* 87
city ville *f* 81
clam palourde *f* 45
classical classique 128
clean propre 61
clean, to nettoyer 29, 76
cleansing cream crème démaquillante *f* 110
clear, to *(cheque)* vérifier 130
cliff falaise *f* 85
cloakroom vestiaire *m* 87
clock pendule *f* 121; horloge *f* 153
clock-radio radio-réveil *m* 119
close *(near)* proche 78, 98
close, to fermer 11, 82, 108, 132
closed fermé(e) 155
cloth toile *f* 118
clothes vêtements *m/pl* 29, 116
clothes peg pince à linge *f* 106
clothing habillement *m* 112
cloud nuage *m* 94
clove clou de girofle *m* 50
coach *(bus)* car *m* 72
coat manteau *m* 116
coconut noix de coco *f* 54
cod morue *f* 45; *(fresh)* cabillaud *m* 44
coffee café *m* 38, 60, 64
coin monnaie *f* 83
cold froid(e) 14, 25, 61, 94
cold *(illness)* rhume *m* 108, 141
cold cuts charcuterie *f* 64
colour couleur *f* 103, 112, 124, 125
colour fast grand teint 114
colour negative négatif couleurs *m* 124
colour rinse coloration *f* 30
colour shampoo shampooing colorant *m* 111
comb peigne *m* 111
come, to venir 36, 92, 95, 137, 146

DICTIONARY

comedy comédie f 86
commission commission f 130
common *(frequent)* courant(e) 154
compact disc disque compact m 127
compartment compartiment m 70
compass boussole f 106
complaint réclamation f 61
concert concert m 88
concert hall salle de concert f 81, 88
conductor *(orchestra)* chef d'or-
    chestre m 88
confectioner's confiserie f 98
confirm, to confirmer 65
confirmation confirmation f 23
congratulation félicitation f 152
connection *(train)* correspondance f
    65, 68
constipated constipé(e) 140
contact lens verre de contact m 123
contain, to contenir 37
contraceptive contraceptif m 109
control contrôle m 16
convent couvent m 81
cookie biscuit m 64
cool box glacière f 106
copper cuivre m 122
copperware objets en cuivre m/pl 127
coral corail m 122
corduroy velours côtelé m 114
cork bouchon m 61
corkscrew tire-bouchons m 106
corn *(Am.)* maïs m 50; *(foot)* cor m
    109
corner angle m 36; *(street)* coin de
    rue m 21, 77
corn plaster emplâtre pour les cors
    m 109
cost coût m 131; prix m 136
cost, to coûter 11, 133
cotton coton m 114
cotton wool coton hydrophile m 109
cough toux f 108, 141
cough, to tousser 142
cough drops pastilles contre la toux
    f/pl 109
counter guichet m 133
country pays m 93
countryside campagne f 85
court house palais de justice m 81
cousin cousin(e) m/f 93
cover charge couvert m 62
crab crabe m 44
cracker biscuit salé m 64
cramp crampe f 141

crayfish écrevisse f 44
crayon crayon de couleur m 104
cream crème f 55, 60, 110
credit crédit m 130
credit, to créditer 130, 131
credit card carte de crédit f 20, 31,
    62, 102, 130
crepe crêpe m 114
crisps chips m/pl 51, 64
crockery vaisselle f 106, 107
cross croix f 121
cross-country skiing ski de fond m 91
crossing *(by sea)* traversée f 74
crossroads carrefour m 77
cruise croisière f 74
crystal cristal m 122, 127
cuckoo clock coucou m 121, 127
cucumber concombre m 49
cuff link bouton de manchette m 121
cup tasse f 36, 60, 107
curler bigoudi m 111
currency monnaie f 129
currency exchange office bureau de
    change m 18, 67, 129
current courant m 90
curtain rideau m 28
curve *(road)* virage m 79
customs douane f 16, 102
cut *(wound)* coupure f 139
cut, to couper 135
cut glass cristal taillé m 122
cuticle remover produit pour enlever
    les cuticules m 110
cutlery couverts m/pl 106, 107,
    121; coutellerie f 127
cutlet escalope f 46
cycling cyclisme m 89
cystitis cystite f 142

D

dairy laiterie f 98
dance, to danser 88, 96
danger danger m 155, 156
dangerous dangereux(euse) 90
dark sombre 25; foncé(e) 101, 112,
    113
date date f 25, 151; *(fruit)* datte f 54
daughter fille f 93
day jour m 16, 20, 24, 32, 80, 151;
    journée f 151
daylight lumière du jour f 124
day off jour de congé m 151
death mort f 155
decade décennie f 149

Dictionnaire

December décembre *m* 150
decision décision *f* 25, 102
deck *(ship)* pont *m* 74
deck-chair chaise longue *f* 91, 106
declare, to déclarer 17
delay retard *m* 69
delicatessen charcuterie *f*, traiteur *m* 98
delicious délicieux 62
deliver, to livrer 102
delivery livraison *f* 102
denim toile de coton *f* 114
dentist dentiste *m/f* 98, 145
denture dentier *m* 145
deodorant déodorant *m* 110
department *(museum)* département *m* 83; *(shop)* rayon *m* 100
department store grand magasin *m* 98
departure départ *m* 65
deposit *(car hire)* caution *f* 20; *(bank)* dépôt *m* 130
deposit, to *(bank)* déposer 130
dessert dessert *m* 37, 55
detour *(traffic)* déviation *f* 79
develop, to développer 124
diabetic diabétique 141
diabetic diabétique *m/f* 37
diaper couche *f* 111
diarrhoea diarrhée *f* 140
dictionary dictionnaire *m* 104
difficult difficile 14
difficulty difficulté *f* 28, 102, 141; peine *f* 141
digital digital(e) 122
dialling code indicatif *m* 134
diamond diamant *m* 122, 127
diarrhoea diarrhée *f* 140
diesel gas-oil *m* 75
diet régime *m* 37
difficult difficile 14
difficulty difficulté *f* 28, 102, 141; peine *f* 141
digital digital(e) 122
dining-car wagon-restaurant *m* 66, 68, 71
dining-room salle à manger *f* 27
dinner dîner *m* 34, 94
direct direct(e) 65
direct, to indiquer 13
direction direction *f* 76
director *(theatre)* metteur en scène *m* 86
directory *(phone)* annuaire *m* 134
disabled handicapé(e) 82
disc disque *m* 77, 127
discotheque discothèque *f* 88, 96
disease maladie *f* 142
dish plat *m* 37

dishwashing detergent produit (à) vaisselle *m* 106
disinfectant désinfectant *m* 109
dislocate, to disloquer 140
display case étalage *m* 100
dissatisfied mécontent(e) 103
district *(town)* quartier *m* 81
disturb, to déranger 155
diversion *(traffic)* déviation *f* 79
dizzy pris(e) de vertige 140
do, to faire 163
doctor médecin *m* 79, 137, 144; docteur *m* 145
doctor's office cabinet (de consultation) *m* 137
dog chien *m* 155
doll poupée *f* 128
dollar dollar *m* 18, 130
door porte *f* 155
double bed grand lit *m* 23
double room chambre pour deux personnes *f* 19, 23
down en bas 15
downhill skiing ski de piste *m* 91
downstairs en bas 15
down there là-bas 77
downtown centre *m* 81
dozen douzaine *f* 120, 149
draught beer bière pression *f* 56
drawing paper papier à dessin *m* 104
drawing pin punaise *f* 104
dress robe *f* 116
dressing gown peignoir *m* 116
drink boisson *f* 40, 59, 60, 61; verre *m* 95
drink, to boire 35, 36
drinking water eau potable *f* 32
drip, to *(tap)* fuire 28
drive, to conduire 21, 76
driving licence permis de conduire *m* 20, 79
drop *(liquid)* goutte *f* 109
drugstore pharmacie *m* 98, 108
dry sec, sèche 30, 59, 111
dry cleaner's teinturerie *f* 29, 98
dry shampoo shampooing sec *m* 111
Dublin bay prawn langoustine *f* 44
duck canard *m* 48
duckling caneton *m* 48
dull *(pain)* sourd(e) 140
dummy tétine *f* 111
during pendant 15, 150, 151
duty *(customs)* droits de douane *m/pl* 17

duty-free shop magasin hors-taxe *m* 19
dye teinture *f* 30, 111

E

each chaque 149
ear oreille *f* 138
earache mal aux oreilles *m* 141
ear drops gouttes pour les oreilles *f/pl* 109
early tôt 14
earring boucle d'oreille *f* 121
east est *m* 77
Easter Pâques *f/pl* 152
easy facile 14
eat, to manger 36, 144
eat out, to aller au restaurant 33
eel anguille *f* 44
egg œuf *m* 38, 64, 120
eggplant aubergine *f* 49
eight huit 147
eighteen dix-huit 147
eighth huitième 149
eighty quatre-vingts 148
elastic élastique 109
elastic bandage bandage élastique *m* 109
Elastoplast sparadrap *m* 109
electrical électrique 119
electrical appliance appareil électrique *m* 119
electrician électricien *m* 98
electricity électricité *f* 32
electronic électronique 125, 128
elevator ascenseur *m* 27, 100
eleven onze 147
embankment *(river)* quai *m* 81
embarkation embarquement *m* 74
emerald émeraude *f* 122
emergency urgence *f* 156
emergency exit sortie de secours *f* 27, 99, 155
emery board lime à ongles *f* 110
empty vide 14
enamel émail *m* 122
end fin *f* 150
endive chicorée *f* 49; *(Am.)* endive *f* 49
engine *(car)* moteur *m* 78
England Angleterre *f* 146
English anglais(e) 12, 80, 84, 104
enjoyable agréable 31
enjoy oneself, to s'amuser 96
enlarge, to agrandir 125

enough assez 15
enter, to entrer 155
entrance entrée *f* 67, 99, 155
entrance fee entrée *f* 82
envelope enveloppe *f* 27, 105
equipment équipement *m* 91; matériel *m* 106
eraser gomme *f* 105
escalator escalier mécanique *m* 100
espresso coffee express *m* 60
estimate estimation *f* 131
Europe Europe *f* 146
evening soir *m* 87, 95, 96, 151, 153; soirée *f* 95
evening dress tenue de soirée *f* 88; *(woman)* robe du soir *f* 116
everything tout 31
examine, to examiner 139
exchange, to échanger 103
exchange rate cours du change *m* 18, 130
excursion excursion *f* 80
excuse, to excuser 11
exercise book cahier *m* 105
exhaust pipe pot d'échappement *m* 78
exhibition exposition *f* 81
exit sortie *f* 67, 79, 99, 155
expect, to attendre 130
expensive cher, chère 14, 19, 24, 101
exposure *(photography)* pose *f* 124
exposure counter compte-poses *m* 125
express par exprès 133
expression expression *f* 10
expressway autoroute *f* 76
extension cord/lead prolongateur *m* 119
external externe 109
extra supplémentaire 27
extract, to *(tooth)* arracher 145
eye œil *m* (pl yeux) 138, 139
eye drops gouttes oculaires *f* 109
eye pencil crayon pour les yeux *m* 110
eye shadow fard à paupières *m* 110
eyesight vue *f* 123
eye specialist oculiste *m/f* 137

F

face visage *m* 138
face-pack masque de beauté *m* 30
face powder poudre *f* 110
factory usine *f* 81
fair foire *f* 81

fall chute f 139; *(autumn)* automne m 150
family famille f 93,
fan ventilateur m 28
fan belt courroie de ventilateur f 75
far loin 14, 100
fare tarif m 21; prix m 68, 73
farm ferme f 85
fashion mode f 127
fast *(film)* ultrarapide 124
fat *(meat)* gras m 37
father père m 93
faucet robinet m 28
fawn fauve f 54
February février m 150
fee *(doctor)* honoraires m/pl 144
feeding bottle biberon m 111
feel, to *(physical state)* se sentir 140
felt feutre m 114
felt-tip pen crayon feutre m 105
fennel fenouil m 50
ferry ferry m 74
fever fièvre f 140
few peu de 14; *(a)* quelques 14
field champ m 85
fifteen quinze 147
fifth cinquième 149
fifty cinquante 147
fig figue f 54
file *(tool)* lime f 110
fill in, to remplir 26, 144
filling *(tooth)* plombage m 145
filling station station-service f 75
film film m 86, 124, 125
film winder levier d'avancement m 125
filter filtre m 125
filter-tipped avec filtre 126
find, to trouver 11, 12, 100, 137
fine *(OK)* d'accord 25
fine arts beaux-arts m/pl 83
finger doigt m 138
finish, to finir 162
fire feu m 156
first premier(ère) 68, 73, 149
first-aid kit trousse de premiers secours f 106
first class première classe f 69
first course entrée f 40
first name prénom m 25
fish poisson m 44
fish, to pêcher 90
fishing pêche f 90
fishing tackle attirail de pêche m 106

fishmonger's poissonnerie f 98
fit, to aller 115, 116
fitting room cabine d'essayage f 115
five cinq 147
fix, to réparer 75, 145
fizzy *(mineral water)* gazeux(euse) 60
flannel flanelle f 114
flash *(photography)* flash m 125
flash attachment glissière du flash f 125
flashlight lampe de poche f 106
flat plat(e) 118
flat tyre crevaison f 75, 78
flea market marché aux puces m 81
flight vol m 65
flight number numéro de vol m 65
flippers palmes f/pl 128
floor étage m 27
floor show spectacle de cabaret m 88
flour farine f 37
flower fleur f 85
flower shop fleuriste m 98
flu grippe f 142
fluid liquide m 75
fog brouillard m 94
folding chair chaise pliante f 106
folding table table pliante f 107
folk music musique folklorique f 128
food nourriture f 37; aliment m 111
food box boîte à conservation f 106
food poisoning intoxication alimentaire f 142
foot pied m 138
football football m 89
foot cream crème pour les pieds f 110
footpath sentier m 85
for pour 15; pendant 143
forbid, to défendre 155
forecast prévision f 94
foreign étranger(ère) 56
forest forêt f 85
forget, to oublier 61
fork fourchette f 36, 61, 107, 127
form *(document)* formule f 133; fiche f 25, 26
fortnight quinze jours m/pl 151
fortress forteresse f 81
forty quarante 147
foundation cream fond de teint m 110
fountain fontaine f 81
fountain pen stylo m 105
four quatre 147
fourteen quatorze 147
fourth quatrième 149

fowl volaille *f* 49
frame *(glasses)* monture *f* 123
France France *f* 146
free libre 14, 70, 82, 96, 155
French français(e) 11, 18, 95, 114
French bean haricot vert *m* 49
french fries (pommes) frites *f/pl* 51, 63
fresh frais, fraîche 54, 61
Friday vendredi *m* 151
fried frit(e) 45, 47
fried egg œuf au plat *m* 38
friend ami(e) *m/f* 93, 95
fringe frange *f* 30
frog grenouille *f* 44
from de 15
front avant 75
frost gel *m* 94
fruit fruit *m* 54
fruit cocktail salade de fruits *f* 54
fruit juice jus de fruits *m* 38, 60
frying-pan poêle *f* 106
full plein(e) 14; complet(ète) 155
full board pension complète *f* 24
full insurance assurance tous risques *f* 20
furniture meubles *m/pl* 83
furrier's fourreur *m* 98

G

gabardine gabardine *f* 114
gallery galerie *f* 81, 98
game jeu *m* 128; *(food)* gibier *m* 48
garage garage *m* 26, 78
garden jardin *m* 85
gardens jardin public *m* 81
garlic ail *m* 50
gas gaz *m* 156
gasoline essence *f* 75, 78
gastritis gastrite *f* 142
gauze gaze *f* 109
gem pierre précieuse *f* 121
general général(e) 27, 100
general delivery poste restante *f* 133
general practitioner généraliste *m/f* 137
gentleman monsieur *m* 155
genuine véritable 118
geology géologie *f* 83
Germany Allemagne *f* 146
get, to *(find)* trouver 11, 19, 21, 32; *(call)* appeler 31, 137; *(obtain)* obtenir 108, 134; se procurer 90; *(go)* se rendre 100

get back, to être de retour 80
get off, to descendre 73
get to, to aller à 19; arriver à 70
get up, to se lever 144
gherkin cornichon *m* 49, 64
gin and tonic gin-tonic *m* 60
ginger gingembre *m* 50
girdle gaine *f* 116
girl fille *f* 112; *(child)* fillette *f* 128
girlfriend amie *f* 93, 95
give, to donner 13, 123, 135
give way, to *(traffic)* céder le passage 79
glad *(to know you)* enchanté(e) 92
gland glande *f* 138
glass verre *m* 36, 59, 60, 61, 143
glasses lunettes *f/pl* 123
gloomy sombre 84
glossy *(finish)* brillant(e) 125
glove gant *m* 116
glue colle *m* 105
go, to aller 96, 162
go away, to s'en aller 156
gold or *m* 121, 122
golden doré(e) 113
gold plate plaqué or *m* 122
golf golf *m* 89
golf course terrain de golf *m* 89
good bon(ne) 14, 101
good-bye au revoir 10
Good Friday Vendredi-Saint *m* 152
goods articles *m/pl* 16
goose oie *f* 48
gooseberry groseille à maquereau *f* 54
gram gramme *m* 120
grammar book grammaire *f* 105
grape raisin *m* 54, 64
grapefruit pamplemousse *m* 54
grapefruit juice jus de pamplemousse *m* 38, 60
gray gris(e) 113
graze éraflure *f* 139
greasy gras(se) 30, 111
great *(excellent)* formidable 95
Great Britain Grande-Bretagne *f* 146
green vert(e) 113
green bean haricot vert *m* 49
greengrocer's primeur *m* 98
green salad salade verte *f* 42
greeting salutation *f* 10
grey gris(e) 113
grilled grillé(e) 45, 47

grocery magasin d'alimentation *m* 98, 120; épicerie *f* 98
groundsheet tapis de sol *m* 106
group groupe *m* 82
guide guide *m/f* 80
guidebook guide (de voyage) *m* 82, 104
guinea fowl pintade *f* 48
gum (teeth) gencive *f* 145
gynaecologist gynécologue *m/f* 137

H

haddock aiglefin *m* 44
hair cheveux *m/pl* 30, 111
hairbrush brosse à cheveux *f* 111
haircut coupe de cheveux *f* 30
hairdresser's coiffeur *m* 30, 98; salon de coiffure *m* 27
hair dryer sèche-cheveux *m* 119
hairgrip pince à cheveux *f* 111
hair lotion lotion capillaire *f* 111
hairpin épingle à cheveux *f* 111
hairspray laque *f* 30, 111
half moitié *f* 149
half a day demi-journée *f* 80
half a dozen demi-douzaine *f* 120
half an hour demi-heure *f* 153
half board demi-pension *f* 24
half price (ticket) demi-tarif *m* 69
hall (large room) salle *f* 81, 88
hall porter concierge *m* 26
ham jambon *m* 38, 46, 63, 64
ham and eggs œufs au jambon *m/pl* 38
hamlet hameau *m* 85
hammer marteau *m* 106
hammock hamac *m* 106
hand main *f* 138
handbag sac à main *m* 116, 156
hand cream crème pour les mains *f* 110
handicrafts artisanat *m* 83
handkerchief mouchoir *m* 116
handmade fait(e) à la main 113
hanger cintre *m* 27
hangover gueule de bois *f* 108
happy heureux 152
harbour port *m* 81
hard dur(e) 123
hard-boiled (egg) dur 38
hardware shop quincaillerie *f* 98
hare lièvre *m* 48
hat chapeau *m* 116
have, to avoir 161; posséder 130; (meal) prendre 38
haversack musette *f* 106

hayfever rhume des foins *m* 108, 141
hazelnut noisette *f* 54
he il 161
head tête *f* 138, 139
headache mal de tête *m* 141
headlight phare *m* 79
headphones casque à écouteurs *m* 119
head waiter maître d'hôtel *m* 61
health santé *f* 56
health food shop magasin de diététique *m* 98
health insurance assurance maladie *f* 144
health insurance form feuille maladie *f* 144
heart cœur *m* 138
heart attack crise cardiaque *f* 141
heat, to chauffer 90
heating chauffage *m* 23, 28
heavy lourd(e) 14, 101
heel talon *m* 118
helicopter hélicoptère *m* 74
hello! (phone) allô! 135
help aide *m* 156
help! au secours! 156
help, to aider 13, 21, 71, 100, 134; (oneself) se servir 120
her son, sa (pl ses) 161
herbs fines herbes *f/pl* 50
herb tea tisane *f* 60
here ici 14; voici 14
herring hareng *m* 44
high haut(e) 90; (blood pressure) élevé(e) 141
high season haute saison *f* 150
high-speed ultrarapide 124
high tide marée haute *f* 90
hill colline *f* 85
hire location *f* 20, 74
hire, to louer 19, 20, 74, 90, 91, 119, 155
his son, sa (pl ses) 161
history histoire *f* 83
hitchhike, to faire l'auto-stop 74
hold on! (phone) ne quittez pas! 136
hole trou *m* 29
holiday jour férié *m* 151
holidays vacances *f/pl* 16, 151
home address lieu de domicile *m* 25
honey miel *m* 38
horse racing courses (de chevaux) *f/pl* 89
horseradish raifort *m* 50

hospital hôpital m 99, 144
hot chaud(e) 14, 25, 38, 94
hotel hôtel m 19, 21, 22
hotel guide guide des hôtels m 19
hotel reservation réservation d'hôtel f 19
hot water eau chaude f 23, 28
hot-water bottle bouillotte f 27
hour heure f 153
house maison f 83, 85
hovercraft aéroglisseur m 74
how comment 11
how far à quelle distance 11, 76, 85
how long combien de temps 11, 24
how many combien 11
how much combien 11, 24, 101
hundred cent 148
hungry, to be avoir faim 13, 35
hurry (to be in a) être pressé(e) 21
hurry up! dépêchez-vous! 13
hurt, to faire mal 139, 145; *(oneself)* se blesser 139
husband mari m 93
hydrofoil hydroptère m 74

I
I je 161
ice glace f 94
ice-cream glace f 55, 64
ice cube glaçon m 27
iced tea thé glacé m 60
ice pack cartouche réfrigérante f 106
ill malade 140, 156
illness maladie f 140
important important(e) 13
imported importé(e) 113
impressive impressionnant(e) 84
in dans 15
include, to comprendre 20, 24, 31, 32, 62, 80
included compris(e) 40, 62
India Inde f 146
indigestion indigestion f 141
inexpensive bon marché 35, 124
infect, to infecter 140
infection infection f 141
inflammation inflammation f 142
inflation inflation f 131
inflation rate taux d'inflation m 131
influenza grippe f 142
information renseignement m 67, 155
injection piqûre f 142, 144
injure, to blesser 139
injured blessé(e) 79, 139

injury blessure f 139
ink encre f 105
inn auberge f 22, 33
inquiry renseignement m 68
insect bite piqûre d'insecte f 108, 139
insect repellent crème anti-insecte f 109
insect spray bombe insecticide f 109
inside dedans 15
instead à la place 37
instrumental *(music)* instrumental(e) 128
insurance assurance f 20, 79, 144
interest intérêt m 80, 131
interested, to be s'intéresser 83, 96
interesting intéressant(e) 84
international international 133, 134
interpreter interprète m 131
intersection carrefour m 77
introduce, to présenter 92
introduction présentation f 92, introduction f 130
investment investissement m 131
invitation invitation f 94
invite, to inviter 94
invoice facture f 131
iodine teinture d'iode f 109
Ireland Irlande f 146
Irish irlandais(e) 92
iron *(laundry)* fer à repasser m 119
iron, to repasser 29
ironmonger's quincaillerie f 99
Italy Italie f 146
its son, sa *(pl* ses) 161
ivory ivoire m 122

J
jacket veston m 116
jam confiture f 38, 63
jam, to coincer 28; bloquer 125
January janvier m 150
jar pot m 120
jaundice jaunisse f 142
jaw mâchoire f 138
jeans jeans m/pl 116
jersey tricot m 116
jewel bijou m 121
jewel box coffret à bijoux m 121
jeweller's bijouterie f 99, 121
joint articulation f 138
journey trajet m 72
juice jus m 38, 41, 60
July juillet m 150
jumper *(sweater)* chandail m 116
June juin m 150

DICTIONARY

Dictionnaire

lost property office bureau des objets trouvés m 67, 156
lot *(a)* beaucoup 14
lotion lotion f 110
loud *(voice)* fort(e) 135
love, to aimer 95
lovely beau, belle 94
low bas(se) 90, 141
lower inférieur(e) 69, 71
low season basse saison f 150
low tide marée basse f 90
luck chance f 135, 152
luggage bagages m/pl 18, 26, 31, 71
luggage locker consigne automatique f 18, 67, 71
luggage trolley chariot à bagages m 18, 71
lump *(bump)* bosse f 139
lunch déjeuner m 34, 80, 94
lung poumon m 138

M

machine machine f 114
mackerel maquereau m 45
magazine revue f 105
magnificent splendide 84
maid femme de chambre f 26
mail, to mettre à la poste 28
mail courrier m 28, 133
mailbox boîte aux lettres f 132
make, to faire 131, 162
make up, to faire 28; préparer 108
make-up remover pad disque démaquillant m 110
man homme m 115, 155
manager directeur m 26
manicure manucure f 30
many beaucoup de 15
map carte f 76, 105; plan m 105
March mars m 150
marinated mariné(e) 45
market marché m 81, 99
marmalade marmelade f 38
married marié(e) 93
mass *(church)* messe f 84
mat *(finish)* mat(e) 125
match allumette f 106, 126; *(sport)* match m 89
match, to *(colour)* s'assortir à 112
material *(cloth)* tissu m 113
mattress matelas m 106
May mai m 150
may *(can)* pouvoir 12, 163

meadow pré m 85
meal repas m 24, 34, 62, 143
mean, to vouloir dire 11; signifier 26
measles rougeole f 142
measure, to prendre les mesures 114
meat viande f 46, 47, 61
meatball boulette f 46
mechanic mécanicien m 78
mechanical pencil porte-mine m 105, 121
medical médical(e) 144
medicine médecine f 83; *(drug)* médicament m 143
medium *(meat)* à point 47
medium-sized moyen(ne) 20
meet, to rencontrer 96
melon melon m 54
memorial monument m 81
mend, to réparer 75; *(clothes)* raccommoder 29
menthol *(cigarettes)* mentholé(e) 126
menu menu m 37, 39; *(printed)* carte f 36, 39, 40
merry joyeux(euse) 152
message message m 28, 136
methylated spirits alcool à brûler m 106
metre mètre m 112
mezzanine *(theatre)* balcon m 87
middle milieu m 69, 87, 150
midnight minuit m 153
mileage kilomètrage m 20
milk lait m 38, 60, 64
milkshake frappé m 60
million million m 148
mineral water eau minérale f 60
minister *(religion)* pasteur m 84
mint menthe f 50
minute minute f 153
mirror miroir m 115, 123
miscellaneous divers(e) 127
Miss Mademoiselle f 10
miss, to manquer 18, 29, 61
mistake erreur f 31, 61, 62, 102
mixed salad salade mêlée f 42
modified American plan demi-pension f 24
moisturizing cream crème hydratante f 110
moment moment m 136
monastery monastère m 81
Monday lundi m 151
money argent m 129, 130
money order mandat m 133

month mois *m* 16, 150
monument monument *m* 81
moon lune *f* 94
moped vélomoteur *m* 74
more plus 15
morning matin *m* 151, 153
Morocco Maroc *m* 146
mortgage hypothèque *f* 131
mosque mosquée *f* 84
mosquito net moustiquaire *f* 106
mother mère *f* 93
motorbike moto *f* 74
motorboat canot à moteur *m* 91
motorway autoroute *f* 76
mountain montagne *f* 85
moustache moustache *f* 31
mouth bouche *f* 138
mouthwash gargarisme *m* 109
move, to bouger 139
movie film *m* 86
movie camera caméra *f* 124
movies cinéma *m* 86, 96
Mr. Monsieur *m* 10
Mrs. Madame *f* 10
much beaucoup 14
mug grosse tasse *f* 107
mulberry mûre *f* 54
muscle muscle *m* 138
museum musée *m* 81
mushroom champignon *m* 49
music musique *f* 83, 128
musical comédie musicale *f* 86
music box boîte à musique *f* 121
mussel moule *f* 45
must, to devoir 31, 37, 61; falloir 95
mustard moutarde *f* 37, 50, 64
my mon, ma *(pl* mes) 161

N

nail *(human)* ongle *m* 110
nail brush brosse à ongles *f* 110
nail clippers coupe-ongles *m* 110
nail file lime à ongles *f* 110
nail polish vernis à ongles *m* 110
nail polish remover dissolvant *m* 110
nail scissors ciseaux à ongles *m/pl* 110
name nom *m* 23, 25, 79, 85, 92
napkin serviette *f* 36, 105, 106
nappy couche *f* 111
narrow étroit(e) 118
nationality nationalité *f* 25, 92
natural naturel(le) 83
nauseous nauséeux(euse) 140

near près 14; près de 15
nearby à proximité 77
nearest le(a) plus proche 78, 98
neat *(drink)* sec 56, 60
neck cou *m* 138; *(nape)* nuque *f* 30
necklace collier *m* 121
need, to avoir besoin de 90; falloir 29
needle aiguille *f* 27
negative négatif *m* 125
nephew neveu *m* 93
nerve nerf *m* 138
nervous nerveux(euse) 138
nervous system système nerveux *m* 138
Netherlands Pays-Bas *m/pl* 146
never ne ... jamais 15
new nouveau, nouvelle 14
newspaper journal *m* 104, 105
newsstand kiosque à journaux *m* 19, 67, 99, 104
New Year Nouvel An *m* 152
New Zealand Nouvelle-Zélande *f* 146
next prochain(e) 14, 65, 68, 73, 76, 149, 151
next time la prochaine fois 95
next to à côté de 15, 77
nice beau, belle 94
niece nièce *f* 93
night nuit *f* 24, 151
nightclub boîte de nuit *f* 88
night cream crème de nuit *f* 110
nightdress chemise de nuit *f* 116
nine neuf 147
nineteen dix-neuf 147
ninety quatre-vingt-dix 148
ninth neuvième 149
no non 10
noisy bruyant(e) 25
nonalcoholic sans alcool 60
none aucun(e) 15
nonsmoker non-fumeurs *m/pl* 36, 70
noodle nouille *f* 51
noon midi *m* 31, 153
normal normal(e) 30
north nord *m* 77
North America Amérique du Nord *f* 146
nose nez *m* 138
nosebleed saignement de nez *m* 141
nose drops gouttes nasales *f/pl* 109
not ne ... pas 15, 163
note *(banknote)* billet *m* 130; coupure *f* 130
notebook bloc-notes *m* 105

DICTIONARY

note paper papier à lettres *m* 105
nothing rien 15, 17
notice *(sign)* écriteau *m* 155
November novembre *m* 150
now maintenant 15
number numéro *m* 26, 65, 135, 136; nombre *m* 147
nurse infirmière *f* 144
nutmeg *(noix)* muscade *f* 50

O

occupation profession *f* 93
occupied occupé(e) 14, 70, 155
October octobre *m* 150
octopus poulpe *f* 45
offer, to offrir 95
office bureau *m* 19, 67, 99, 132, 133, 156
oil huile *f* 37, 75, 111
oily gras(se) 30, 111
old vieux, vieille 14; ancien(ne) 14
old town vieille ville *f* 81
olive olive *f* 41
omelet omelette *f* 42
on sur 15
once une fois 149
one un, une 147
one-way *(ticket)* aller *m* 65, 69
on foot à pied 76
onion oignon *m* 50
on request sur demande 73
on time à l'heure 68
only seulement 80
onyx onyx *m* 122
open ouvert(e) 14, 82, 155
open, to ouvrir 11, 17, 82, 108, 131, 132, 142
open-air en plein air 90
opera opéra *m* 88
opera house opéra *m* 81, 88
operation opération *f* 144
operator opérateur m, opératrice *f* 134
operetta opérette *f* 88
opposite en face (de) 77
optician opticien(ne) *m/f* 99, 123
or ou 15
orange orange 113
orange orange *f* 54, 64
orange juice jus d'orange *m* 38, 60
orchestra orchestre *m* 88; *(seats)* parterre *m* 87
orchestral music musique symphonique *f* 128

order *(goods, meal)* commande *f* 40, 102
order, to *(goods, meal)* commander 61, 102, 103
oregano origan *m* 50
ornithology ornithologie *f* 83
our notre *(pl* nos) 161
out of order hors service 155
out of stock épuisé(e) 103
outlet *(electric)* prise *f* 27
outside dehors 15, 36
oval ovale 101
overalls salopette *f* 116
overdone trop cuit(e) 61
overheat, to *(engine)* chauffer 78
overnight *(stay)* d'une nuit 24
overtake, to doubler 79
owe, to devoir 144
owerwhelming imposant(e) 84
oyster huître *f* 44

P

pacifier tétine *f* 111
packet paquet *m* 120, 126
page *(hotel)* chasseur *m* 26
pail seau *m* 106, 128
pain douleur *f* 140, 141, 144
painkiller calmant *m* 140, 144
paint peinture f 155
paint, to peindre 83
paintbox boîte de couleurs *f* 105
painter peintre *m* 83
painting peinture *f* 83
pair paire *f* 116, 118, 149
pajamas pyjama *m* 116
palace palais *m* 81
pancake crêpe *f* 63
panties slip *m* 116
pants *(trousers)* pantalon *m* 116
panty girdle gaine-culotte *f* 116
panty hose collant *m* 116
paper papier *m* 105
paperback livre de poche *m* 105
paperclip trombone *f* 105
paper napkin serviette en papier *f* 105, 106
paraffin *(fuel)* pétrole *m* 106
parcel colis *m* 132
parents parents *m/pl* 93
park parc *m* 81
park, to garer 26, 77
parking stationnement *m* 77, 79
parking disc disque de stationnement *m* 77

Dictionnaire

parking meter parcomètre *m* 77
parliament parlement *m* 81
parsley persil *m* 50
part partie *f* 138
partridge perdrix *f* 48
party *(social gathering)* réception *f* 95
pass, to *(car)* doubler 79
passport passeport *m* 16, 17, 25, 26, 156
passport photo photo d'identité *f* 124
pass through, to être de passage 16
pasta pâtes *f/pl* 51
paste *(glue)* colle *f* 105
pastry pâtisserie *f* 64
pastry shop pâtisserie *f* 99
patch, to *(clothes)* rapiécer 29
path chemin *m* 85
patient patient *m* 144
pay, to payer 31, 62, 102
payment paiement *m* 102, 131
pea petit pois *m* 50
peach pêche *f* 54
peak sommet *m* 85
peanut cacahouète *f* 54
pear poire *f* 54
pearl perle *f* 122
pedestrian piéton *m* 79
peg *(tent)* piquet *m* 107
pen plume *f* 105
pencil crayon *m* 105
pencil sharpener taille-crayon *m* 105
pendant pendentif *m* 121
penicillin pénicilline *f* 143
penknife canif *m* 106
pensioner retraité(e) *m/f* 82
people gens *m/pl* 93
pepper poivre *m* 37, 38, 51, 64
per cent pour cent 149
perch perche *f* 45
per day par jour 20, 32, 89
perfume parfum *m* 110, 127
perfume shop parfumerie *f* 108
perhaps peut-être 15
per hour horaire 77; par heure 89
period *(monthly)* règles *f/pl* 141
period pains règles douloureuses *f/pl* 141
permanent wave permanente *f* 30
permit permis *m* 90
per night par nuit 24
per person par personne 32
person personne *f* 32, 36
personal personnel(le) 17

personal call communication avec préavis *f* 135
personal cheque chèque à ordre *m* 130
person-to-person call communication avec préavis *f* 135
per week par semaine 20, 24
petrol essence *f* 75, 78
pewter étain *m* 122
pheasant faisan *m* 48
phone téléphone *m* 28, 78, 79, 134
phone, to téléphoner 134
phone booth cabine téléphonique *f* 134
phone call appel *m* 135; communication *f* 136
phone number numéro de téléphone *m* 96, 134, 135
photo photo *f* 82, 124, 125
photocopy photocopie *f* 104, 131
photograph, to photographier, prendre des photos 82
photographer photographe *m/f* 99
photography photographie *f* 124
phrase expression *f* 12
pick up, to prendre 80, 96
picnic pique-nique *m* 63
picture tableau *m* 83; *(photo)* photo *f* 82
piece morceau *m* 120
pig cochon *m* 46
pigeon pigeon *m* 48
pike brochet *m* 44
pill pilule *f* 141, 143
pillow oreiller *m* 27
pin épingle *f* 110, 111, 121
pineapple ananas *m* 54
pink rose 113
pipe pipe *f* 126
pipe cleaner nettoie-pipe *m* 126
pipe tool cure-pipe *m* 126
place place *m* 25; endroit *m* 76
place of birth lieu de naissance *m* 25
plaice carrelet *m* 44; plie *f* 45
plane avion *m* 65
planetarium planétarium *m* 81
plaster plâtre *m* 140
plastic plastique *m* 107
plastic bag sac en plastique *m* 107
plate assiette *f* 36, 61, 107
platform quai *m* 67, 68, 69, 70
platinum platine *f* 122
play *(theatre)* pièce *f* 86
play, to jouer 86, 88, 89, 93

playground terrain de jeu m 32
playing card carte à jouer f 105
please s'il vous plaît 10
plimsolls tennis m/pl 118
plug (electric) fiche f 29
plum prune f 54
pneumonia pneumonie f 142
poached poché(e) 45
pocket poche f 117
point, to (show) montrer 12
poison poison m 109
poisoning intoxication f 142
pole (ski) bâton m 91
police police f 78, 156
police station poste de police m 99, 156
polish (nails) vernis m 110
pond étang m 85
pop music musique pop f 128
poplin popeline f 114
poppy pavot m 64
porcelain porcelaine f 127
pork porc m 46
port port m 74; (wine) porto m 60
portable portatif(ive) 119
porter porteur m 18, 71; (hotel) bagagiste m 26
portion portion f 37, 55, 61
possible possible 137
post (letters) courrier m 28, 133
post, to mettre à la poste 28
postage tarif (d'affranchissement) m 132
postage stamp timbre m 28, 126, 132
postcard carte postale f 105, 126, 132
post office bureau de poste m 99, 132
potato pomme de terre f 51
pothole nid de poule m 79
pottery poterie f 83, 127
poultry volaille f 48
pound (money) livre f 18, 130; (weight) livre f 120
powder poudre f 110
powder compact poudrier m 122
powder puff houppette f 110
prawns scampi m/pl 45
preference préférence f 101
pregnant enceinte 141
premium (gasoline) super m 75
preparation préparation f 51
prescribe, to prescrire 143
prescription ordonnance f 108, 143
press, to (iron) repasser à la vapeur 29

press stud bouton-pression m 117
pressure pression f 75
price prix m 24
priest prêtre m 84
print (photo) copie f 125
private privé(e) 91, 155
processing (photo) développement m 124
profession profession f 25
profit bénéfice m 131
programme programme m 87
prohibit, to interdire 79
pronunciation prononciation f 6
propelling pencil porte-mine m 105, 122
propose, to proposer 40
Protestant protestant(e) 84
provide, to procurer 131
prune pruneau m 54
public holiday jour férié m 152
pull, to tirer 155
pullover pull(over) m 117
puncture crevaison f 75
purchase achat m 131
pure pur(e) 114
purple violet(te) 113
push, to pousser 155
put, to mettre 24
pyjamas pyjama m 117

Q

quail caille f 48
quality qualité f 103, 113
quantity quantité f 14, 103
quarter quart m 149; (part of town) quartier m 81
quarter of an hour quart d'heure m 153
question question f 11
quick rapide 14; vite 156
quickly vite 137, 156
quiet tranquille 23, 25

R

rabbi rabbin m 84
rabbit lapin m 48
race course/track champ de courses m 90
racket (sport) raquette f 90
radiator radiateur m 78
radio (set) poste de radio m 23, 119; radio f 28
radish radis m 50
railroad crossing passage à niveau m 79

railway chemin de fer *m* 154
railway station gare *f* 19, 21, 67, 70
rain pluie *f* 94
rain, to pleuvoir 94
raincoat imperméable *m* 117
raisin raisin sec *m* 54
rangefinder télémètre *m* 125
rare *(meat)* saignant(e) 47, 61
rash éruption *f* 139
raspberry framboise *f* 54
rate tarif *m* 20; taux *m* 131
razor rasoir *m* 110
razor blade lame de rasoir *f* 110
reading-lamp lampe de chevet *f* 27
ready prêt(e) 29, 118, 123, 125, 145
real véritable 121
rear arrière 75
receipt quittance *f* 103, 144
reception réception *f* 23
receptionist réceptionnaire *m* 26
recommend, to recommander 35, 36; indiquer 35, 88, 137, 145; conseiller 80, 86
record *(disc)* disque *m* 127, 128
record player tourne-disque *m* 119
rectangular rectangulaire 101
red rouge 59, 113
redcurrant groseille *f* 54
red mullet rouget *m* 45
reduction réduction *f* 24, 82
refill recharge *f* 105
refund remboursement *m* 103
regards salutations *f/pl*, amitiés *f/pl* 152
register, to *(luggage)* faire enregistrer 71
registered mail recommandé(e) 133
registration enregistrement *m* 25
registration form fiche *f* 25, 26
regular *(petrol)* normale *f* 75
religion religion *f* 83
religious service service religieux *m*, culte *m* 84
rent, to louer 19, 20, 74, 90, 91, 119, 155
rental location *f* 20, 74
repair réparation *f* 125
repair, to réparer 29, 118, 119, 121, 123, 125, 145
repeat, to répéter 12
report, to déclarer 156
require, to exiger 88
reservation réservation *f* 19, 23, 65, 69

reservations office bureau de réservation *m* 19, 67
reserve, to réserver 19, 23, 36, 87
restaurant restaurant *m* 19, 32, 34, 35, 67
return *(ticket)* aller-retour *m* 65, 69
return, to *(give back)* rendre 103
reverse the charges, to téléphoner en P.C.V. 135
rheumatism rhumatisme *m* 141
rhubarb rhubarbe *f* 54
rib côte *f* 46, 138
ribbon ruban *m* 105
rice riz *m* 51
right droite 21, 63, 69, 77; *(correct)* juste 14
ring *(on finger)* bague *f* 122
ring, to sonner 155; téléphoner 134
river rivière *f* 85, 90; *(major)* fleuve *m* 85
road route *f* 76, 77, 85
road assistance assistance routière *f* 78
road map carte routière *f* 105
road sign panneau routier *m* 79
roast rôti(e) 47
roast beef rosbif *m* 46
roll *(bread)* petit pain *m* 38, 64
roller skate patin à roulettes *m* 128
roll film bobine *f* 124
roll-neck à col roulé 117
room chambre *f* 19, 23, 24, 25, 28; *(space)* place *f* 32
room service service d'étage *m* 23
rope corde *f* 107
rosary chapelet *m* 122
rosemary romarin *m* 51
rouge fard à joues *m* 110
round rond(e) 101
round *(golf)* partie *f* 89
round-neck à col rond 117
roundtrip *(ticket)* aller-retour *m* 65, 69
rowing-boat barque à rames *f* 91
royal royal(e) 82
rubber *(material)* caoutchouc *m* 118; *(eraser)* gomme *f* 105
ruby rubis *m* 122
rucksack sac de montagne *m* 107
ruin ruine *f* 81
ruler *(for measuring)* règle *f* 105
rum rhum *m* 60
running water eau courante *f* 23
rye seigle *m* 64

DICTIONARY

S

saddle selle f 46
safe (not dangerous) sans danger 90
safe (coffre-fort) m 26
safety pin épingle de sûreté f 110
sage sauge f 51
sailing-boat voilier m 91
salad salade f 42
sale vente f 131; (bargains) soldes m/pl 100
sales tax T.V.A. f 24, 102
salmon saumon m 45
salt sel m 37, 38, 64
salty salé(e) 61
sand sable m 90
sandal sandale f 118
sanitary towel/napkin serviette hygiénique f 109
sapphire saphir m 122
Saturday samedi m 151
sauce sauce f 51
saucepan casserole f 107
saucer soucoupe f 107
sauerkraut choucroute f 47
sausage saucisse f 46, 64
sautéed sauté(e) 45, 47
scallop coquille St-Jacques f 45; (meat) escalope f 46
scampi langoustines f/pl 44
scarf foulard m 117
scarlet écarlate 113
scenery paysage m 92
scenic route route touristique f 85
school école f 79
scissors ciseaux m/pl 107, 110
Scotland Ecosse f 146
sculptor sculpteur m 83
sculpture sculpture f 83
sea mer f 23, 85, 90
sea bream daurade f 44
seafood fruits de mer m/pl 44
season saison f 40, 150
seasoning condiments m/pl 37
seat place f 69, 70, 87
seat belt ceinture de sécurité f 75
second deuxième 149
second seconde f 153
second class deuxième classe f 69
second hand trotteuse f 122
second-hand d'occasion 104
secretary secrétaire m/f 27, 131
see, to voir 12, 163

send, to envoyer 102, 103, 133; expédier 132
send up, to faire monter 26
sentence phrase f 12
separately séparément 62
September septembre m 150
seriously (wounded) grièvement 139
service service m 24, 62, 98, 100; (religion) culte m 84
serviette serviette f 36
set (hair) mise en plis f 30
set menu menu (à prix fixe) m 36, 40
setting lotion fixatif m 30, 111
seven sept 147
seventeen dix-sept 147
seventh septième 149
seventy soixante-dix 148
sew, to coudre 29
shade (colour) ton m 112
shallot échalote f 50
shampoo shampooing m 30, 111
shape forme f 103
share (finance) action f 131
sharp (pain) aigu(e) 140
shave, to raser 31
shaver rasoir (électrique) m 27, 119
shaving brush blaireau m 111
shaving cream crème à raser f 111
she elle 161
shelf étagère f 120
ship navire m 74
shirt chemise f 117
shivery pris(e) de frissons 140
shoe chaussure f 118
shoelace lacet m 118
shoemaker's cordonnerie f 99
shoe polish cirage m 118
shoe shop magasin de chaussures m 99
shop magasin m 98
shopping achats m/pl 97
shopping area quartier commerçant m 82, 100
shopping centre centre commercial m 99
short court(e) 30, 116, 117
shorts short m 117
short-sighted myope 123
shoulder épaule f 46, 138
shovel pelle f 128
show spectacle m 86, 87, 88
show, to montrer 13, 76, 100, 101, 103, 119, 124; indiquer 12
shower douche f 23, 32

shrimp crevette f 44
shrink, to rétrécir 114
shut fermé(e) 14
shutter *(window)* volet m 29; *(camera)* obturateur m 125
sick *(ill)* malade 140, 156
sickness *(illness)* maladie f 140
side côté m 30
sideboards/burns favoris m/pl 31
sightseeing visite touristique f 80
sightseeing tour visite guidée f 80
sign *(notice)* écriteau m 155; *(road)* panneau m 79
sign, to signer 26, 131
signature signature f 25
signet ring chevalière f 122
silk soie f 114
silver argenté(e) 113
silver argent m 121, 122
silver plate plaqué argent m 122
silverware argenterie f 122
since depuis 15, 150
sing, to chanter 88
single célibataire 93
single *(ticket)* aller m 65, 69
single room chambre pour une personne f 19, 23
sister sœur f 93
sit down, to s'asseoir 95
six six 147
sixteen seize 147
sixth sixième 149
sixty soixante 147
size format m 124; *(clothes)* taille f 114; *(shoes)* pointure f 118
skate patin m 91
skating rink patinoire f 91
ski ski m 91
ski, to faire du ski 91
ski boot chaussure de ski f 91
skiing ski m 89, 91
ski lift remonte-pente m 91
skin peau f 138
skin-diving plongée sous-marine f 91
skirt jupe f 117
ski run piste de ski f 91
sky ciel m 94
sled luge f 91
sleep, to dormir 144
sleeping bag sac de couchage m 107
sleeping-car wagon-lit m 66, 68, 69, 70
sleeping pill somnifère m 109, 143, 144
sleeve manche f 117

slice tranche f 120
slide *(photo)* diapositive f 124
slip jupon m 117
slipper pantoufle f 118
slow lent(e) 12, 14, 135
slow down, to ralentir 79
small petit(e) 14, 25, 101, 118, 130
smoke, to fumer 95
smoked fumé(e) 45
smoker fumeurs m/pl 70
snack casse-croûte m 63
snack bar buffet-express m 34, 67
snail escargot m 44
snap fastener bouton-pression m 117
sneakers tennis m/pl 118
snorkel tuba m 128
snow neige f 94
snow, to neiger 94
snuff tabac à priser m 126
soap savon m 27, 111
soccer football m 89
sock chaussette f 117
socket *(outlet)* prise f 27
soft drink boisson non alcoolisée f 64
soft-boiled *(egg)* mollet 28
sold out *(theatre)* complet 87
sole semelle f 118; *(fish)* sole f 45
soloist soliste m/f 88
some de, de la, du *(pl* des) 15
someone quelqu'un 95
something quelque chose 36, 55, 108, 112, 113, 125, 139
son fils m 93
song chanson f 128
soon bientôt 15
sore *(painful)* douloureux(euse) 145
sore throat mal de gorge m 141
sorry désolé(e) 11, 87; *(I'm)* excusez-moi 16
sort genre m 86; sorte f 120
sound-and-light show spectacle son et lumière m 86
soup soupe f, potage m 43
south sud m 77
South Africa Afrique du Sud f 146
souvenir souvenir m 127
souvenir shop magasin de souvenirs m 99
Soviet Union Union soviétique f 146
spade pelle f 128
Spain Espagne f 146
spare tyre roue de secours f 75
sparking plug bougie f 76
sparkling *(wine)* mousseux(euse) 59

spark plug bougie f 76
speak, to parler 12, 135, 162
speaker *(loudspeaker)* haut-parleur m 119
special spécial(e) 20, 37
special delivery par exprès 133
specialist spécialiste m/f 142
speciality spécialité f 40, 59
specimen *(medical)* prélèvement m 142
spectacle case étui à lunettes m 123
spell, to épeler 12
spend, to dépenser 101
spice épice f 50
spinach épinard m 49
spine colonne vertébrale f 138
spiny lobster langouste f 44
sponge éponge f 111
spoon cuillère f 36, 61, 107
sport sport m 89
sporting goods shop magasin d'articles de sport m 99
sports jacket veste de sport f 117
sprain, to fouler 140
spring *(season)* printemps m 150; *(water)* source f 85
square carré(e) 101
square place f 82
squid calmar m 44
stadium stade m 82
staff personnel m 26
stain tache f 29
stainless steel inox m 107, 122
stalls *(theatre)* parterre m 87
stamp *(postage)* timbre m 28, 126, 132
staple agrafe f 105
star étoile f 84
start, to commencer 80, 87, 88; *(car)* démarrer 78
starters hors-d'œuvre m 41
station *(railway)* gare f 19, 21, 67, 70; *(underground, subway)* station f 73
stationer's papeterie f 99, 104
statue statue f 82
stay séjour m 31, 92
stay, to rester 16, 24, 26; loger 93
steal, to voler 156
steamed cuit(e) à la vapeur 45
stew ragoût m 47
stewed à l'étouffée 47
stiff neck torticolis m 141
still *(mineral water)* non gazeux (euse) 60

sting piqûre f 139
sting, to piquer 139
stitch, to *(clothes)* recoudre 29; *(shoes)* coudre 118
stock *(in shop)* stock m 103
stock exchange bourse f 82
stocking bas m 117
stomach estomac m 138
stomach ache maux d'estomac m/pl 141
stools selles f/pl 142
stop *(bus)* arrêt m 72, 73
stop, to s'arrêter 21, 68, 70, 72
stop thief! au voleur! 156
store magasin m 98
straight *(drink)* sec 56, 60
straight ahead tout droit 21, 77
strange étrange 84
strawberry fraise f 54
street rue f 25
streetcar tram m 72
street map plan de ville m 19, 105
string ficelle f 105
strong fort(e) 143
student étudiant(e) m/f 82, 93
study, to étudier 93
stuffed farci(e) 41
sturdy solide 101
subway *(railway)* métro m 73
suede daim m 114, 118
sugar sucre m 37, 63, 64
suit *(man)* complet m 117; *(woman)* tailleur m 117
suitcase valise f 18
summer été m 150
sun soleil m 94
sunburn coup de soleil m 108
Sunday dimanche m 151
sunglasses lunettes de soleil f/pl 123
sunny ensoleillé(e) 94
sunshade *(beach)* parasol m 91
sunstroke insolation f 141
sun-tan cream crème solaire f 111
sun-tan oil huile solaire f 111
super *(petrol)* super m 75
superb superbe 84
supermarket supermarché m 99
supplement supplément m 40
suppository suppositoire m 109
surfboard planche de surf f 91
surgery *(consulting room)* cabinet (de consultation) m 137
surname nom (de famille) m 25
surroundings environs m/pl 35

suspenders *(Am.)* bretelles *f/pl* 117
swallow, to avaler 143
sweater chandail *m* 117
sweatshirt sweatshirt *m* 117
sweet *(food)* sucré(e) 61; *(wine)* doux, douce 59
sweet bonbon *m* 126
sweet corn maïs *m* 50
sweetener édulcorant *m* 37
swell, to enfler 139
swelling enflure *f* 139
swim, to nager, se baigner 90
swimming natation *f* 89; baignade *f* 91
swimming pool piscine *f* 32, 90
swimming trunks maillot de bain *m* 117
swimsuit costume de bain *m* 117
Swiss suisse 18
switch interrupteur *m* 29
switchboard operator standardiste *m/f* 26
switch on, to *(light)* allumer 79
Switzerland Suisse *f* 146
swollen enflé(e) 139
synagogue synagogue *f* 84
synthetic synthétique 114
system système *m* 138

T

table table *f* 36, 107
tablet comprimé *m* 109
tailor's tailleur *m* 99
take, to prendre 18, 25, 72, 73, 102; porter 114
take away, to *(carry)* emporter 63, 102
talcum powder talc *m* 111
tampon tampon hygiénique *m* 109
tangerine mandarine *f* 54
tap *(water)* robinet *m* 28
tape recorder magnétophone *m* 119
tapestry tapisserie *f* 127
tarragon estragon *m* 50
tart tarte *f*, tartelette *f* 55
taxi taxi *m* 19, 21, 31
tea thé *m* 38, 60, 64
team équipe *f* 89
tear, to déchirer 140
tearoom salon de thé *m* 34
teaspoon cuillère à café *f* 107, 143
telegram télégramme *m* 133
telegraph office bureau du télégraphe *m* 99, 133

telephone téléphone *m* 28, 78, 79, 134
telephone, to téléphoner 134
telephone booth cabine téléphonique *f* 134
telephone call appel *m* 135; communication *f* 136
telephone directory annuaire téléphonique *m* 134
telephone number numéro de téléphone *m* 96, 135, 136
telephoto lens téléobjectif *m* 125
television *(set)* poste de télévision *m* 23; télévision *f* 28; téléviseur *m* 119
telex télex *m* 133
telex, to envoyer un télex 130
tell, to dire 13, 73, 136; indiquer 76, 153
temperature température *f* 90, 142; *(fever)* fièvre *f* 140
temporary provisoire 145
ten dix 147
tendon tendon *m* 138
tennis tennis *m* 89
tennis court court de tennis *m* 89
tennis racket raquette de tennis *f* 90
tent tente *f* 32, 107
tenth dixième 149
tent peg piquet de tente *m* 107
tent pole montant de tente *m* 107
term *(word)* terme *m* 131
terrace terrasse *f* 36
terrifying effrayant 84
terrycloth tissu-éponge *m* 114
tetanus tétanos *m* 140
than que 15
thank you merci 10
that ce, cette 160; cela 11, 100
the le, la *(pl* les) 159
theatre théâtre *m* 82, 86
theft vol *m* 156
their leur *(pl* leurs) 161
then ensuite 15
there là 14; voilà 14
thermometer thermomètre *m* 109, 144
these ces 160; ceux-ci 63
they ils, elles 161
thief voleur *m* 156
thigh cuisse *f* 138
thin mince 113
think, to penser 94; croire 62
third troisième 149
third tiers *m* 149
thirsty, to be avoir soif 13, 35
thirteen treize 147

thirty trente 147
this ce, cette 160; ceci 11, 100
those ces 160; ceux-là 63, 120
thousand mille 148
thread fil *m* 27
three trois 147
throat gorge *f* 138, 141
throat lozenge pastille pour la gorge *f* 109
through à travers 15
through train train direct *m* 68, 69
thumb pouce *m* 138
thumbtack punaise *f* 105
thunder tonnerre *m* 94
thunderstorm orage *m* 94
Thursday jeudi *m* 151
thyme thym *m* 51
ticket billet *m* 65, 69, 87, 89, 156; *(bus)* ticket *m* 72
ticket office guichet *m* 67
tide marée *f* 90
tie cravate *f* 117
tie clip pince à cravate *f* 122
tight *(clothes)* étroit(e) 116
tights collant *m* 117
time temps *m* 80; *(clock)* heure *f* 137, 153; *(occasion)* fois *f* 143
timetable horaire *m* 68
tin *(can)* boîte *f* 120
tinfoil papier d'aluminium *m* 107
tin opener ouvre-boîtes *m* 107
tint coloration *f* 111
tinted teinté 123
tire pneu *m* 75, 76
tired fatigué(e) 13
tissue *(handkerchief)* mouchoir en papier *m* 111
to à 15
toast pain grillé *m* 38
tobacco tabac *m* 126
tobacconist's bureau de tabac *m* 99, 126
today aujourd'hui 29, 151
toe orteil *m* 138
toilet paper papier hygiénique *m* 111
toiletry articles de toilette *m/pl* 110
toilets toilettes *f/pl* 27, 32, 37, 67
toilet water eau de toilette *f* 111
toll péage *m* 75, 79
tomato tomate *f* 50
tomato juice jus de tomate *m* 41, 60
tomb tombe *f* 82
tomorrow demain 29, 151
tongs pince *f* 107

tongue langue *f* 46, 138
tonic water Schweppes *m* 60
tonight ce soir 29, 86, 87, 96
tonsil amygdale *f* 138
too trop 15; *(also)* aussi 15
tooth dent *f* 145
toothache mal de dents *m* 145
toothbrush brosse à dents *f* 111, 119
toothpaste dentifrice *m* 111
top haut *m* 30, 145
torch *(flashlight)* lampe de poche *f* 107
torn déchiré(e) 140
touch, to toucher 155
tough dur(e) 61
tourist office syndicat d'initiative *m* 22, 80; office du tourisme *m* 80
tourist tax taxe de séjour *f* 32
towards vers 15
towel serviette *f* 27, 111
tower tour *f* 82
town ville *f* 19, 21, 76, 93, 105
town hall mairie *f* 82
tow truck dépanneuse *f* 78
toy jouet *m* 128
toy shop magasin de jouets *m* 99
tracksuit survêtement *m* 117
traffic circulation *f* 79
traffic light feu *m* 77
trailer caravane *f* 32
train train *m* 66, 68, 69, 70; *(underground, subway)* rame *f* 73
tram tram *m* 72
tranquillizer tranquillisant *m* 109, 143
transfer *(bank)* transfert *m* 131
transformer transformateur *m* 119
translate, to traduire 12
transport transport *m* 74
travel, to voyager 92
travel agency agence de voyages *f* 99
traveller's cheque chèque de voyage *m* 18, 62, 102, 130
travelling bag sac de voyage *m* 18
travel sickness mal du voyage *m* 108
treatment traitement *m* 143
tree arbre *m* 85
tremendous formidable 84
trim, to *(beard)* rafraîchir 31
trip voyage *m* 93, 152; trajet *m* 72
tripe tripes *f/pl* 47
trolley chariot *m* 18, 71
trousers pantalon *m* 117
trout truite *f* 45

truck camion *m* 79
truffle truffe *f* 50
try, to essayer 115; *(sample)* goûter 60
T-shirt teeshirt *m* 117
tube tube *m* 120
Tuesday mardi *m* 151
tuna thon *m* 45
Tunisia Tunisie *f* 146
tunny thon *m* 45
turbot turbot *m* 45
turkey dinde *f* 48
turn, to tourner 21, 77
turnip navet *m* 50
turquoise turquoise *f* 122
turtleneck à col roulé 117
tweezers pince à épiler *f* 111
twelve douze 147
twenty vingt 147
twice deux fois 149
twin bed lits jumeaux *m/pl* 23
two deux 147
typewriter machine à écrire *f* 27, 105
typing paper papier à machine *m* 105
tyre pneu *m* 75, 76

U

ugly laid (e) 14, 84
umbrella parapluie *m* 117; *(beach)* parasol *m* 91
uncle oncle *m* 93
unconscious évanoui(e) 139
under sous 15
underdone *(meat)* saignant(e) 47; pas assez cuit(e) 61
underground *(railway)* métro *m* 73
underpants caleçon *m*, slip *m* 117
undershirt maillot de corps *m* 117
understand, to comprendre 12, 16
undress, to déshabiller 142
United States Etats-Unis *m/pl* 146
university université *f* 82
unleaded sans plomb 75
until jusqu'à 15
up en haut 15
upper supérieur(e) 69
upset stomach indigestion *f* 108
upstairs en haut 15
urgent urgent(e) 13, 145
urine urine *f* 142
use usage *m* 17, 109
use, to utiliser 134; se servir de 78
useful utile 15
usual habituel(le) 143

V

vacancy chambre disponible *f* 23
vacant libre 14, 155
vacation vacances *f/pl* 151
vaccinate, to vacciner 140
vacuum flask thermos *m* 107
vaginal vaginal(e) 141
valley vallée *f* 85
value valeur *f* 131
value-added tax T.V.A. *f* 24, 102, 154
vanilla vanille *f* 55
VAT *(sales tax)* T.V.A. *f* 24, 102, 154
veal veau *m* 46
vegetable légume *m* 49
vegetarian végétarien *m* 37
vein veine *f* 138
velvet velours *m* 114
velveteen velours de coton *m* 114
venereal disease maladie vénérienne *f* 142
venison cerf *m*, chevreuil *m* 48
very très 15
vest maillot de corps *m* 117; *(Am.)* gilet *m* 117
video cassette vidéocassette *f* 119, 124, 127
video recorder magnétoscope *m* 119
view vue *f* 23, 25
village village *m* 76, 85
vinegar vinaigre *m* 37
vineyard vignoble *m* 85
visit visite *f* 92
visit, to visiter 84
visiting hours heures de visite *f/pl* 144
vitamin pills vitamines *f/pl* 109
V-neck à col en V 117
volleyball volley-ball *m* 89
voltage voltage *m* 27, 119
vomit, to vomir 140

W

waistcoat gilet *m* 117
wait, to attendre 21, 95, 162
waiter garçon *m* 26, 36
waiting-room salle d'attente *f* 67
waitress serveuse *f* 26; mademoi-selle *f* 36
wake, to réveiller 27, 71
Wales Pays de Galles *m* 146
walk, to marcher 74; aller à pied 85
wall mur *m* 85
wallet portefeuille *m* 156
walnut noix *f* 54

DICTIONARY

want, to (wish) vouloir, désirer 13
warm chaud(e) 94
wash to laver 29, 114
washable lavable 114
wash-basin lavabo m 28
washing powder lessive f 107
watch montre f 121, 122, 127
watchmaker's horlogerie f 99, 121
watchstrap bracelet de montre m 122
water eau f 23, 28, 32, 38, 75, 90
watercress cresson m 49
waterfall chute d'eau f 85
water flask gourde f 107
watermelon pastèque f 54
water-ski ski nautique m 91
wave vague f 90
way route f, chemin m 76
we nous 161
weather temps m 93
weather forecast prévisions météo f/pl 94
wedding ring alliance f 122
Wednesday mercredi m 151
week semaine f 16, 20, 24, 80, 151
weekend week-end m 151
well (healthy) bien 10, 140
well-done (meat) bien cuit(e) 47
west ouest m 77
what quoi, que, comment 11; quel(e) 20, 21
wheel roue f 78
when quand, à quelle heure 11
where où 11
which lequel, laquelle 11
whipped cream crème Chantilly f 55
whisky whisky m 17, 60
white blanc, blanche 59, 113
whitebait blanchaille f 44
whiting merlan m 45
Whit Sunday Pentecôte f 152
who qui 11
why pourquoi 11
wick mèche f 126
wide large 118
wide-angle lens grand-angulaire m 125
wife femme f 93
wig perruque f 111
wild boar sanglier m 48; (young) marcassin m 48
wind vent m 94
window fenêtre f 28, 36, 69; (shop) vitrine f 100, 112
windscreen/shield pare-brise m 76

wine vin m 57, 59, 61
wine list carte des vins f 59
wine merchant marchand de vin m 99
winter hiver m 150
winter sports sports d'hiver m/pl 91
wiper essuie-glace m 76
wish vœu m 152
with avec 15
withdraw, to (bank) retirer 131
without sans 15
woman femme f 115
wonderful merveilleux(euse) 96
wood bois m 85
wood alcohol alcool à brûler m 107
woodcock bécasse f 48
woodgrouse coq de bruyère m 48
wool laine f 114
word mot m 12, 15, 133
work, to (function) fonctionner 28, 119
working day jour ouvrable m 151
worse pire 14
worsted peigné m 114
wound blessure f 139
wrinkle resistant infroissable 114
write, to écrire 12, 101
writing pad bloc m 105
writing-paper papier à lettres m 27
wrong faux, fausse 14, 135

X

X-ray (photo) radio f 140

Y

year an m, année f 149
yellow jaune 113
yes oui 10
yesterday hier 151
yet encore 15
yield, to (traffic) céder le passage 79
yoghurt yaourt m, yoghourt m 38, 64
you tu, vous 161
young jeune 14
your ton, ta (pl tes) 161; votre (pl vos) 161
youth hostel auberge de jeunesse f 22, 32

Z

zero zéro m 147
zip(per) fermeture-éclair f 117
zoo jardin zoologique m 82
zoology zoologie f 83
zucchini courgette f 49

Dictionnaire

Index français

Say BERLITZ

... and most people think of outstanding language schools. But Berlitz has also become the world's leading publisher of books for travellers – Travel Guides, Phrase Books, Dictionaries – plus Cassettes and Self-teaching courses.

Informative, accurate, up-to-date, Books from Berlitz are written with freshness and style. They also slip easily into pocket or purse – no need for bulky, old-fashioned volumes.

Join the millions who know how to travel. Whether for fun or business, put Berlitz in your pocket.

BERLITZ®

Leader in
Books and Cassettes
for Travellers

A Macmillan Company

BERLITZ Books for travellers

TRAVEL GUIDES

They fit your pocket in both size and price. Modern, up-to-date, Berlitz gets all the information you need into 128 lively pages – 192 or 256 pages for country guides – with colour maps and photos throughout. What to see and do, where to shop, what to eat and drink, how to save.

AFRICA	Algeria (256 pages)* Kenya Morocco South Africa Tunisia
ASIA, MIDDLE EAST	China (256 pages) Hong Kong India (256 pages) Japan (256 pages) Nepal* Singapore Sri Lanka Thailand Egypt Jerusalem & Holy Land Saudi Arabia
AUSTRAL-ASIA	Australia (256 pages) New Zealand
BRITISH ISLES	Channel Islands London Ireland Oxford and Stratford Scotland
BELGIUM	Brussels
FRANCE	Brittany France (256 pages) French Riviera Loire Valley Normandy Paris
GERMANY	Berlin Munich The Rhine Valley
AUSTRIA and SWITZER-LAND	Tyrol Vienna Switzerland (192 pages)
GREECE, CYPRUS & TURKEY	Athens Corfu Crete Rhodes Greek Islands of Aegean Peloponnese Salonica/North. Greece Cyprus Istanbul/Aegean Coast Turkey (192 pages)
ITALY and MALTA	Florence Italian Adriatic Italian Riviera Italy (256 pages) Rome Sicily Venice Malta
NETHER-LANDS and SCANDI-NAVIA	Amsterdam Copenhagen Helsinki Oslo and Bergen Stockholm

*in preparation

PORTUGAL	Algarve Lisbon Madeira	NORTH AMERICA	New York Canada (256 pages) Toronto Montreal
SPAIN	Barcelona / Costa Dorada Canary Islands Costa Blanca Costa Brava Costa del Sol & Andalusia Ibiza and Formentera Madrid Majorca and Minorca	CARIBBEAN, LATIN AMERICA	Puerto Rico Virgin Islands Bahamas Bermuda French West Indies Jamaica Southern Caribbean Mexico City Brazil (Highlights of) Rio de Janeiro
EASTERN EUROPE	Budapest Dubrovnik & S. Dalmatia Hungary (192 pages) Istria and Croatian Coast Moscow & Leningrad Prague Split and Dalmatia Yugoslavia (256 pages)	EUROPE	Business Travel Guide – Europe (368 pages) Pocket guide to Europe (480 pages) Cities of Europe (504 p.)
NORTH AMERICA	U.S.A. (256 pages) California Florida Hawaii Miami	CRUISE GUIDES	Caribbean cruise guide (368 pages) Alaska cruise guide (168 p) Handbook to Cruising (240 pages)

DELUXE GUIDES

combine complete
travel guide, phrase
book and dictionary in
one book.
Titles available:
Amsterdam, Barcelona,
Budapest, Florence,
French Riviera, Madrid,
Mexico, Munich, Paris,
Rome, Venice.

SKI GUIDES

Top resorts rated,
where to ski, colour
maps:
Austria
France
Italy
Switzerland
Skiing the Alps*

BLUEPRINT GUIDES

Imaginative new large size guide with mapped itineraries,
special interest checklists, selected restaurant and hotel
recommendations, large-scale road atlas, all in full colour.

France, Germany*, Great Britain*, Greece*, Italy, Spain*.

MORE FOR THE $

Over $ 4'000 worth of discount coupons and gift certificates
from the finest hotels and restaurants for each country
covered.

France, Italy.

*in preparation

PHRASE BOOKS

World's bestselling phrase books feature all the expressions and vocabulary you'll need, and pronunciation throughout. 192 pages, 2 colours.

Arabic	Hebrew	Russian
Chinese	Hungarian	Serbo-Croatian
Danish	Italian	Spanish (Castilian)
Dutch	Japanese	Spanish (Lat. Am.)
Finnish	Korean	Swahili
French	Norwegian	Swedish
German	Polish	Turkish
Greek	Portuguese	European Phrase Book
		European Menu Reader

All of the above phrase books are available with C60 or C90 cassette and miniscript as a "**cassettepak**".

Cassette and miniscript only are also available in the major languages as a "**phrase cassette**".

DICTIONARIES

Bilingual with 12,500 concepts each way. Highly practical for travellers, with pronunciation shown plus menu reader, basic expressions and useful information. Over 330 pages.

Danish	French	Norwegian
Dutch	German	Portuguese
Finnish	Italian	Spanish
		Swedish

TRAVEL VIDEO

Travel Tips from Berlitz are now part of the informative and colourful videocassette series of over 80 popular destinations produced by Travelview International. Ideal for planning a trip, Travelview videos provide 40 to 60 minutes of valuable destination briefing and a Reference Guide to local hotels and tourist attractions. Available from leading travel agencies and video stores everywhere in the U.S.A. and Canada or call 1-800-325-3108 (Texas, call (713) 975-7077; (403) 248-7170 in Canada; 908-66 9422 in UK; (5) 531-8714 in Mexico City).